THE PROBLEM OF REFUGEES IN THE CONTEMPORARY INTERNATIONAL LAW

NIJHOFF LAW SPECIALS

Volume 12

The titles published in this series are listed at the end of this volume.

Graduate Institute of International Studies — Geneva

The Problem of Refugees in The Light of Contemporary International Law Issues

Papers presented at the Colloquium organized by the
Graduate Institute of International Studies
in collaboration with the Office of the
United Nations High Commissioner for Refugees,
Geneva, 26 and 27 May, 1994

Edited by

Vera Gowlland-Debbas

MARTINUS NIJHOFF PUBLISHERS
THE HAGUE / BOSTON / LONDON

Library of Congress Cataloging-in-Publication Data

The problem of refugees in the light of contemporary international law
  issues / edited by Vera Gowlland-Debbas.
      p.   cm. -- (Nijhoff law specials ; 12)
  "Papers presented at the colloquium organized by the Graduate
Institute of International Studies in collaboration with the Office
of the United Nations High Commissioner for Refugees, Geneva, 26 and
27 May, 1994."
   Includes index.
   ISBN 9041100857 (pb)
   1. Refugees--Legal status, laws, etc.   2. Refugees--International
cooperation.   I. Gowlland-Debbas, Vera, 1943-   II. Graduate
Institute of International Studies (Geneva, Switzerland)
III. Office of the United Nations High Commissioner for Refugees.
IV. Series.
JX4292.R4P76   1995
341.4'86--dc20   95-20419

ISBN 90-411-0085-7

Published by Kluwer Law International,
P.O. Box 85889, 2508 CN The Hague, The Netherlands.

Sold and distributed in the U.S.A. and Canada
by Kluwer Law International,
675 Massachusetts Avenue, Cambridge, MA 02139, U.S.A.

In all other countries, sold and distributed
by Kluwer Law International,
P.O. Box 85889, 2508 CN The Hague, The Netherlands.

Printed on acid-free paper

Printed in the Netherlands

Table of Contents

Preface

The Colloquium took place May 26–27, 1994 under the auspices of UNHCR and the Graduate Institute of International Studies. It was a contribution to the Decade of International Law as well as part of the Graduate Institute's activities in celebration of the United Nations 50th Anniversary in 1995.

Although the title of the Colloquium and the papers focused on legal issues, there were at least two sub-themes in the organization and discussions that warrant mentioning.

The first aspect is the relationship between practitioners and scholars. Those working at UNHCR are overwhelmed with an increasing number of immediate and practical problems that call for instant action. Many of these problems are logistical, but even more important, many of the problems involve practical decisions that may have enormous consequences for future human-itarian activities. While the problems call for immediate solutions, the long-term implications of those solutions are not at all evident at the time of their implementation.

Thus, in the midst of their daily activities, it is important for those working at UNHCR to be exposed to outside input and scholarly reflection. The dichotomy between the practitioners and scholars is a false dichotomy; those who are in practice must understand the deeper background of their activi-ties, and those involved in scholarly research must understand the daily practical problems confronting the practitioners. It is in this sense that the Colloquium tried to introduce a dialogue between practitioners and scholars.

The second aspect of the Colloquium I would like to mention is the rela-tionship between refugees and international relations in general. If the specific subject of the Colloquium was the problem of refugees in the light of con-temporary law issues, the larger problem was to reconcile the specificity of refugees with international relations. By their very nature, refugees are on the borderline between traditional international relations as involving rela-tions between states and a more nuanced understanding of international relations issues at large. Refugees confront international lawyers with a host of questions involving state succession, state responsibility, human rights, inter-national jurisdiction, and UN mandates. The subjects of the discussion, however, were not merely traditional international legal questions. Rather, and this is my privileged comment as a non-jurist, the subjects discussed raise enormous issues in contemporary international relations beyond the legal ones. Refugees, in this sense, can be seen as the prism through which a host of exploding issues confront traditional international law and international relations.

For example, it has been argued by me that the refugee situation of home-lessness and homesickness is paradigmatic of our modern dilemma. Without prejudicing the necessity of placing certain persons in the category of refugees for their protection, it can be argued that the homeless are not necessarily those without territorial place, that the situation of the stranger that characterizes refugees is not totally dissimilar to Nietzsche's description of the modern condition in which we are all strangers to ourselves. In other words, interest in the refugee definition might be re-interpreted as part of an entire process that seeks to redefine differences and similarities between a range of categories and identities. The refugee is on the borderline between traditional international law with its fixed borders and domains of control and new international relations issues like the environment which demand new understandings of concepts like territoriality and sovereignty.

Those two aspects of the Colloquium – the relationship between scholars and practitioners as well as refugees and international relations in general – highlight the enlargement of refugee issues from what they were when UNHCR began. Indeed, if an article in the *Economist* noted that it was so much simpler then, referring to the smaller number of refugees at the end of World War II than now, one could also look back to a time when the issues raised by refugees were indeed simpler. It is because the issues raised by refugees are so complex today that it is important for practitioners and scholars, refugee lawyers and international lawyers and international relation specialists as well, to meet to compare perspectives.

The organizers of the Colloquium would like to thank UNHCR and the Graduate Institute of International Studies for their support in organizing the Colloquium. Special thanks to Mr. Jean-François Durieux, Chief, Promotion of Refugee Law, Division of International Protection, UNHCR for his assistance and encouragement throughout the project. Valerie van Daeniken of the Graduate Institute was most cheerfully helpful.

Geneva, October 1994   Daniel Warner
Deputy to the Director for
External Relations and Special
Programs, GIIS

VERA GOWLLAND-DEBBAS

Introduction

The contributions in this book go beyond the confines of traditional refugee law in situating the problem of refugees within the broader framework of contemporary international law. The colloquium at which these papers were originally presented in the Spring of 1994, sprang from two premises.

The first was that international lawyers concerned with humanitarian issues should be responsive both to the increasing need of practitioners for a conceptual framework that will make – if only marginally – a little more sense out of the seemingly chaotic and senseless sequence of events in the field, and to the impact of policy on law. The colloquium therefore brought together the differing but complementary approaches of scholars and practitioners to a major and exponentially expanding contemporary problem. The second premise was based, to paraphrase Sir Robert Jennings,[1] on the need to move from an awareness of the problem of refugees which requires a solution, to an awareness of the place of the refugee problem within the international legal system through which alone such legal solutions may be found.

It is only fairly recently that refugee law, in its strict sense, was introduced into university curricula as an academic discipline in its own right. More usually, international law courses and manuals refer only fleetingly to refugees, *if at all*, in connection with the status of aliens, questions of nationality or statelessness. No sooner however has this discipline asserted itself, than it is requiring a change of focus and a reassessment of its place in the framework of international law. For the stalemate engendered by post-war refugee law – which is largely centred on questions of durable asylum, therefore addressing the problem of only a small tranche of the asylum-seeking population – has made it imperative to encompass the broader issues relating to prevention,

---

[1] Jennings, Sir Robert, "International Law and the Citizen", *in Le droit international au service de la paix, de la justice et du développement. Mélanges Michel Virally*, Paris 1991, pp. 341–347, at p. 346, who states, with reference to human rights law: "these topics which thus do capture the imagination of the public in general show an awareness of certain particular problems which necessitate a solution rather than awareness of an international legal system through which alone such solutions may be found".

ix

V. Gowlland-Debbas (ed.), The Problem of Refugees in the Light of Contemporary International Law Issues, ix–xvii.
© 1996 *Kluwer Academic Publishers. Printed in the Netherlands.*

containment and solution of coerced movements of peoples at large. As highlighted by the High Commissioner, Mrs. Sadako Ogata, in her Keynote
Address, the protection of refugees is increasingly viewed by international
protection agencies and States, as a continuous process, going beyond the
attainment of short-term interim objectives.

But in moving beyond asylum law, refugee law has become inextricably
entangled with the broader framework of human rights and humanitarian law
from which it was originally isolated, as well as with other fields of international law such as State responsibility and peace maintenance. This poses a
dilemma for refugee lawyers. For on the one hand it is important that they seek
to systematize the emerging range of norms, recommendations and guidelines directed at a broader class of individuals who have lost or are in imminent
danger of losing the protection of their home State. On the other hand, this
broadening of refugee law must be obtained neither at the expense of those
traditional rules relating to durable asylum for those fleeing from a well-
founded fear of persecution (considered by some to be the only raison d'être
of refugee law), nor at the risk of losing the specificity of the refugee
condition.

The Initial Segregation of Refugee Law as "Asylum Law"

Initially, refugee law was segregated from the development of international
human rights law, even though it may seem to be fairly self-evident that refugee
law *is* and *should be* part of human rights law, since it is ultimately concerned with protection of the human person, albeit of a more vulnerable kind.
"Refugeehood" however, which is premised on the crossing of borders, is
distinguished from general human rights law in that proposed solutions to
the problem collide with the walls of domestic jurisdiction of not one, but
two sets of states: the country of origin of the refugee and the country of
asylum. Hence, although the 1951 Convention on the Status of Refugees
(which, with its update – the 1967 Protocol – remains the cornerstone of the
international protection system), has frequently been called the first postwar
universal human rights instrument, refugee law was hooked on to traditional
concepts of state territorial jurisdiction, i.e., the sovereign right of states to
decide on admission and expulsion of all those not linked by the bonds of
nationality.

Of course, this discretionary right of States was tempered by important
limitations, such as the principle of *non-refoulement* (the obligation of States
not to return a refugee to a territory where her/his life or freedom would be
threatened on certain defined grounds). This principle, embedded in Article
33 of the 1951 Convention, lies at the core of refugee protection and is
considered to have a basis outside conventional law. But such limitations
did not automatically imply an *absolute* obligation to admit *on a durable
basis*.

The irony of the system, therefore, lay in the fact that while the right to leave any country including one's own became well established in international human rights law – albeit circumscribed as Guy Goodwin-Gill and Kay Hailbronner point out – and was central to demands made of Eastern Europe in Western European cold-war propaganda, one corollary of this right, namely the right to asylum, did not succeed in establishing itself as an unconditional subjective right of the individual. In short, if, in the words of Article 14 of the Universal Declaration of Human Rights, the individual had the right "to seek and to enjoy in other countries asylum from persecution", she/he continued to lack an enforceable right to be granted it.

Again, although the 1951 Convention regulated not only the personal status of refugees as a special category of aliens, but also dealt with certain human rights, such as non-discrimination and freedom of movement, that were subsequently developed in regional and universal instruments, this link with human rights law arose solely from the obligations of the receiving State to mete out certain standards of treatment to those who were granted refugee status on the basis of the Convention's criteria.

Within this framework, therefore, there was no room for concern with the human rights situation prevailing in the State of origin: 1) the system only began to operate once a person had crossed an international border; 2) though the criterion of a "well-founded fear of persecution" based on race, religion, nationality, membership of a particular social group or political opinion, was central to the Convention definition of a refugee, it had relevance only with respect to determination of status in the country of asylum and in no way implied concern with the human rights situation prevailing in the State of origin or engaged that State's legal responsibility (although it had certain political implications, which explains the hesitations of States to grant asylum to the nationals of "friendly" States); 3) the "exilic" bias[2] of the system with its sole solution of integration into a new community, meant that there was no need for concern with the root causes of flight for purposes of determining the conditions propitious to repatriation.

The 1951 Convention regime based on the concept of durable asylum remains of course central to the protection of a particular – albeit narrow – segment of asylum-seekers. However, the danger lies in the erosion of even this modicum of international protection. For paradoxically, the more this branch of law develops as "positive law" and the more universal becomes the 1951 Convention in terms of State ratifications, the more its increasingly restrictive application by States in the form of policies serving only to deflect, not to stem the flow, narrows even further this segment of the asylum-seeking population covered by the traditional legal regime. It is indeed ironical at a

---

[2] Gervase Coles in coining the term, has been paramount in pointing to the underlying weaknesses of such an approach. See, *inter alia*, Coles, G., "Approaching the Refugee Problem Today", in Loescher, G. and Monahan, L. (eds.), *Refugees and International Relations*, Oxford 1989, pp. 373–410, at pp. 390–393.

time when it has become fashionable to speak of the withering away or erosion of State sovereignty that we are witnessing a reinforcement of that last bastion of State sovereignty which is the right to decide who to admit and who to expel. This is reflected in the way States are establishing defence of their borders in areas outside or increasingly remote from these borders – for instance through interdiction at sea, control at foreign airport departure points by means of visa requirements and sanctions on carriers, and the creation of international airport zones – in other words asserting jurisdiction in order to deny jurisdiction and the obligations which flow from it.

The Need in Policy Terms for Broadening the Approach to the Refugee Problem

This is not to say that the fundamentally important function of traditional refugee law must not continue to be reaffirmed, and George Okoth-Obbo forcefully underlines in his contribution the dangers inherent in a contrary approach, for in his view, that "refugee law *must* necessarily be 'exilic' is its strength . . . as it is the *failure* of any effective protection in the country of origin that kicks it into gear".

But for those who lie outside the net of protection of the 1951 Convention, and in respect of those cases it was never intended to encompass, e.g. the mass uprooting of a population resulting from ruthless governmental policies, or a total breakdown in the State system itself, or again, where large-scale voluntary repatriation schemes are seen as the only viable alternatives, it becomes evident that any meaningful solution can only be found by building bridges. These require moving out of the confines of the traditional regime, by implicating also the State of origin as well as the international community as a whole, and by addressing the entire spectrum of the problem from before flight to after return.

In short, it is not a question of substitution of one legal regime by another, but the recognition that the sheer magnitude and complexity of the contemporary refugee problem cannot *solely* be tackled from the narrow base of the international system of protection that has been inherited, and the practice of recent decades has illustrated this gradual broadening of the approach.

The Legal Issues Raised by a Comprehensive Approach

To state, however that a comprehensive approach is in *policy* terms the only viable approach, and that such policies have been pursued by international agencies *de facto* and in the field, does not necessarily mean that in terms of the academic discipline itself the broadening of the ambit of refugee law can be done without raising certain problems.

First, it may be argued, the anchorage of refugee law in asylum law preserves its specificity and enables protection to develop as part and parcel of positive international law. This includes a solid treaty basis and a growing body of case law at the domestic and regional levels.

Secondly, the "rediscovery" that refugee law is part and parcel of human rights law, in other words the recognition that a refugee as a human being is entitled first and foremost to all the panoply of human rights protection, creates certain legal pitfalls. One is the risk of merging the refugee conundrum with the traditional thorny problems of human rights law. These include the domestic *versus* international jurisdiction debate, the pitting of traditional concepts of state sovereignty against the imperatives of humanitarian intervention, the tensions between political/security and humanitarian concerns, issues of State responsibility in areas where reciprocity does not play its traditional role, and the problem of institutional coordination and overlapping mandates, to name only a few. Another problem is that current efforts to develop within human rights law a body of legal principles affording incremental protection and aimed at the specificity of the refugee condition, are producing increasingly "softer" soft law – not only in the form of resolutions and declarations of representative international bodies, but also as conclusions of subsidiary organs of subsidiary organs, NGO guidelines, etc. . . . .

This reorientation of refugee law may therefore raise objections by legal purists. It can be argued that attempts to identify points of convergence between refugee, human rights and humanitarian law, as well as connecting problems such as state succession, state responsibility, international security, and even development and environmental questions, are artificial exercises, as Pellet points out in respect of the link between creation and dissolution of States and refugee flows. No one doubts that there may be factual, practical or policy links but, as it may quite rightly be argued, it is not always easy to establish *juridical* links between these fields.

THE ESTABLISHMENT OF JURIDICAL LINKS BETWEEN REFUGEE LAW AND OTHER AREAS OF INTERNATIONAL LAW

The Interwar Period

We are not, however, dealing with a new phenomenon, for the focus on asylum as the be-all and end-all of refugee law is of post-1951 vintage, and the issues raised during the interwar period, at least in Europe, strangely resemble the contemporary debate. That the facilitation of international movement of persons deprived of the juridical protection of their state of origin, rather than immigration, was the crux of the problem is shown by the emphasis on arrangements for the issue of certificates of identity for the refugees of the early inter-war period.[3] That removal of root causes creating refugee flows was

---

[3] See, e.g., Hathway, James C., "The Evolution of Refugee Status in International Law:

not unthought of during this period is illustrated by James McDonald's letter of 27 December, 1935 regarding his resignation from the office of High Commissioner for Refugees coming from Germany, in which he states: "It will not be enough to continue the activities on behalf of those who flee from the Reich. Efforts must be made to remove or mitigate the causes which create German refugees."[4] That state responsibility of the country of origin was not far from the minds of the writers of the period is reflected in the words of Robert Jennings, who is well worth quoting at some length. He wrote in 1939 and well before the development of modern human rights law, with refugees from Germany in mind:

> But there is one aspect of the refugee problem to which the general and customary international law is relevant, and that is the consideration of the legality or illegality of the conduct of the state which creates a refugee population. . . .
>
> *Prima facie* the treatment accorded by a state to its own subjects, including the conferment or deprivation of nationality, is a matter of purely domestic concern. But there is some authority for the proposition that even this comes within the ambit of international law when the treatment in question offends against those principles of justice and humanity which are recognized by civilized nations. . . .
>
> (However a) sounder line of approach would appear to be one which has regard not so much to the ethics of domestic policy as to the repercussions of that policy on the material interests of third states. Even if the state whose conduct results in the flooding of other states with refugee populations be not guilty of an actual breach of law, there can be little doubt that states suffering in consequence would be justified in resorting to measures of *retorsion* . . .
>
> But there seems to be good ground for stating that the wilful flooding of other states with refugees constitutes not merely an inequitable act, but an actual illegality, and *a fortiori* where the refugees are compelled to enter the country of refuge in a destitute condition . . . (A)s soon as the persecution of a minority does in fact result in a refugee movement which causes embarrassment to other states, the matter clearly becomes one of international concern. . . . And for a state to employ these (domestic) rights with the avowed purpose of saddling other states with unwanted sections of its population is as clear an abuse of right as can be imagined.
>
> Not only is it an abuse of right, it is an evasion of the undoubted duty of a state to receive back its own nationals.[5]

1920–1950", 33 *ICLQ* (1984), pp. 348–380; Holborn, L., "The Legal Status of Political Refugees, 1920–1935", 32 *AJIL* (1938), pp. 680–703.
  [4] League document C.13, M.12, 1936, Annex, cited in Jennings, R. Yewdall, "Some International Law Aspects of the Refugee Question", 20 *BYIL* (1939), pp. 98–114.
  [5] *Ibid.*, pp. 10–12.

The interwar arrangements also emphasized, as a decisive criterion in determination of refugee status, the presence or lack of effective protection by the governments concerned, not the crossing of an international border. In fact, the Constitution of the International Refugee Organization of 1946 extended the competence of the organization also to victims of Nazi persecution who had never left Germany or Austria.[6] Finally, humanitarian law, which antedated human rights law, has specifically provided for some protection of refugees during armed conflict situations.

Thus we can see in these interwar developments all the ingredients of the so-called "new" holistic approach which UNHCR among others is urging.

The Contemporary Practice

Bringing refugee law out of the narrow confines in which it has been isolated also has a number of advantages and this has been reflected in the practice of the last few decades.

This body of law is enriched and strengthened when it is combined with norms drawn from other areas and thus better able to offer some measure of substitute protection to those individuals who have lost in one way or another the protection of their home state. This is particularly so in the area of human rights.

With respect to normative enrichment, the fact is often overlooked that refugee law as traditionally conceived was only meant to provide *incremental* protection to a particularly vulnerable category of individuals. Today, however, human rights law has itself departed from its initial monolithic treatment of individuals (barring some distinctions between aliens and nationals), and has come to recognize that certain vulnerable groups, such as children, minorities, or indigenous peoples, require the specific reiteration of general and fundamental principles of human rights law in their respect, and this is reflected in a series of recent conventions and United Nations declaratory resolutions. It is going in the same sense, therefore, to insist on the importance of identifying, within the mass of human rights norms, those principles and obligations that when violated have a direct or indirect bearing on the creation of refugee flows. Emphasis on such human rights as the right to leave and to return, the right to freedom of movement, the right to a nationality, the right to due process, and the corresponding responsibility of states to ensure such rights, has particular significance in the current world climate, where on the one hand, receiving States practice policies of detention, refoulement and other treatment of asylum-seekers that violate elementary considerations of humanity, appearing to regard refugee law (restrictively interpreted) as the only applicable framework; and on the other, situations of state disintegration, dissolution and succession, internal and external conflicts, and gross violations of human

---

[6] This has been pointed out by Luke T. Lee, chairman of the International Law Association Committee on Internally Displaced Persons, in an unpublished paper sent to the author.

rights, in some cases tantamount to genocide, lay the groundwork for mass exodus from countries of origin.

In terms of individual redress, it is also important to provide access for individual asylum seekers to the regular channels provided by the international human rights system, in the absence of similar mechanisms established specifically for refugees. This can only be done by building bridges and the process has begun, at least on the regional level. Thus, links have been forged – albeit indirect ones – with the European Convention of Human Rights, despite the absence in this instrument of any references to immigration law or asylum law.[7] In certain respects, it has also been done at the universal level, for example, through the Human Rights Committee which, in the process of examining country reports, has begun to address the question of asylum-seekers and illegal entrants, *inter alia*, in the context of Article 13 of the CCPR dealing with expulsion.

Finally, an international legal platform is being forged by the United Nations to ground action by the international community, as the contributions of Claire Palley and Richard Plender show. The problem of mass exodus and its root causes, and that of internal displacement, have found their way into the United Nations human rights and peace maintenance agendas. They have not only become a matter of international concern, which is a political concept, but have also been reflected in the links forged by the Security Council under Chapter VII of the Charter between threats to international peace and security, violations of human rights and humanitarian law, and state and individual responsibility. This has given the international community a broad platform for action, whether in the form of access to displaced persons, humanitarian assistance, internal protection of refugees in so-called "safe areas", or the inflicting of collective sanctions on recalcitrant states (although whether such action may be considered effective or not in policy terms is another matter).

*   *   *

The Colloquium was a means of discovering the extent to which juridical links can be established, whether directly or indirectly, by exploring areas of international law which are relevant to the refugee condition. It is with these issues in mind that the contributions in this book have been made, in an attempt to address questions that have become central to the debate on coerced movements of people.

This debate is initially set, in Part I, against the background of UNHCR field operations in Africa, Former Yugoslavia, and the States of the former Soviet Union, discussed by key UNHCR persons who speak from the vantage of their direct involvement and experience: Leonardo Franco, George Okoth-Obbo, Wilbert van Hövell and Michel Iogna-Prat.

---

[7]   See the case-law surrounding the application, *inter alia*, of Articles 3 and 8 of the European Convention on Human Rights: e.g., *Case of Cruz Varas and others v. Sweden*, ECHR, Judgment of 20 March 1991, Series A., vol. 201, and *Case of Vilvarajah and others v. the United Kingom*, ECHR, Judgement of 30 October 1991, Series A., Vol. 215.

The second part of the book is placed in an international law perspective. Václav Mikulka and Alain Pellet have analyzed one of the most difficult problems in the law of State succesion – that of the effect of a change of sovereignty upon the nationality of the inhabitants of the territories concerned – from the perspective of the potential creation of stateless persons and hence of refugee flows. They look in particular at the legal incidence of such changes on the obligations of successor States and on refugee status in receiving states.

Christian Tomuschat and Brigitte Stern have proposed how the traditional and emerging rules on state responsibility may be applied within the framework of the creation of refugee flows, analyzing the legal consequences of such responsibility both within the interstate and the human rights framework. They have also touched on the question of obligations owed to the international community as a whole.

Guy Goodwin-Gill and Kay Hailbronner have looked at the true meaning, legal status and scope of the right to leave as an aspect of the freedom of movement, as well as the right to return, and they have questioned the emerging concept developed in the practice of UNHCR, of a "right to remain".

Broadening the concept of "refugee" to one beyond exile, so as to encompass the notion of an individual without the protection of her/his home State, even in the absence of the crossing of an international border, Richard Plender and Ved Nanda have focussed on the internally displaced and explored the legal bases of action by the international community on their behalf.

Claire Palley places herself within the framework of institutionalized action by the international community, showing the inherent difficulties in reconciling, whether in terms of legal mandate or action in the field, the potential incompatibility between humanitarian concern and political action; the pursuit at one and the same time of a policy of humanitarian assistance dependent on impartiality, and one of coercive action dependent on the designation of a guilty party.

Finally, Virginia Leary in her concluding remarks gives the flavour of the discussion which ensued in which all the participants to the Colloquium took part, and synthesizes and reflects comments that would otherwise have gone unrecorded. George Abi-Saab's commentary on Claire Palley's paper considerably enriched this discussion.

The issues discussed in this book are part and parcel of a new focus on those problems of human rights law and other areas of international law that are directly linked to the creation of the refugee condition. However, whatever the conclusions on the merits or demerits of this broadening of the ambit of refugee law, international lawyers should keep in mind first the bearing of international relations on the subject, highlighted by Daniel Warner in his preface, and secondly the concluding words of the High Commissioner in her Keynote Address: whatever the gaps and uncertainties in the law, operational agencies have to continue their daily work in the field of surmounting the momentous practical obstacles which arise.

SADAKO OGATA

Keynote Address

I am very pleased to have the opportunity to address the Colloquium on the Problems of Refugees in the Light of Contemporary International Law Issues. I should like to congratulate the Graduate Institute of International Studies and its Director, Professor Swoboda, for bringing together such an eminent group of experts. At a time when each day witnesses a new surge in the number of people uprooted by persecution and violence, the opportunities for practitioners and scholars to meet and reflect together on the foundations of humanitarian action are indeed precious.

The Office of the United Nations High Commissioner for Refugees was created in 1951 to provide protection and assistance to refugees and to find solutions to their problem. At that time there were about one million refugees, mainly Europeans fleeing communist persecution. Today, there are over 20 million refugees, displaced and other persons of concern to UNHCR. From Burundi to Bosnia, Tajikistan to Tanzania, Rwanda to Russia, in some 110 countries across the globe UNHCR is helping refugees and displaced persons, responding to their emergency needs for food, shelter and health, or helping them to return home. Within the space of a few days, more than 200,000 people fled the massacres in Rwanda to seek refuge in one of the most remote areas of Tanzania. The human misery of the uprooted is as poignant today, their need for protection and assistance, for finding new homes or returning to old ones, are as real and urgent now as it was almost half a century ago, when my Office was first established.

The problems of refugees have not changed. But the refugee problem has. In so doing, it has challenged the basic assumptions underlying refugee law.

Within the universe of international law, what has become known as refugee law developed as a largely autonomous body of human rights law in order to protect the victims of persecution and generalized violence. At the same time, this development was made possible because of the inter-State dimension of the refugee problem, signified by the crossing of an international border. Refugee law thus lies at a confluence, which marks, on the one hand, concern for the individual and his most fundamental rights, and, on the other, concern for international peace and security, and harmonious relations between States.

V. Gowlland-Debbas (ed.), The Problem of Refugees in the Light of Contemporary International Law Issues, xix–xxiv.

UNHCR can give meaning to its mandate of international protection and solutions only to the extent that States themselves are willing to meet their responsibilities, either through the grant of asylum or through the creation of conditions conducive to voluntary repatriation.

Because of the strong political and ideological context in which refugee law was initially nurtured, it has tended in the past to downplay the responsibility of the country of origin. Its focus was primarily on victims after they crossed the border. The emphasis of the 1951 Convention, for instance, is on protection and integration of refugees in the countries of asylum, and it does not refer to their voluntary repatriation.

Today, that approach is neither adequate nor justifiable in the face of spiralling humanitarian emergencies. Indeed, as the Colloquium so rightly sets out to do, we must look beyond refugee law to broader issues of international law to find answers to some fundamental questions. What are the responsibilities inherent in Statehood which not only promote respect for the right to seek asylum, but also the right to return, and perhaps most significantly, the right to remain in one's home in safety? What are the responsibilities of the international community to meet humanitarian needs, not only across borders but also within them? How should the parameters be drawn, and content developed, so that international responsibility does not usurp State obligations but rather promotes the restoration of responsible Statehood?

I do not intend to provide the answers but rather to provoke you into debate and discussion. Let me stress however that, in discussing these questions, it is important to keep in mind the nature of today's humanitarian problem. The reality today is that despite the growing opportunities for voluntary repatriation, despite the return of more than 5 million refugees in recent years to Cambodia, Tajikistan, Ethiopia, South Africa, Mozambique and El Salvador, the prospects for solutions remain fragile. The conditions to which refugees are returning are far from ideal. They are often going back to uncertainty and instability, sometimes even open conflict, to villages which have been devasted, and homes which have been destroyed, with little hope of reconstruction or economic development. Even in Cambodia or central America, where there has been some progress towards reconciliation, peace remains fragile.

In such circumstances, returning refugees remain without effective national protection even after they have returned home. They may become internally displaced as a result of conflict, or be cut off from humanitarian assistance and international monitoring by moving front lines, as has happened to many of the 1.5 million Afghan returnees who have gone back to Afghanistan from Pakistan and Iran. Those who return in the midst of conflict and insecurity need to be protected and assisted. UNHCR considers it has a legitimate interest in their welfare until they have been reintegrated.

The other fact to note is that there are more refugees today than ever before, and possibly an even larger number of internally displaced persons in refugee-like conditions. The predominant cause is internal conflict and tensions. The end of Superpower control has rekindled ethnic, religious and tribal hatreds. It has revived many ancient feuds, often exacerbated by the problems of poverty, population pressures and environmental degradation. Resurgent nationalism is sowing seeds of strife among insecure minorities in some States, particularly in the former Soviet Union. "Ethnic cleansing" has become the new euphemism for persecution. Former Yugoslavia has provided a tragic and painful example of vicious war, torture, rape and murder to force one group of people to leave territory shared with another. Rwanda provided yet another example, as hundreds of thousands of men, women and children were ruthlessly massacred in 1994, simply because of their ethnic origin. In many other parts of the world, fundamental principles of international human rights and humanitarian law are being flouted with impunity, and violations have reached levels of brutality rarely known before.

Even refugees who believed they had found sanctuary in exile are finding themselves at risk when the country of asylum is itself engulfed in conflict, as is currently happening to the Somalis in Yemen and the Burundi refugees in Rwanda.

Equally compelling are the protection needs of the internally displaced, whose global numbers might well exceed that of refugees. Frequently, the internally displaced cannot obtain effective protection from their own government, either because it has lost control of part of its territory or because it perceives them as a threat. The plight of internally displaced persons in conflict is comparable to that of refugees. Yet, because they have not left their country, internally displaced persons cannot benefit from the mechanisms and instruments which have been developed for the international protection of refugees. What is needed is a combination of new approaches and mechanisms to improve implementation of existing humanitarian law and gradual development of new standards to meet the special needs of the internally displaced.

Although UNHCR does not have a general mandate for this group of persons, we have assisted in specific cases, at the request of the Secretary General, particularly when there is a link to an existing or potential refugee problem. For example, in Bosnia-Herzegovina, we are providing humanitarian assistance and protection to some 2.7 million persons who have been internally displaced or otherwise affected by the war. Our action on behalf of internally displaced persons has been encouraged and endorsed by the 48th session of the UN General Assembly, giving us a selective and limited mandate for this group of persons.

It is against this background of conflict, dissolution or decline of State power, crisis of States and emergence of sub-State actors, that I hope this Colloquium will examine the norms of international law which guide the prospects and parameters of international protection and assistance of refugees, returnees and internally displaced persons.

First and foremost, there is an urgent need to improve the implementation of existing principles of humanitarian law. The international community must examine the ways and means of strengthening respect for the provisions of the Geneva Conventions and Additional Protocols, which, if heeded, would go a long way towards reducing human suffering and uprooting of civilian populations. States have a primary and collective responsibility to redress this appalling situation. Their responsibility does not diminish as a result of their non-involvement in, or their remoteness from, a conflict. This responsability cannot be over-emphasized. It should also extend to non-State entities, as well as to States which have considerable influence, if not control, over them. No belligerent must be allowed to behave as if it were immune from the imperatives of humanity and exempt from national and international accountability. Aspirants to modern Statehood cannot expect international recognition while flouting the minimum norms on which the law of war is based. How can a people or its leadership seek admission to the community of civilized nations if its practices are nothing but a display of barbarity? The quest for national identity is not compatible with the exercise of unbounded hatred and mass felony.

Secondly, an international consensus should be developed around the notion of humanitarian access. The presence of UNHCR staff and other international organizations has been of critical importance in protecting and assisting refugees and displaced and affected populations in such places as northern Iraq, Bosnia-Herzegovina, Somalia, El-Salvador, Tajikistan, Sri Lanka and Cambodia. Such presence has usually been based on negotiation, improvisation and innovation. Although there is increasing acceptance of the value of international presence by all parties to a conflict, it is based on pragmatic and political considerations, rather than a legal framework.

One obstacle to agreement is the view of many governments that access to population on their territory is a fundamental question of national sovereignty. If sovereignty constrains the ability of the international community to reach refugees and displaced and other affected persons, so can the corollary decline of State power. This was precisely the problem faced in Somalia and now in Rwanda. The existing inter-State system is based on the concept of viable States. As countries break up into republics, and republics into territories ruled by warlords, who should bear responsibility for the protection of peoples, particularly of civilians? What are the international legal norms to deal with situations where the State is in crisis? How can we bring some order, without which responsible humanitarian action is paralysed?

Increasing international attention to the issue has focussed around the debate on humanitarian intervention and the use of military force for humanitarian purposes. On 5 April 1991, the UN Security Council adopted Resolution 688, linking for the first time human rights violations to threats to international peace and security. In Bosnia, Somalia and now Rwanda, the Security Council has gone even further, justifying the deployment of military troops for humanitarian purposes.

There is clearly an effort to find a balance between sovereign rights and individual needs, as well as between principle and practice. General Assembly

Resolution 46/182 of 19 December 1991 allows humanitarian assistance to be provided with "the consent of the affected country", rather than at its request. Humanitarian law and human rights provisions create a strong presumption in support of such a principle when civilian lives are in danger. During the course of recent years creative humanitarian strategies have indeed succeeded in building some practice.

A concept of humanitarian access should serve to affirm two complementary principles: that a claim to sovereignty implies certain unavoidable humanitarian obligations; and that there exists a collective duty of the international community to assist people in distress. By prohibiting interference with neutral and impartial humanitarian action, a commitment to humanitarian access would emphasize that, in the final analysis, State sovereignty is to be judged by its responsible, that is humane, exercise.

Thirdly, the responsibility of a State towards its own citizens should be stressed. It is through such responsibility that solutions to refugee problems can be found, because inherent in that concept is the notion of restoration of national protection. UNHCR's responsibility towards returning refugees should end when the state of displacement has ended. Yet, in some situations, as in Tajikistan, there is a risk that the need for international protection, or at least monitoring of human rights, will persist even after the returnees have been materially integrated in their communities. How can the international community help States to resume their responsibility? It may be necessary for the international community, though not necessarily UNHCR, to undertake a whole range of activities aimed at fostering national reconstruction, healing inter-communal wounds, and building democratic institutions and human rights protection mechanisms. The challenge is to translate the rhetoric of human rights into practical measures, to establish more representative and responsible forms of government, which respect human rights and adequately protect minorities. How do we promote tolerance for diversity? How do we control abuse of State power? How do we foster responsibility as well as accountability of States as regards the treatment of their own citizens? These are not easy tasks.

In conclusion, let me say that as international concern for human rights expands, on the one hand, and the nature of States changes on the other, the challenge will be to strike a balance between individual and collective responsibilities of States. The role of the international community, including UNHCR, is two-fold: on the one hand, to devise more effective means to address humanitarian needs, and on the other, to recognize, emphasize and encourage the responsibility of States for their own citizens.

The unfolding tragedy in Rwanda has starkly exposed the failure of State responsibility as well as the limits of international responsibility. Whatever the gaps in law or the uncertainties on interpretation and application, operational agencies such as mine must continue to work, in a practical and pragmatic manner, to address urgent protection and assistance needs of the victims. I hope that our action on the ground, and its endorsement by the international community, will contribute to the work of legal experts and scholars as they seek to develop legal norms and establish new standards for addressing the protection of uprooted populations and solutions to their plight. I see this Colloquium as an important expression of that dynamic and most crucial relationship. I wish you a lively and fruitful discussion.

PART I

UNHCR Perspective

LEONARDO FRANCO

Legal Issues Arising from Recent UNHCR Operations: Introduction*

The Office of the United Nations High Commissioner for Refugees (UNHCR) has been charged with the functions of providing international protection to refugees, under the auspices of the United Nations, and of seeking solutions to refugee problems. These functions include ensuring, with and through governments, the legal and practical protection of refugees, mobilizing and coordinating the deployment of the resources required to ensure their survival and well-being, and promoting conditions in countries of origin that will be conducive to the ideal solution of voluntary repatriation and help prevent further refugee problems.

There are over 20 million refugees throughout the world today, and the refugee problem continues to grow in size and complexity. The situations addressed by the Office in performing its functions during these past years have all too frequently involved irreparable human suffering and loss of life. In the centre of Africa, sudden and massive new refugee flows fuelled by murderous ethnic and political conflict have overwhelmed the reception capacity of neighbouring countries and outpaced the capacity of the international community to respond effectively and in time. As with Bosnia and Somalia, the situation in Rwanda demonstrates the limits of humanitarian action in the midst of conflict, as well as the great cost in human misery that can result when early warning is not followed by timely action to avert or contain the outbreak of violence.

In other parts of the world, as well as in Africa, longstanding refugee situations persist despite international efforts to resolve the conflicts that were at their source and which continue to impede solutions. The ongoing conflict in former Yugoslavia has led to the largest refugee crisis in Europe since the Second World War, displacing more than 2.5 million people and threatening many more who remain trapped inside conflict areas. UNHCR has provided material assistance to refugees and, at the request of the Secretary-General, to internally displaced persons in the former Yugoslavia since

* The views expressed in this and the following contributions are of a personal nature and do not necessarily represent the official position of UNHCR.

V. Gowlland-Debbas (ed.), The Problem of Refugees in the Light of Contemporary International Law Issues, 3–6.
© 1996 *Kluwer Academic Publishers. Printed in the Netherlands.*

November 1991. Extremely dangerous security conditions have been a major constraint in aid deliveries in Bosnia-Herzegovina. The extent of UNHCR's future involvement in the region is dependent upon political and military developments. With the ongoing peace initiatives, a consolidation of the cease-fires and return to normalization, the formulation of preliminary plans for rehabilitation and recovery has commenced. Conditions in Bosnia-Herzegovina are, however, not yet conducive to the promotion and implementation of large-scale voluntary repatriation.

UNHCR is also carefully monitoring potential disruptive developments in regions where its involvement is recent, and its implantation still modest. In the newly independent States of the former Soviet Union, UNHCR is primarily guided by an effort to engage in preventive actions as the most effective long-term activity, taking into account the specific situation of each country. Its activities in Armenia, Georgia, Russia, Azerbaijan and Tajikistan aim to provide humanitarian assistance where needed, while, wherever possible, seeking solutions to the conflict. Timely interventions to effect negotiations have helped contain conflict which might otherwise spread regionally, and pave the way for voluntary return to home areas.

The distinguishing feature of all refugees is the lack of national protection of their fundamental rights and freedoms, which creates a need for international protection in order to secure the enjoyment of those rights. The vulnerabilities and needs of refugees are vast and various in scope, ranging from the need for personal security and means of subsistence, through legal status and respect for fundamental human rights, to finding durable solutions to their plight. Whilst the needs and corresponding content of international protection vary according to the circumstances, the universal and paramount objectives of international protection, as contained in the fundamental refugee instruments, are admission to a country of refuge, security from forcible return and respect for basic human rights without discrimination.

The 1951 Convention and 1967 Protocol relating to the Status of Refugees provide the legal framework for the international protection of refugees. Due to their universal character, their provisions are the standard against which any measures for the protection of refugees must be judged. The 1969 Organization of African Unity (OAU) Convention Governing the Specific Aspects of Refugee Problems in Africa, the 1984 Cartagena Declaration on Refugees and other regional instruments reaffirmed the irreplaceable value of asylum for refugees and broadened the refugee definition to meet the needs of asylum seekers in the regions in which they are applied.

The papers presented hereafter (all three written in May 1994) examine the challenges of protection amid the dynamics of changing political economic and social realities. The continuation and intensification of old conflicts, the violent outbreak of new clashes and the ongoing global recession have placed formidable demands on the High Commissioner's office. Each of the papers represents an example of UNHCR's implementation of the various tools of protection available to it in order to meet the particular needs of the region concerned. The traditional tools of protection range from legal and diplomatic, to material and practical, requiring international presence and access to refugees in the field. Other tools include: resettlement to third countries or return home when remaining in the country of refuge is not possible; public information and training to promote understanding; information on countries of origin to ensure that refugees are identified; and dissemination programs on the needs of refugees, including those of particularly vulnerable groups such as women and children.

Given the complexities of UNHCR's task in providing international protection, one of the major issues confronting the Office is the adequacy of the available tools of protection, in particular the legal tools. The papers point to examples of the strengths and limitations of international legal instruments to cover those in need of protection, and suggest how they could be improved.

In Africa, for example, the instruments have adequately covered situations of mass influx caused by armed conflict as they have, for the most part, been applied in the generous spirit in which their provisions were conceived. In some European countries, on the other hand, restrictive interpretations of the 1951 Convention by States and inconsistencies in interpretation have led to the exclusion of persons in need of international protection, including many refugees fleeing the massive violations of human rights involved in internal conflict. Whilst in practice States have offered some form of protection to victims in such circumstances, at times the protection offered has been inconsistent and subject to the goodwill of States.

The gaps in legal protection afforded to all categories of refugees under the principal instruments have necessitated efforts to broaden the scope of international protection, involving broadening of the mandate of the High Commissioner, reliance on regional instruments and ad hoc arrangements. Resort must also increasingly be had to international law instruments and mechanisms not specifically designed for the protection of refugees and displaced persons.

In parts of Africa, and most ostensibly in former Yugoslavia, armed conflict dictated the need for UNHCR to provide protection and assistance in a situation of armed conflict. This has presented the need to develop new tools of protection. Measures taken by UNHCR to meet this need, include: humanitarian diplomacy; closer coordination with political and military organs of the UN in peace operations; increased cooperation with human rights machinery; and military protection of humanitarian assistance. Protection activities within countries of origin have proved essential to containing future refugee flows and encouraging voluntary repatriation, without prejudice to the fundamental right to seek and enjoy asylum in other countries. This has resulted in UNHCR's direct involvement in providing protection to persons in need of such protection within the territory of the former Yugoslavia, including returning refugees, internally displaced persons, members of the local population who are at risk, and stateless persons.

The international protection functions performed by international organizations such as UNHCR cannot, however, provide an adequate substitute for the protection which should be accorded by States to their citizens and other persons on their territory. One of the principal goals of UNHCR's prevention strategies is to ensure that States fulfill their obligation to provide national protection. To this end, in the newly independent States, UNHCR has actively promoted nationality laws that do not marginalize or exclude individuals who might otherwise become stateless and therefore vulnerable to abuses. UNHCR considers that by assisting countries to draft and implement generous citizenship and nationality laws, the destabilizing effect of large numbers of stateless persons in the country may be avoided, thereby preventing future refugee flows.

In its broadest sense, international protection implies complex and collaborative efforts of the international community as a whole. The strategies required to ensure a global approach to admission and granting of asylum, together with activities in countries of origin which will prevent refugee flows and permit solutions to refugee problems, require comprehensive and far-ranging action. In keeping with its mandate and in a spirit of cooperation with other international organizations, concerned governments and NGO's, UNHCR will continue to strive to develop innovative and effective responses to the needs of all those requiring international protection.

GEORGE OKOTH-OBBO

Coping with a Complex Refugee Crisis in Africa: Issues, Problems and Constraints for Refugee and International Law*

INTRODUCTION

In Africa, the activities and operations of UNHCR have not, with a few exceptions, differed in nature and character from what the organization has undertaken before, namely, to provide protection and assistance to refugees and to promote durable solutions.

The Office has, however, encountered principal and important challenges to the way in which it carries out these responsibilities. For purposes of these notes, at least four sources of such challenges may be mentioned. The first is that the *context* for the discharge of the mandate and operations of the Office has changed dramatically as summarized in the paragraphs which follow. Secondly, a plethora of other humanitarian needs, not necessarily of a refugee nature, are increasingly being juxtaposed to the mandate, responsibilities and activities of the Office. Thirdly, a clear shift in the political and policy outlook towards the refugee problem can be discerned throughout the continent, most particularly in the attitude of States. Finally, and related to the preceding point, difficulties in achieving solutions, particularly for long-standing refugee caseloads, are more and more coming to the fore of the preoccupations of UNHCR, States and the refugees themselves.

These factors have been viewed by some as pointing to gaps or inadequacies in the regime of law which provides the framework and basis for the protection of refugees and for UNHCR's activities. At any rate, they have necessitated at least some sophistication in the policies, approaches, strategies and operations of the Office in discharging its mandate in Africa. Nevertheless, it is the view of this paper that the complexities arising from an admittedly expanding and increasingly more complex humanitarian crisis do not necessarily reflect an inadequacy of either *refugee law* as such, or the mandate of UNHCR, when seen from the perspective of the *need* for and delivery of international protection.

* The views expressed in this paper are personal to the author and do not necessarily represent the official position of the United Nations High Commissioner for Refugees.

V. Gowlland-Debbas (ed.), The Problem of Refugees in the Light of Contemporary International Law Issues, 7–17.
© 1996 *Kluwer Academic Publishers. Printed in the Netherlands.*

THE NEW CHALLENGES, CONSTRAINTS AND COMPLEXITIES

The humanitarian crises associated with the upheavals in Somalia, Liberia and Rwanda typify some of the examples which have driven calls to "rethink" "traditional" legal regimes, mandates and approaches. In these situations, an almost comprehensive breakdown of any semblance of civic society has occurred. Most particularly, the state structure has disintegrated and the system of national law and order lies in ruins. An effective national, political and executive authority does not exist any more. Instead, a motley crew of "liberation movements", armed bands, warlords or chieftaincies, militias and, often, plain thugs, compete violently with each other on differentiated levels of ability, ideology and objectives.

In all these cases, national protection, most particularly the ability to guarantee the personal physical protection of the national population, has failed or is not viable and a state of anarchy will usually have replaced that of normalcy. *Material* safety will also be unachievable as the political, social and economic activities and institutions necessary to sustain populations on both a personal and national level will also, respectively, be impossible to carry out or are heaped in ruin. Thus, in a situation such as that which prevails in Rwanda, where it is generally feared that the loss of lives is taking place on a genocidal scale, *displacement*, whether internal or external, is but only one of the indicators of the comprehensive destruction and crisis which engulfs the whole society. Flight to another territory and to another authority capable of ensuring safety often becomes the only way to ensure survival, both physical and material.

Turning to the point about other needs, in several African countries, a certain amount of political and structural normalcy exists alongside a serious dysfunction in some of the other major institutions or sectors of society, particularly the social and economic. Whereas this crisis may not necessarily compromise the legal and physical protection of populations, it will usually jeopardize their *material* and *social* security at a most basic human level. In many countries, this crisis of poverty is manifested by the inability of populations to have access to food, public health facilities, or communal and social services such as education. More and more of the national population thus starts to increasingly exhibit material needs similar to those of groups, such as refugees or returnees, that benefit from international humanitarian assistance in a systematic and institutionalized way. From the point of view of UNHCR, which is mandated to protect and assist refugees and returnees, this is referred to as the "mix-factor".

With respect to the changing political and policy outlook towards refugees, several factors may be considered. The typically massive and sudden refugee flows which occur in Africa, caused by violent civil strife and the disintegration of societies, are increasingly accompanied by – or considered to contribute to – serious security problems in the host countries. Among the principal reasons for this is the preponderance of dangerous weapons which are brought into the refugee-hosting communities as displacement takes place. Furthermore, as the continent experiences the slackening of authoritarian government control over most aspects of national affairs, there is more frequent and overt competition between refugees and nationals over such matters as land, grazing ranges, water, fuel wood and education and public health facilities. Similarly, as more and more countries are gripped by open, adversarial politics, suspicions develop that refugees may be unscrupulously manipulated to illegally participate in, and thereby influence, the result of elections, referenda or constitutional votes in favour of one or another party. Additionally, amid the particularly desperate economic performance of African nations in the post Cold War economic "order", there is more and more consciousness by asylum states and their populations of the economic and resource burdens of hosting large numbers of refugees. All these factors contribute to an increase in the *politicization* of the refugee issue.

As far as intractable refugee problems are concerned, the Rwandan refugee situation demonstrates the challenges and indeed hazards of the inability to find solutions to refugees in an expeditious and effective way. Along with other constraints on the achievement of solutions which are considered later in this paper, the longer a refugee situation continues to defy solutions, the more likely the prospect that it will ultimately unravel in a very chaotic and uncontrollable manner.

What are the implications for refugee policy, law and practice of all the aforementioned factors?

THE REAFFIRMATION OF THE FUNDAMENTALLY IMPORTANT ROLE OF REFUGEE LAW AND PROTECTION

As the carnage taking place in Rwanda illustrates, the ability to seek and obtain the physical and material safety of another authority, and particularly another state, is often the only real option available to populations caught in many of the ethnic, political and other upheavals taking place in Africa, to ensure their survival and safety. Philosophically, it is, of course, a truism that, in all such cases, it is far more effective to prevent the "root causes" of the upheavals and, as a result, refugee flows, before they occur or attenuate them after they have begun. However, as long as a refugee flow is in progress, the opportunity for such interventions has long passed and, in any case, such measures in practice do not, for a host of reasons, appear to be feasible.

In this sense, it is submitted that the substitute protection of another community, of the UNHCR and the whole regime of international refugee law, are positioned precisely where national protection and prevention have failed, or are not possible or feasible, and people have been forced to seek refuge elsewhere. In this precise, strict way of viewing refugee law and the mandate of the UNHCR, it is clear that both were intended to serve a likewise *very strict* and *precisely defined* need. In other words, the legal lineaments ·

of the "refugee problem" as viewed from this vantage point are quite different from those of the "refugee problem" as viewed in broad, political terms. It is submitted that the gamut of multifarious and varied tasks involved in responding to, let alone resolving, the refugee problem in this latter sense were never envisaged in the purposes of refugee law, the system of international protection and the institution of asylum. The reality is that their material scope is in any case far short of the tasks of tackling and preventing the root causes of refugee flows.

It is indeed this combination of empirical and philosophical observations which jurisprudentially counterpoise asylum and international protection on one hand and notions of prevention and in-country protection on the other. Most particularly, for an organization such as UNHCR, it becomes extremely delicate to articulate and embrace both concepts within a seamless, undifferentiated frame of "new approaches" to the "refugee problem". Even more delicate would be the appearance that within this policy and legal matrix, the two concepts are assimilated or that one (prevention) is considered to provide a greater and better capacity to solve refugee problems than the other (asylum). For some of the reasons mentioned earlier, such a conjoinment becomes particularly attractive to states as a rationale validating a shift away from the obligations of asylum, to concepts of "prevention" whose articulation and definition has to date not attained the clarity and concreteness that would justify this substitution as a materially functional solution to refugee problems or, in particular, protection requirements. A historically well-established and essentially functional facility is thus eroded without being replaced by any which compares in definition or effectiveness.

Asylum, refugee law, and international protection and the mandate of UNHCR are thus very *specific* and unique tools available to the international community to respond to likewise very specific and only limited aspects of humanitarian emergencies such as the Rwandese refugee crisis, that is, the refugee aspect. The failure, in legal, institutional and operational terms, of the international system to respond to *other* aspects of the crisis, including the political, military and humanitarian, thereby does not translate into an inadequacy of these specific tools, although, of course, they may be critiqued vis-à-vis their specific functions. This point, that is, the need to define precisely and to understand the scope and limits of the respective legal regimes and international institutions, is a point upon which insistence is not misplaced. It is only in this way that the real gaps, legal, institutional and operational, can be properly understood and be addressed effectively for purposes of dealing with the 'refugee problem' in its broader, political sense. More particularly, the critique now weighted strongly against asylum and refugee law would hopefully find more legitimate targets in other fields of application.

With these considerations in mind, I consider it to be fundamental for legal scholars and practitioners in the refugee area to reaffirm the importance of asylum, refugee protection and refugee law. Of course, such a re-affirmation does not, and should not, invalidate initiatives to deal with all other aspects of the humanitarian emergencies of today, not necessarily or directly implicating refugee law properly so-called. In particular, it is crucial to guarantee that persons seeking safety as refugees on the territory of another State are admitted into such territory, protected from forcible return to danger, and treated in line with the relevant standards. This reaffirmation is particularly urgent and essential because:

(i)   for political and other reasons, states are seeking all kinds of legal and other polemical rationalizations to weaken the institution of asylum and refugee protection;

(ii) in Africa in particular, without this reaffirmation, the political, security and socioeconomic tensions described in paragraph 7 above would tend to seriously compromise asylum and refugee protection policy;

(iii) above all, no real substitutes, including those that are, or appear to be, frequently counterposed to asylum and refugee protection such as prevention, human rights monitoring, in-country protection, humanitarian intervention, etc. have been demonstrated to be *implementable* in a way that would in practical terms either remove the factors compelling the search for safety elsewhere or at least provide such safety and protection within a national context so as to meet squarely the need(s) for protection.

The very strict way in which refugee law and the need for international protection have been viewed here mean that we do not readily accept as correct the terms of the critique of refugee law that is currently in vogue. This critique often points to the "shortcomings" of "traditional" refugee law in that it is "centered too much on the obligations of the asylum state", that it has "no concern with the situation in the country of origin" or on the responsibilities of that State.

It is doubtful if some of these observations are legally tenable, the main point being that not all these questions needed to be disposed of within the scope of refugee law. Moreover, the specific principles which may be elicited in other spheres of human rights and international law would further expose the narrowness of such critiques. The core of the approach taken in this paper, is that refugee law *must* necessarily be "exilic". It must emphasize the obligations of an asylum state and the international community as it is the *failure* of any effective protection in the country of origin that kicks it into gear. It must emphasize protection and security from forcible return to danger. In view of the circumstances outlined earlier, these are *not* the weaknesses, but the very *strengths*, of refugee law, the system of international protection and the mandate of UNHCR.

It is, nevertheless, clear that the institutions of asylum and refugee protection are under tremendous strain, particularly given the political and ideological shifts in the perception of the "refugee problem" that have followed the end of the Cold War. It is also clear, therefore, that the reaffirmation of asylum and refugee protection cannot be merely a rhetorical exercise. The several other measures which need to underpin and complement this exercise could not possibly all be described here. However, on a point of legal theory, it is considered that the current trend of employing the magnitude or character of the refugee problem, its problems, burdens and other legal notions such as state responsibility, to calibrate on a unilateral basis the nature and extent of a state's obligations under refugee law is legally incorrect. Both the political and legal solutions of the problems given rise to by these properly lie, in my view, in the concepts of international solidarity and burden-sharing on which the solution of refugee problems has historically been predicated. These are two areas to which attention may need increasingly to be paid, with a view to expanding and articulating the way in which the concepts can be used to solidify asylum, refugee protection and solutions. At the same time, of course, attention needs to continue to be paid to the other legal, political, economic and military fields relevant to the "refugee problem" as understood in its broader, more global and political sense. Clearly, an interface exists between all these fields. However, and not to belabour the point, there can be no question that the province of refugee law and refugee protection is itself not the ultimate crossroad, but only one of the grids, in a much larger and more complex mosaic.

APPLICATION OF LEGAL NORMS VERSUS INABILITY TO OPERATE

In discussions concerning operations by international organizations in "complex emergency situations", the application or not of legal norms, their nature and scope, the mandates of the various organizations and other questions of an incremental nature tend to predominate. The ongoing situation in Rwanda, however, also illustrates that such questions are not nearly as important as the *ability to operate*, even by organizations or entities which otherwise have a clear legal obligation to act.

In the case of UNHCR, it has been impossible, at one point or another, to gain *access* to *refugees or returnees* in Rwanda, Burundi, Somalia and Liberia, and to be able to discharge legal and assistance responsibilities which in themselves are fairly clear and well-known. But this essentially non-legal constraint nevertheless throws forth several important practical and notional factors as far as the international system of protection is concerned.

First of all, the protection which UNHCR can offer is premised on the existence of basic conditions of civic stability, law and order. Conditions of war, conflict and the kind of insecurity which has been witnessed in Rwanda compromise, indeed make impossible, the ability of UNHCR to operate. Moreover, even if it were able to operate, it is not clear if the kind of protection UNHCR could offer would be effective to meet the safety requirements of the populations at risk. The other way of making this point is to consider whether the tools, experience, methodologies, expertise and personnel which UNHCR possesses are geared to responding to such needs. At the most, they could do so with only the greatest difficulties.

Secondly, in situations such as these, an entire population, or substantial cross-sections of it, within a given situation, geographical area, ethnic grouping, etc. are in need either of protection or humanitarian assistance,or both. This fact underscores the shortcomings of the formulaistic approach of international humanitarian law which, in defining needs, relies on category-based parameters (refugees, civilian victims of war, etc.) and the attribution of organizational responsibilities on a mandate basis likewise governed by such categorizations.

In purely *legal* terms, there may be various ways to redress these shortcomings, including, possibly, by juxtaposing and rationalizing all legal regimes and mandates into a systematic and consistent "collectivity" addressing the full range of needs and responsibilities at all the different levels. Most particularly, this would imply the interaction of human rights law in general, nationality, minorities and self-determination laws, the humanitarian law of armed conflicts, refugee law, the law of international peace and order, what may be grouped together as the law of a fair economic and development order, as well as the way in which all these norms are expressed within a specific domestic legal and political order.

On the abovementioned interface, an obvious chasm may be noted in the way the "refugee problem" is viewed today. Whereas much has been done to underline the connection of human rights and political and governance issues to displacement questions and solutions, (i.e. essentially domestic-based questions) there is not as much readiness to recognize the role of economic factors, and, most particularly, the implications of an extremely unjust international economic system. Yet, few would deny that in Africa today, social and economic considerations, particularly the lack of progress and a state of general poverty and decline, occupy an important place in the conflicts, human rights abuses and social disintegration being witnessed on this continent.

In *practical* terms, we would suggest that the utilization of *typologies* for *each situation* could also be considered as the more feasible and useful approach to the issue under discussion in this part of the paper. By this approach, problems and needs would be identified specifically and the necessary responses determined accordingly, including the question of which particular legal principles are at stake, the measures that need to be taken and which organization would be best qualified to undertake the necessary actions. Needless to say, such a system would need a certain amount of standing rationality and predictability to avoid being entirely *ad hoc* and disorganized.

The ways to achieve this rationality and predictably, particularly as far as the United Nations system is concerned, are not considered in this paper.

INTERNALLY DISPLACED PERSONS (IDPs)

The limitations of the categorical approach mentioned above are quite clear in the current approach to the question of IDPs. The emphasis in this approach is on *displacement* and on *locus*, i.e. the fact that populations are displaced within national borders, and it is these elements which create the need for protection or assistance, or both.

While, indeed, these facts will often suffice in certain situations as the sole indicators of needs and problems, the Rwandan and Somali situations illustrate the need for more sophistication in aggregating the nature and extent of the protection and assistance needs that might exist under specific circumstances. In situations of conflict and strife, populations are often threatened as a result of a complex interplay of several factors (including ethnic grouping, age, political affiliation, socio-economic standing, etc.) which places them in a *situation* of danger or need as opposed merely to being in a specific *location* or being in danger or need as a result only of being in such a specific location. Moreover, under certain conditions,particularly those approximating anarchy, all populations, whether displaced or not, may be placed in jeopardy, and persons displaced elsewhere may indeed by that fact alone be in a relatively more secure situation. This concrete, *situational* approach could then perhaps be used to develop certain general legal and assistance typologies in which displacement may or may not be only one of the factors. (It is conceded, of course, that under certain circumstances, safety and basic necessities may indeed be guaranteed but the problem of displacement, per se, remains. In other words, the concern in this situation would relate to the need to find solutions which may include return to former places of residence, local settlement, relocation, etc.).

The methodological approach argued in the preceding paragraph would, as indicated earlier, have the advantage of bringing into much clearer focus the nature and scope of protection that the concerned populations, including internally displaced persons, would require and from what source, and by what methodologies, such protection could be expected to be delivered. As far as internally displaced persons, as defined, for example, in the initiatives undertaken by the Special Representative of the United Nations Secretary-General, Dr. Francis Deng, are concerned, it is not clear, as said earlier, that the type of protection provided by UNHCR would be relevant as an effective measure to ensure safety or, conversely, that an organization such as UNHCR would, using its mandate, tools, expertise and staff, be able to provide effectively the protection called for.

As has been remarked, the kind of protection that UNHCR can provide is primarily of a diplomatic nature and assumes the existence of basic conditions of civic law and order, authority and continuity. While, clearly, even under conditions of conflict UNHCR would be able to provide specific diplomatic, legal and material services that would benefit both refugees and other populations caught in such a situation, the dramatic situations of the Rwanda, Somalia and Liberia type are probably beyond even the best efforts UNHCR would be able to offer so as to ensure safety in real terms.

The fundamental challenge in such a situation is to stop the massacres and the killings, in other words to re-establish conditions of law and order.

While this task may be framed in legal nomenclature somewhat euphemistically as "ensuring or promoting the observance of human rights, or humanitarian law", in practice, measures of enforcement, of disarmament, of separation of warring forces and, indeed, often, of combat, may be called for. These tasks, of course, cannot be performed by UNHCR. Moreover, until such conditions are created, UNHCR, and indeed many other humanitarian organizations, would be able to operate only with maximum difficulty and minimum effectiveness.

For international law and scholarship, it is in this area, of re-establishing *law and order*, (that is, the restoration of the ability to extend, within a specific national formation, national protection) and particularly its enforcement in an effective manner, which to my mind is a particularly important subject for further thought. Presently, the challenges and indeed weaknesses of this "system" are being demonstrated in a dramatic and particularly sad way in Rwanda. Whether these challenges and weaknesses arise essentially from the present state of the international *legal* regime may not be quite evident to those of us who are not specialized in the area. Few would deny, however, that the political will of States to act, and to act with measures that go effectively to the heart of the causes, have as much, if not more, to do with the problem. Nevertheless, if legal elucidation can contribute to the elaboration of imperatives that will countervail this lack of will, and organize the system of response to disasters such as Rwanda in a systematic, predictable way, the effort will have been worth it.

THE MIX-FACTOR: THE CROSS-MANDATE APPROACH IN THE HORN OF AFRICA

To respond to the "mix-factor" mentioned earlier, UNHCR has developed the cross-mandate approach for its operations in the Horn of Africa. In simple terms, this means that the relevant government, UN system agencies and NGOs active in the humanitarian field would pool their respective administrative, human, financial and material resources to meet the humanitarian and development needs of all needy populations within a given area in which (as far as UNHCR is concerned) refugees or returnees may be. It is an approach that relies extensively on effective local integration to promote stability and self-reliance among the needy populations.

A detailed study of the cross-mandate approach has, to date, not been undertaken. Nevertheless, the Office has been aware of several issues and difficulties which arise from the concept including among others,those to do with the challenges of inter-agency cooperation and coordination, the lack of a focalized action-forcing and decision-making system, the fact that agency systems (administrative, budgetary and management) are in reality not pooled, and the lack of clear entry and exit criteria.

From a legal point of view, the relevant issues may be elicited in the following series of questions:

(i)   In general terms, how is UNHCR to continue to discharge its protec-
       tion mandate where the legal distinctions have been abandoned (general
       human rights monitoring?);
(ii)   Are the distinctions abandoned only for assistance purposes but not for
       protection? If so, what mechanisms shall be utilized for purposes of
       the protection requirements where populations are indistinguishably inter-
       mingled?
(iii) Is local integration in the cross-mandate approach only a programme
       or also a legal notion? If so, what is the legal status of refugees under
       the cross-mandate approach (quasi-nationals?);
(iv)   If refugee status continues under the cross-mandate approach, how is it
       brought to an end? If new asylum-seekers arrive, is refugee status deter-
       mination nevertheless an important consideration?
(v)   What are the legal arrangements for access to, settlement on and
       utilization of land?
(vi)   Is there a recognition of "acquired rights" for purposes of acquisition
       of citizenship or property rights such as land?
These and other questions are the subject of an ongoing review of the cross-
mandate approach.

VOLUNTARY REPATRIATION

While, philosophically, voluntary repatriation continues to be considered as
the best solution for refugees, in at least some situations its feasibility is
more and more questionable. Four cases may be considered.

The case of Rwanda mentioned in the introduction to these notes represents the first problem area. For several years, the Rwandan government's
official position concerning refugees from that country was that any possible
solution for them would not include return from exile. As is known, among
other factors, the failure by the refugees to exercise authorized return resulted
in several attempts to return by forcible means which culminated in the invasion
of Rwanda by Rwandese exilees in October 1991.

Although the refugees continued to insist on their *right* to return to their
country of origin, the implications of this policy for them was made particularly serious by the fact that no country of asylum was willing to embark on
a massive exercise of granting citizenship as a way of solving their problem.
In other words, the policy of their country of origin, seen in combination
with attitudes in the countries of asylum meant that, in effect, they had been
condemned to permanent exile.

A related constraint concerns the significant political, ethnic and even
geographical reordering of countries or communities of origin in such a way
that refugees could not possibly return even if they earnestly yearned to do
so. In these cases the refugees may not have a country or even a place to return
to; certainly they would not, even if they were able to return to a place, be

returning to the same historical, cultural and social situation as that prior to their seeking exile. As is known, these associations are quite important in practical and emotional terms for the effectiveness of return as a durable solution.

Thirdly, the destruction, decline and decay that may have been suffered by the communities of origin or of potential return mean that dignified return would require a massive investment in recovery and rehabilitation. Conversely, if persons are returned without assuring the means of sustainability, relief assistance would have to be continued to ensure that they have not merely been translocated from one situation of emergency to another, possibly worse, one.

Finally, in many societies, while the original source of persecution (for example a state authority) or of danger (such as a situation of war or conflict) may have changed, return in safety may not be possible, as in the case of Angola and North-West Somalia, because of a high preponderance of land mines and other unexploded munitions.

In all these cases, a gap exists between the formal legal criteria for repatriation and the regime of obligations which would ensure the most optimal conditions to realize a right to return to one's country, and to do so in conditions of both material and physical security. In what legal situation are refugees placed if, because of a fundamental political, ethnic or regional restructuring, an effective country or place of return no longer exists? What are the principles of law that then apply in terms of a lost or forcibly attributed nationality? What principles shall apply and how is the international community to approach solutions for these refugees? What obligations, if any, accrue upon the international community to provide resources for and support the re-creation, recovery or rehabilitation of a country or area of return? What is the legal threshold for such an obligation, if it does exist? Is a country entitled, as the Eritrean authorities in effect did between 1991 and 1993, to both demand the fulfilment of such an obligation and make it the condition for the return of refugees? Who has the responsibility to ensure mine clearance and eradication? Where in the legal doctrine relating to voluntary repatriation does this problem fit and with what consequences? Finally, in what way does the international law of armed conflict connect to the aspects of refugee law governing repatriation in these situations?

This paper has not included an attempt to answer these questions. They are however of fundamental importance to the whole area of solutions for refugees, and presently dominate the academic and policy thinking of UNHCR, as well as the practical reality on the ground. The resolution of these questions, one way or another, will, without a doubt, be decisive to how far refugee repatriation continues to be the "best and most feasible solution for refugee problems" in Africa. Refugee and general international law may contribute to this process by elucidating the applicable legal principles, rights and obligations.

WILBERT VAN HÖVELL

Issues Arising from the UNHCR Operation in Former Yugoslavia

INTRODUCTION

In November 1991, the then Secretary-General of the United Nations, Mr. Perez de Cuellar, asked the United Nations High Commissioner for Refugees to assist the displaced persons in the Socialist Federal Republic of Yugoslavia. At that time it was difficult to foresee that in May 1994 UNHCR would be coordinating international relief efforts in favour of 4.2 million persons in the five States which emerged from the former Yugoslavia. This became one of the most complex operations ever conducted by UNHCR. To date it continues to be essentially an emergency operation, in the absence of a peaceful settlement of the conflicts in Croatia and Bosnia-Herzegovina. In the latter country, since June 1992 (UN Security Council Resolution 758) a sizeable United Nations military presence has been built, through different stages, around the UNHCR – led humanitarian operation, first to protect the delivery of aid and later also to protect six designated "safe areas". The cooperation with the military brought new challenges to both UNHCR and the military. Rather than explaining the nuts and bolts, and kilos and metric tonnes of assistance through food, shelter, health and community services, the following paragraphs aim to give an impression of some of the issues arising from UNHCR's activities in former Yugoslavia.

UNHCR's MANDATE

A striking feature of the operation has been the flexibility of UNHCR's mandate. The Office is currently coordinating, and to a considerable extent, implementing the international relief effort for some 700,000 refugees and 1.6 million internally displaced persons (of whom 1.3 million are in Bosnia and 0.35 million in Croatia, including the United Nations Protected Areas). But it is also providing assistance to ensure the survival of the entire civilian population of besieged cities such as Sarajevo and Gorazde; it is assisting 325,000 destitute and socially vulnerable citizens of regional countries of

19

V. Gowlland-Debbas (ed.), The Problem of Refugees in the Light of Contemporary International Law Issues, 19–24.

asylum (including 120,000 persons in Serbia who are particularly vulnerable to international sanctions); and finally, it is trying to assist and monitor the human rights of minority populations at risk in many areas of Bosnia-Herzegovina. In the case of former Yugoslavia the international community has sanctioned the considerable extension of UNHCR's competence *ratione personae*, by assigning to the Office the lead agency role for humanitarian assistance to the victims of conflict. Less evident would seem the basis for the de facto extension of UNHCR's authority *ratione materiae*, to undertake efforts of international protection in favour of internally displaced persons, and of non-displaced minority or other populations at risk, in addition to the provision of humanitarian relief.

But should it be different? In such a situation, should a United Nations agency "just" carry food, and watch? Especially in the absence of international human rights protection machinery on the ground, the Office felt that it should not lose the opportunity to use its humanitarian presence to monitor the treatment of minority populations and to expose abuses, however moderate the impact would be in areas of virulent persecution. In so doing, UNHCR cooperated closely with the ICRC, and with the UN Special Rapporteur on Human Rights (who, however, until recently had no field staff in Bosnia-Herzegovina). There should not be an absolute and artificial distinction between life-saving assistance and protection. As the government of Bosnia-Herzegovina controlled only 30% of its territory, there was a 70% gap in legitimate State protection of internally displaced persons and of other vulnerable citizens. The authorities did not dispute UNHCR's concern over the treatment of these groups in the whole of Bosnian territory. The Office was also supported by General Assembly Resolution 48/116 (1993), which encouraged the High Commissioner "to continue to explore and to undertake protection and assistance activities aimed at preventing conditions that give rise to refugee outflows, . . ." and ". . . to provide humanitarian assistance and protection to persons displaced within their own country . . .".

DEALING WITH NON-STATE ENTITIES

Whether in the context of extending assistance or protection, UNHCR has had frequent contacts with the "authorities" of entities aspiring to statehood, the recognition of which is opposed by the international community. To what extent does this assist in or amount to legitimizing the illegitimate? This should not be a main issue of concern for impartial, humanitarian organizations addressing vital human needs. Dealing with belligerent parties is a matter of necessity for providing humanitarian assistance on all sides of a conflict, and under international law does not confer legality upon non-State belligerents. Under common Article 3 of the 1949 Geneva Conventions the latter principle also applies with regard to special "agreements" which the parties to non-international armed conflicts are encouraged to conclude regarding the applicability of provisions of those Conventions.

It is important to realize that in the case of Bosnia-Herzegovina, the UN Security Council has opted for a humanitarian "intervention" based precisely on negotiated presence and passage. It is therefore indeed a matter of necessity to conclude agreements with de-facto authorities (whatever their legal force), and humanitarian organizations must be in a position to remind non-recognized belligerents of basic humanitarian norms.

Recently UNHCR was even involved in the conclusion of an agreement with de facto Abkhaz authorities in Georgia about the return of displaced persons to Abkhazia. Even in the case of Chapter VII action authorizing enforcement action, it may be necessary to make arrangements with the parties concerned. On the other hand, although humanitarian concerns should have precedence, attempts should be made, especially by a UN agency, to avoid as much as possible giving any semblance of legality. It is obvious that UNHCR would not enter into an *accord de siège* or Branch Office agreement for the establishment (and protection) of offices in "capitals" of self-proclaimed "Republics", however important the liaison and other functions of such offices may be. Such agreements would be legally void and politically unacceptable.

THE PROVISION OF HUMANITARIAN ASSISTANCE

The large-scale provision of humanitarian assistance amidst violence and disrespect for the impartial and humanitarian character of relief operations has given rise to several questions. First, there does not seem to exist an absolute right of access for humanitarian organizations. A related question is the definition of humanitarian assistance. The Second Protocol Additional to the Geneva Conventions of 12 August 1949 (Article 18.2) mentions supplies essential for the survival of the civilian population, "such as foodstuffs and medical supplies". But what about stoves and fuel to keep hospital patients warm in the freezing Balkan winter? It took great efforts to let the Bosnian parties agree to the principle that it was for UNHCR and the ICRC to determine the content of humanitarian assistance.

At the same time the conflicting parties were obliged not to divert humanitarian assistance to the military. But what about situations when monitoring the end-use of relief is not possible and when relief is probably also feeding combatants: should this lead to the discontinuation of humanitarian assistance? Should relief operations in general, or specific attempts to gain access to victims in need, be continued if the granting of humanitarian passage for convoys, planes and staff is manipulated by the parties and linked to quid pro quos, such as medical evacuation, the transfer of civilians based on ethnicity alone, or the release of prisoners? And, how should security risks for (unarmed) humanitarian personnel be weighed against the needs of the victims? Is there an acceptable threshold of staff insecurity?

A recurrent and thorny question has been whether military force should be used to gain access and to ensure the delivery of humanitarian assistance. UN Security Council Resolution 770 of 13 August 1992 called upon States, under Chapter VII, "to take . . . all measures necessary to facilitate . . . the delivery of humanitarian assistance". However, subsequently it was made clear that the humanitarian operation would be carried out on the basis of negotiated safe passage. UNPROFOR would provide "protective support", "at UNHCR's request" (Secretary General's report S/24540 of 10 September 1992). This concept was then endorsed through UN Security Council Resolution 776 of 14 September 1992. It has served as a basis for many life-saving operations. It has also brought with it moments of tension between humanitarian, political and military mandates and decision-making, as well as confusion among the parties on the ground.

THE PROTECTION OF INTERNALLY DISPLACED PERSONS

This subject, with its multiple aspects, rightly draws much attention including from UNHCR's own Executive Committee during this year's debate. In Bosnia-Herzegovina, UNHCR has clearly experienced that there are three dimensions to the plight of internally displaced persons and their protection. They are human beings whose human rights must be respected. In situations of armed conflict they must, moreover, benefit from the special protection of international humanitarian law. Thirdly, in the specific context of their uprootedness they are in need of additional care and measures of protection, such as admission to safety, registration (as a precondition for shelter and assistance), non-discrimination particularly with regard to assistance, and family reunification. In conflicts often characterized by de- and re-population tactics, an important protection activity consists of countering pressure on unsafe or premature return to areas of origin. There may also be undue pressure to relocate to other areas, or such relocation, if preferred by the displaced themselves as a solution to their plight, can be prevented by the authorities for political reasons (which raises questions related to the scope of the human right of freedom of movement and of abode).

Protective measures aimed specifically at displaced persons are therefore important, even if there is no ethnic or other distinction or hostility between the displaced and the receiving government or de facto authorities. To what extent there should be international protection – in addition to, in support of, or as a substitute for legitimate national protection – is a different question. Second, the example of Bosnia-Herzegovina again confirms that in situations of armed conflict displaced persons have one primordial need in common with non-displaced populations: to be protected, as much as possible, against the effects of war. The UN-declared "safe area" of Gorazde, which has recently been the theatre of serious fighting, is a case in point: it accommodates local residents as well as large numbers of displaced persons, who as civilians all share the same need for protection against armed attack, starvation and forcible displacement. It would therefore seem important, especially in situations of armed conflict and of widespread violations of human rights, not to examine the situation of internally displaced persons in isolation. This is neither right vis-à-vis non-displaced populations nor would it help to bring about effective protection against the effects of war and of persecution in general.

SOME ISSUES OF REFUGEE PROTECTION

Turning now to more traditional aspects of its mandate, UNHCR has had to deal with many issues of refugee protection. Admission to safety and non-rejection at borders of adjacent States have been matters of constant concern. In 1992 this was even an issue with UNPROFOR, which under UN Security Council Resolution 769 of 7 August 1992 had obtained authority to control the entry of civilians into the United Nations Protected Areas in Croatia. As these areas are controlled by local Serbs, UNPROFOR was, for security reasons, concerned about the entry and stay of undocumented Muslim and ethnic Croat refugees pending negotiation, by UNHCR, of their admission to Croatia proper. The Office has had to intervene several times to prevent the *refoulement*, after admission, of male refugees to Bosnia-Herzegovina, because a "Friendship Agreement" concluded in 1992 between the Croatian and Bosnian government allowed for forcible return to areas declared "safe" by the Bosnian authorities. Another aspect was UNHCR's position advocating international protection, at least on a temporary basis, for draft evaders and deserters fearing punishment or mobilization by force for refusing to participate in war action condemned by the international community (for violating *ius in bello* and/or *ius ad bellum*).

An important component of the Comprehensive Humanitarian Response to the Humanitarian Crisis in Former Yugoslavia, launched by UNHCR in July 1992, was the provision of at least temporary protection to victims of conflict and of gross violations of human rights fleeing across international borders. This concept was intended to serve as a practical and flexible tool, in situations of mass influx and at a time of overburdened refugee determination procedures in many western European countries, to ensure the protection of all victims of conflict and persecution. This would notably include the category of "war refugees", who risked being denied status under the refugee definition of the 1951 Refugee Convention because of varying interpretations of that definition. As intensive and hopeful efforts at political mediation and peacemaking were under way, a central theme was indeed the granting of protection pending a political settlement allowing for return. But how temporary should temporary protection be? When and how can it be terminated? As the situation in Bosnia-Herzegovina shows, hopes for an early safe return are not always realized, despite the active involvement of the international community from an early stage. UNHCR has therefore advocated the improvement over time of the standards of treatment attached to temporary protection, leading to a set of rights close to those enjoyed by refugees with refugee status. It has welcomed the conversion, by some European States, of temporary protection into refugee status or humanitarian status, while emphasizing the need to promote conditions that would permit repatriation in safety and dignity. In practice, the implementation of temporary protection (eligibility criteria, standards of treatment and link with asylum procedures) has varied. The concept of temporary protection is therefore certainly a subject for further study and discussion.

CONCLUDING REMARKS

The foregoing by no means covers all issues which UNHCR continues to face to date in the former Yugoslavia. It should, however, demonstrate that UNHCR is rapidly expanding its experience and expertise, in a complex (and dangerous) environment. Existing international law or practice does not provide clear answers to many questions. What is regrettably clearer still: humanitarian assistance and protection are necessary, but cannot stop war and persecution.

MICHEL IOGNA-PRAT

Nationality and Statelessness Issues in the Newly Independent States

BACKGROUND

UNHCR has been actively involved since 1991 in addressing refugee-related problems in the States of the former Soviet Union. Already, large numbers of people are on the move, either displaced by conflicts or returning to their places of origin. The new States lack the resources and the institutional capacity both to absorb flows of peoples and to deal effectively with the problems associated with population movements.

Over 200 different ethnic groups lived for centuries within the cultural mosaic of the Russian Empire. The Soviet Federal system that emerged from the Bolshevik revolution was based on a hierarchy of different ethnic groups, meting out cultural and linguistic rights and differences at random. Artificial borders were drawn to divide national groups, decreasing the likelihood of threats to the central government in Moscow. Stalin's policies of relocation and colonization still have repercussions today. Balts, Poles, Chechens, Germans, Kalmyks and the Crimean Tatars, to name a few, were among those forcibly relocated in Central Asia and Siberia. At the same time, Stalin and subsequent Soviet leaders encouraged large numbers of Russians to settle in the non-Russian republics of the former USSR. These population movements had the effect of diluting the ethnic homogeneity of each republic and of reducing the titular nationality and other non-Russian minorities to quasi-lesser status.

The breakup of Russia's hegemony has created a myriad of ethnic tensions. The Soviet legacy has left the new States with a total population of ethnic minorities of more than 60 million people. This includes an estimated 25 million Russians, 6.7 million Ukrainians, 2.5 million Uzbeks and about a million each of Armenians and of Tadjiks, all suddenly living abroad.

According to information available, ethnic Russians comprise one-third of the population in Latvia (34%), Estonia (30%) and Kazakhstan (38%), over one-fifth in Ukraine (22%) and Kyrgyzstan (21.5%), and over one-tenth in Belarus (13%) and Moldova (13%).

The potential for massive displacements arising from man-made causes is

25

V. Gowlland-Debbas (ed.), The Problem of Refugees in the Light of Contemporary International Law Issues, 25–31.
© 1996 Kluwer Academic Publishers. Printed in the Netherlands.

immense. New States must develop an entire new legal system, bearing in mind that discriminatory legislation could have disastrous consequences.

Problems Relating to Nationality and Statelessness

With the formal dissolution of the Soviet Union in December 1991, the Soviet nationality ceased to exist. Most of the new States have already adopted their own citizenship laws and thus defined who should be the nationals of the State. The citizenship laws of Azerbaijan, Kyrgyzstan and Tadjikistan, which were adopted under Soviet rule, are still in force and have not so far been amended. Citizenship law is still under discussion in Armenia. All the other States have already adopted their citizenship laws. Most of them passed them before the formal dissolution of the Soviet Union, except for Estonia, Turkmenistan and Uzbekistan.

A substantive analysis of the various citizenship laws leads to the conclusion that the problem of statelessness is of actual concern in the context of the changes in the former Soviet Union. By analysing the various citizenship laws of the new States, it is clear that significant groups of people have not been included in the initial body of citizens, do not meet the requirements of the various laws to acquire the nationality of one of the States, and are left stateless. Such a situation in the volatile context of the former USSR, where a number of conflicts have erupted and where tensions could lead to more conflicts, means that statelessness could result in massive displacements of persons as these unprotected individuals will eventually feel coerced to move from the countries of their habitual residence to seek refuge and protection elsewhere.

The developments in the region over the recent period have either generated new and complex problems of statelessness or have the strong potential to do so. Problems of statelessness in the former Soviet Union are to be seen either as a result of specifically targeted discriminatory legislation under which groups of persons cannot meet the criteria for the granting of nationality in their country of residence, or as a result of territorial and sovereignty changes.

Since the breakup or dissolution of the Soviet Union in December 1991, various public international law aspects of the situation arising from these changes, in particular those dealing with the identity and continuity of States or State succession in relation to citizenship, have come under the scrutiny of the international community. These changes are in many ways unique and call for an innovative reflection. For the first time since the end of the Second World War, the international community has experienced the emergence of new States in a non-colonial context where previous solutions are not relevant.

OPEN QUESTIONS IN THE CONTEXT OF INTERNATIONAL LAW

There are two sets of questions which call for deeper reflection in the context of public international law.

1. The first area of issues centres around international law aspects of nationality matters. In international law, is there a recognized right to a nationality? If the answer is positive, which State has an obligation to grant nationality? How is the genuine link between the State and the individual established by the nationality laws? What are the contemporary functions of the law of nationality? What is the content of the right to a nationality as a human right? Are there common international standards in regard to the elimination/ reduction/prevention of statelessness? How are such efforts to eliminate/reduce/ prevent statelessness compatible with the concept of national sovereignty?

2. The second area of issues is related to the qualification under public international law of the disintegration of the Soviet Union and the consequences for nationality matters.

The disintegration of the Soviet Union raises some questions concerning its qualification under public international law. Has the Soviet Union ceased to exist as a subject of international law? Is it dismemberment or secession that has happened to the Soviet Union?

The answer is unclear and rather confusing. Basically, there are two schools of thought:

a. The first one bases itself on the concept of the legal continuity of the former Soviet Union and the partial succession of those States which broke away and became independent, bearing in mind that in this context the Baltic States would be considered as restored States as the Soviet annexation was considered largely as a breach of international law.

In support of this theory, two arguments could be used. Firstly, in case of major changes in the State territory or in the form of the government, the existence of the State as a subject of international law is not affected and these changes do not necessarily lead to its extinction.

The question of membership in the United Nations is a key indication of how the whole process of the breakup of the Soviet Union may be interpreted under public international law. The Russian Federation made a declaration of continuation to the Secretary General on 24 December 1991 which was circulated to all Member States by a *note verbale* of the same date. This declaration was tacitly accepted by the Security Council at its informal consultations on 27 December 1991 and its formal meeting on 31 December 1991. Similarly this declaration was accepted by the General Assembly at the 80th plenary meeting of its 46th session, held on 4 February 1992.

By a *note verbale* dated 26 December 1991, the Ministry of Foreign Affairs of the Russian Federation stated that "the participation of the Union of the Soviet Socialist Republics [. . .] in all conventions, agreements and other legal instruments, concluded in the framework of the United Nations shall be continued by the Russian Federation and in this connection the name Russian Federation shall be used instead of the name Union of the Soviet Socialist Republics in the United Nations".

Moreover, the Russian Federation took over most of the Union's institutions, including the permanent seat in the Security Council and embassies, and never declared independence.

All these elements would suggest that the Russian Federation should be considered in legal continuity to the Soviet Union as a personality of international law.

b. According to the second school of thought, with the Declaration of Alma Ata, dated 21 December 1991, an agreement was reached among the Soviet Union's component members that the Union has ceased to exist as a subject of international law and that on its territory 15 new States have emerged. As the Commonwealth of Independent States established by the Alma-Ata Declaration is not a State, continuity between the Soviet Union and the CIS is not legally possible. Consequently, the dissolution of the Soviet Union should be seen as a dismemberment and all the 15 new States, including the Russian Federation, should then have to be regarded as successor States.

In that context, it is then essential to consider what are the consequences concerning nationality matters. What is the scope of international rights and duties of a new State with regard to the population in its territory?

Depending on what theory is followed, consequences for nationality matters will differ.

a. In regard to State succession, there is a lot of uncertainty and confusion as to the obligations under international law of the successor State in nationality matters.

The classical view is that, in principle, questions of nationality fall within the domestic jurisdiction of each State. According to Brownlie,[1] the evidence is overwhelmingly in support of the view that the population follows the change of sovereignty. In view of the State practice analysed by Brownlie, there is a general presumption that persons attached to a territory will *ipso facto* lose their former nationality and acquire the nationality of the new State. Nationality would change when sovereignty changed hands. Attachment generally means a substantial connection with the territory concerned by citizenship, residence or family relations to a qualified person. The link of the people with the territory is said to be in accord with human and political reality.

This view is not shared by other scholars. O'Connell[2] argues that, undesirable as it may be for any person to become stateless as a result of a change of sovereignty, it cannot be asserted with any measure of confidence that

---

[1]   Brownlie, I., *Principles of International Law*, 4th ed., Oxford 1990.
[2]   O'Connell, D., *State Succession in Municipal and International Law*, I, 2nd ed., Cambridge 1967 (chapter 20).

international law, at least in its present stage of development, imposes any duty on the successor State to grant its nationality.

Weis[3] holds the view that there is no rule of international law under which the nationals of the predecessor State shall acquire the nationality of the successor State. There is only a presumption in international law that the acquiring State would, through municipal law, confer its nationality on the former nationals of the predecessor State.

Looking from a different angle, Chan[4] considers that, upon a change of sovereignty, all persons who have a genuine and effective link with the new State will automatically acquire the nationality of the new State. It is within the competence of each State to determine what constitutes a genuine and effective link in the granting of its nationality, subject to the presumption of avoidance of statelessness and the duty not to apply any law on a discriminatory basis which would be in contradiction with Article 15 (paragraph 2) of the Universal Declaration of Human Rights. It is also a settled rule of customary international law that residents of the transferred territory who have a nationality other than that of the predecessor State are not affected by the change of sovereignty.

b. On the other hand, if one follows the theory that the Russian Federation has to be seen in legal continuity with the former Soviet Union, then the question arises of how to define the relationship between the predecessor and the successor State in respect of nationality matters. Weis states in this connection that "one may speak of a positive rule of international law on nationality to the effect that, under international law and provided the territorial transfer is based on a valid title, the predecessor State is under the obligation vis-à-vis the successor State to withdraw its nationality from the inhabitants of the transferred territory if they acquire the nationality of the successor State."

Therefore, and in line with the theory of legal continuity, one could argue that the predecessor State has, under certain conditions, a subsidiary responsibility for all inhabitants of its former territory in regard to nationality matters.

This subsidiary responsibility could be formulated as follows: If and only if the individuals concerned have not obtained the nationality of any of the new States and no obligations under international law would impose the granting of a nationality on these individuals, then one might conclude that a genuine link of a secondary nature could be re-established with the Russian Federation because of their ex-Soviet citizenship. Since the Russian Federation assumes the legal continuity to the former Soviet Union, it is then bound by all international obligations of the former Soviet Union, including obliga-

[3]   Weis, P., *Nationality and Statelessness in International Law*, 2nd rev. ed., Alphen aan den Rijn 1979.

[4]   Chan, J.M., "The Right to a Nationality as a Human Right", 12 *Human Rights Law Journal* (1991), pp. 1–14.

tions under international human rights principles, especially Article 15 of the Universal Declaration of Human Rights.

Consequently, one could argue in this case that the Russian Federation has a subsidiary responsibility for the "left-overs" i.e., for those who fall through the net of nationality laws of the successor States, otherwise they would remain stateless.

We know that these issues are currently being considered by the International Law Commission and are under discussion in various international and regional fora as well as in the academic world. Given its specific mandate for stateless persons, UNHCR is trying to strengthen its efforts and to contribute, with others, to the solution of these problems and to finding an answer to the open questions which have been raised.

UNHCR's Involvement in Nationality Matters

UNHCR has a worldwide responsibility for refugees but is, more and more, being called to take responsibility for persons having been displaced either externally or internally upon request of the United Nations Secretary General. In the former USSR, UNHCR is presently actively involved in emergency operations where massive displacements of persons occurred in Georgia, Armenia, Azerbaijan and Tadjikistan. In the course of its activities in the region, UNHCR is then confronted with situations of persons being stateless and of their need to be protected. In these countries, UNHCR is also frequently requested to provide support in building up legal systems aimed at protecting refugees, displaced persons and stateless persons and has been associated with the drafting process of nationality laws or amendments to the existing nationality laws.

UNHCR's mandate regarding statelessness derives from United Nations General Assembly Resolutions. Resolution 3274 (XXIX) of 10 December 1974 provides a specific mandate to UNHCR in this matter:

> Considering the Convention on the Reduction of Statelessness of 28 August 1961 and, in particular, articles 11 and 20 requiring the establishment of a body to which a person claiming the benefit of the Convention may apply for the examination of his claim and for assistance in presenting it to the appropriate authority,
> 1. Requests the Office of the United Nations High Commissioner for Refugees provisionally to undertake the functions foreseen under the Convention on the Reduction of Statelessness in accordance with its article 11 after the Convention has come into force . . .

Resolution 31/36 of 30 November 1976 has requested the United Nations High Commissioner for Refugees to continue to perform these functions.

So far, activities undertaken under this mandate have been limited, but given the magnitude and the complexity of the problem, especially in the former

USSR, it appears essential for UNHCR to strengthen its efforts to provide adequate solutions. However it would require primarily, a clearer definition of its mandate. The United Nations General Assembly, through a resolution, should define the content of the mandate given to UNHCR to act as the body established under article 11 of the 1961 Convention. It would imply that UNHCR should be given a supervisory role in the implementation of that Convention and to report on a regular basis to the General Assembly on statelessness.

It would also imply giving UNHCR a similar supervisory function concerning the implementation of the 1954 Convention on the Status of Stateless Persons as both Conventions are clearly interlinked. With a more clear and precise mandate, UNHCR would then be in a position to be more active on the one hand to promote these two international instruments, and on the other hand to find solutions to prevent and to reduce statelessness, as part of the comprehensive approach advocated in numerous instances by the High Commissioner.

It will also require that the Executive Committee of the High Commissioner's programme adopt a Conclusion to strenghten the Office's mandate concerning statelessness as part of the overall strategy in preventing movements of unprotected persons.

Finally, it will also require a closer link with other organs of the United Nations system dealing with nationality matters and particularly, the International Law Commission and the United Nations Center for Human Rights.

PART II

International Law Perspective

VÁCLAV MIKULKA

Legal Problems Arising from the Dissolution of States in Relation to the Refugee Phenomenon

This paper deals with two specific questions relating to the refugee phenomenon in the context of the dissolution of States in Eastern Europe, in particular Yugoslavia, namely:
– State succession in respect of international treaties concerning refugees, and
– State nationality after dissolution with regard to refugees.
Rather than providing answers, this paper, namely its second part, attempts to define the problems which should be solved through concerted international efforts.

I. State Succession in Respect of International Treaties Concerning Protection of Refugees

The main body of law concerning refugees is treaty law. While general principles on the protection of refugees have become an integral part of customary international law, most of the rules aimed at solving the problem of refugees are contained in a number of treaty instruments. Some of these are of a universal character, as in the case of the Convention Relating to the Status of Refugees of 28 July 1951, the Protocol Relating to the Status of Refugees of 31 January 1967, the Agreement Relating to Refugee Seamen of 23 November 1957 and the Protocol of 12 June 1973 to this Agreement, just to mention a few. Several other instruments were concluded to enhance international cooperation in the field of refugee protection in different regions.[1]

The emphasis on the universal participation of States in conventions providing for the protection of refugees was already included in UN General Assembly Resolution 428 (V) of 14 December, 1950, through which the Assembly adopted the Statute of the Office of the UN High Commissioner for Refugees. In paragraph 2 the General Assembly:

---

[1] For the texts of these and other instruments, see *Collection of International Instruments Concerning Refugees*, HCR/IP/1/Eng., Geneva 1979.

V. Gowlland-Debbas (ed.), The Problem of Refugees in the Light of Contemporary International Law Issues,
35–49.

> Calls upon Governments to co-operate with the United Nations High
> Commissioner for Refugees in the performance of his functions concerning
> refugees [. . .] especially by:
> a) Becoming parties to international conventions providing for the pro-
>   tection of refugees, and taking the necessary steps of implementation
>   under such conventions; [. . .].

The responsibilities of the High Commissioner in this respect are spelled
out in the Statute of his/her Office annexed to the said resolution. Paragraph
8 of the Statute requests the High Commissioner:

> . . . [to] provide for the protection of refugees falling under the compe-
> tence of his Office by:
> a) Promoting the conclusion and ratification of international conventions
>   for the protection of refugees, supervising their application and
>   proposing amendments thereto;

It would not be an exaggeration to presume that the promotion of the
uninterrupted application of these instruments by successor States resulting
from the dissolution of a State which was a treaty party should also fall under
the mandate of the High Commissioner.

As far as the Eastern European region is concerned, the reluctant position
of former communist governments towards the instruments concerning refugees
is well-known. It corresponded with their reserved position towards the whole
body of human rights instruments based primarily on the Western concept of
fundamental rights and freedoms which were incompatible with the Marxist-
Leninist philosophy of law. While, as a matter of pragmatism, communist
governments acceded to the main instruments of human rights protection, such
as the two International Covenants on Human Rights which contained rather
general rules, they remained outside the conventional framework establishing
specific mechanisms for monitoring compliance (see, for example, the Optional
Protocol to the International Covenants on Civil and Political Rights).

It is even less surprising that, except for Yugoslavia where at the time the
political climate was more liberal, Eastern European States did not join the
instruments concerning the protection of refugees. The permanent flow of
opponents of the communist regime towards the West was a continuous characteristic of the political system during the whole history of its existence.
Shortly after the installation of the communist regime, as well as several
times thereafter when the regime was in crisis, it resorted to oppressive action
(Soviet military interventions to suppress the 1956 uprising in Hungary and
the Czechoslovak reformation movement in 1968) resulting in a flow of
refugees comparable to the major refugee movements in any other part of
the world. No wonder it was politically difficult for the regime to accept
specific international obligations in this field.

The attitude of Eastern European countries towards the treaties regulating
the status and protection of refugees changed only after the fall of communism

in 1989, when some of them acceded to the 1951 Convention and to the 1967 Protocol Relating to the Status of Refugees – namely Hungary in 1989 and Czechoslovakia, Poland and Romania in 1991. Yugoslavia had been a party to these instruments since 1959.[2]

The fall of communism in Eastern Europe resulted in the disintegration of three multinational federal States: Yugoslavia, the USSR and Czechoslovakia. The dissolution of Yugoslavia, accompanied by a violent military conflict, gave rise to a huge wave of refugees looking for a safe place in neighbouring and other European countries which have, thus, been suddenly confronted with a considerable number of problems. Their solution requires close cooperation among the States concerned, the number of which has increased as a result of the dissolution.

The treaties concerning refugees, no doubt, provide the necessary legal basis for concerted international action. But to what extent do these treaties bind the States emerging from the dissolution? Are they *ipso facto* applicable vis-à-vis all successor States of former Yugoslavia or is consent of these States necessary?

According to Article 34 of the Vienna Convention on Succession of States in Respect of Treaties of 1978:[3]

1. When a part or parts of the territory of a State separate to form one or more States, whether or not the predecessor State continues to exist:
a) any treaty in force at the date of the succession of States in respect of the entire territory of the predecessor State continues in force in respect of each successor State so formed.
b) [. . .]
2. Paragraph 1 does not apply if:
a) the States concerned otherwise agree; or
b) it appears from the treaty or is otherwise established that the application of the treaty in respect of the successor State would be incompatible with the object and purpose of the treaty or would radically change the conditions for its operation.

The Vienna Convention is not a treaty in force. Thus, in order to clarify the fate of multilateral treaties, including those concerning refugees or human rights protection, to which Yugoslavia, the USSR and Czechoslovakia were parties, it is important to reveal the character of the rule contained in Article 34; namely, whether it comprises a mere codification of customary law, which applies to the cases of the dissolution of States in Eastern Europe irrespective of the Vienna Convention, or rather a progressive development of

---

[2] See *Multilateral treaties deposited with the Secretary General, Status as at 31 December 1993*, New York 1994.
[3] For the text see *United Nations Conference on the Succession of States in Respect of Treaties, Official Records*, vol. III, Doc. A/CONF.80/16/Add.2.

international law which, due to the fact that the Vienna Convention is not in force, does not operate.[4]

In its commentary to the 1974 draft of this provision (at that time Article 33) the International Law Commission concluded that:

> . . . although some discrepancies might be found in State practice, still that practice was sufficiently consistent to support the formulation of a rule which, with the necessary qualifications, would provide that treaties in force at the date of the dissolution should remain in force *ipso iure* with respect to each State emerging from the dissolution. The fact that the situation may be regarded as one of 'separation of part or parts of a State' rather than one of 'dissolution' does not alter this basic conclusion.[5]

The key to how the Commission came to adopt that position lay in what, in 1972, were two different articles (Art. 27 and 28) dealing separately with the dissolution of a State, when the continuity principle should apply, and separation of part of a State, in which event the "clean slate" principle was established because a new State emerging from such a separation was considered to be in the same position as a newly independent State.

Some governments, in their written comments relating to the 1972 draft, raised doubts concerning the soundness of this distinction, pointing out that the "clean slate" concept in the event of separation of part of a State had been largely based on old precedents, while there had been little State practice in the United Nations period to justify it. For this reason, the Commission amalgamated the two situations and opted for a continuity principle as a uniform rule for all cases (dissolution as well as separation).

The only exception to the continuity principle that the Commission envisaged in the event of a separation was reflected in paragraph 3 of the final draft article (Art. 33) which provided that:

> . . . if a part of the territory of a State separates from it and becomes a State in circumstances which are essentially of the same character as those existing in the case of the formation of a newly independent State, the successor State shall be regarded [. . .] in all respects as a newly independent State.

---

[4]   In the meantime, this question has lost much of its practical importance. As far as Croatia, Slovenia and Bosnia-Herzegovina or the Czech Republic and Slovakia are concerned, these countries have already notified the UN Secretary General of their succession in respect of multilateral treaties concerning the protection of refugees as well as in respect of other human rights instruments which could be of relevance in relation to refugee problems. See *op. cit.* (note 2). The problem of State succession in respect of treaties concerning protection of refugees does not arise for successor States of the former Soviet Union because the USSR was not a party to them.

[5]   For the text of the 1974 draft articles see *op. cit.* (note 3).

In other words, it is not the principle of continuity, but the "clean slate" rule that shall apply.

As the expert consultant explained to the Conference:

> . . . from the wording of article 33 and the commentary to it, it was clear that paragraph 3 was not intended to apply to the case where a predecessor State ceased to exist. Consequently it would not apply to the case of dissolution of a State.[6]

The International Law Commission's approach was, in principle, approved by the Vienna Conference held in 1977–78. Two major proposals to alter the basic principle of this article were rejected by the Conference.[7]

In defending the Commission's approach and in agreement with the prevailing view, the delegate of the United States said that:

> . . . article 33 accorded with the bulk of international practice. [. . .] [R]ights freely accorded under a treaty should not be cut off because one State united with another [. . .] or separated into two or more parts [. . .]. The central question for the Conference's consideration therefore, was why the right of reliance should disappear.[8]

While the view that the continuity principle was justified irrespective of whether the dissolution of a State or the separation of part of a State was involved was shared by the majority of (though not all) delegations, there was a quasi consensus among delegations that in situations of dissolution of a State or a union, and, in particular, in the case where the constituent parts

[6] See Sir Francis Vallat, *op. cit.* (note 3), vol.II, Doc.A/CONF.80 /16/Add.1, 48th meeting, para. 1.

[7] See amendments to Article 33 submitted by Switzerland and France (A/CONF.80/C.1/L.41/ Rev.1) and by the Federal Republic of Germany (A/CONF/.80/C.1/L.52).

According to the delegate of Switzerland, the ILC in its draft of Article 33 departed from existing international law while "[. . .] the 'clean slate' rule [. . .] was the basic principle of classic international law concerning the succession of States in respect of treaties [. . .] generally applied in international relations long before decolonization. [. . .]" (See *op. cit.* (note 3), vol. II, 40th meeting, paras. 27–31).

France, nevertheless, stated the difference between its and the Swiss position concerning the place of the 'clean slate' principle in classic international law when it recognized "[. . .] that in customary international law the 'clean slate' principle co-existed with the principle of continuity and that both were found in practice. France had opted for a mixed system applying the 'clean slate' principle to treaties concluded *intuitu personae* and the principle of continuity to other treaties." (See *ibidem.*, 40th meeting, para. 44.) The Swiss – French proposal was rejected by the Conference (See *ibidem.*, 49th meeting, para. 38).

The amendment submitted by Germany was aimed at limiting the application of the principle of *ipso iure* continuity in cases of dissolution or separation only to multilateral treaties, while bilateral treaties would be considered to remain in force only if the successor State and the other State party expressly so agreed, or, by reason of their conduct were to be considered as having so agreed. It received the support of some delegations; nevertheless, it was also rejected by the Conference (see *ibidem*, 48th meeting, para. 39).

[8] *Ibidem*, 41st meeting, para. 16.

which separated had to some extent participated in the formulation of international relations or were given limited international personality, the continuity principle was based on sufficient State practice.[9]

Nevertheless, as far as the distinction between the events of the dissolution of a State and the separation of a part of a State is concerned, it has rightly been pointed out by some authors that apart from objective factors, subjective factors become important and a solution depends largely on recognition.[10]

In general, the principle of continuity in cases of separation of part or parts of the territory of a State received strong support at the conference.[11] The role of this principle was further strengthened by the decision of the conference to delete paragraph 3 of Art. 33 establishing the 'clean slate' rule for cases of separation in circumstances similar to decolonization.

As J. Crawford has pointed out: "The process of evolution towards a general regime of treaty continuity [. . .] was, remarkably, completed at the Second Session of the Vienna Conference."[12]

According to the State Department Legal Adviser's opinion expressed as early as 1980, the rules of the Vienna Convention were ". . . generally regarded as declarative of existing customary law by the United States."[13]

This position was not maintained in the Restatement (Third) of the Foreign Relations Law of the United States which favoured giving all new States (regardless of whether or not they were dependent colonies) freedom to start afresh.[14] Nevertheless the Restatement itself, in this respect, became a target of criticism and was finally determined not to reflect the practice of the United States, including in recent years. Thus E. Williamson (Legal Adviser to the US Department of State from 1990–1993) and J. Osborn find that:

> [H]owever, the Department viewed State practice as falling along a continuum. At one end of this continuum, where a portion of the State breaks away from the primary, predecessor State, the practice tends to support a 'clean slate' approach. At the other extreme, where a State divides into its constituent parts, the practice supports the continuity of existing treaty rights and obligations.[15]

As O. Schachter observes in respect of the State policy likely to be followed in recent cases:

[9]   *Ibidem*, see the debate at the 40th–42nd and 48th meetings.
[10]   Compare e.g. Crawford, J., *The Creation of States in International Law*, Oxford 1979, p. 406.
[11]   *Op. cit.* (note 3), vol. II, 48th meeting, par. 40.
[12]   Crawford, J., "The Contribution of Professor D.P. O'Connell to the Discipline of International Law", *BYIL* (1980), I, p. 40.
[13]   See 43 *Digest of United States Practice in International Law* (1980), p. 1041.
[14]   *Restatement (Third) of the Foreign Relations Law of the United States*, 210 cmt.f (1987).
[15]   Williamson, E.D., Osborn, J.E., "A U.S. Perspective on Treaty Succession and Related Issues in the Wake of the Breakup of the USSR and Yugoslavia", 33 *Virg. JIL* (1993), p. 263.

[I]t seems probable that a general presumption of continuity of the obligations of a predecessor State will be accepted for new States that have come into being by secession or by dissolution of existing States. This is in accord with the position of the United States [. . .]. Most other countries may be expected to follow. Thus it is unlikely that the Restatement's rule of a clean slate for all new States will prevail in practice or theory.[16]

In relation to the recent cases of dissolution of States in Eastern Europe, on the basis of their attitudes towards the treaty obligations of their predecessors, the same author concludes:

The experience thus far with respect to [these] cases [. . .] supports a general presumption of continuity. [. . .]
An especially strong case for continuity can be made in respect of multilateral treaties of a so-called 'universal' character that are open to all States. Such treaties include the codification conventions like those on the law of treaties and on diplomatic and consular relations. In addition, there is good reason to include in this category other law making treaties that have been widely accepted, even though they fall in the category of 'development' of new law rather than codification of preexisting law. [. . .] [M]ost such treaties of a general 'legislative' character will be treated in the future as automatically binding on new States on the basis of adherence by their respective predecessor States.[17]

What conclusions could be drawn from all this about the status of refugee instruments and other relevant multilateral treaties vis-à-vis the successor States of the former Yugoslavia, the USSR or Czechoslovakia?

1) Even if the outcome of the debate at the Conference on the question of the extent to which the principle of continuity applies in case of separation of a part or parts of a State was not unanimously accepted, it can be concluded that in situations such as the disintegration of Yugoslavia, the Soviet Union or Czechoslovakia, the application of the principle of the continuity of treaties, in particular of multilateral treaties of universal character, is supported by more convincing reasons than that of the 'clean slate'.
2) Even if this principle was not yet fully embodied in customary law at the time of the Vienna Conference, without any doubt it had already entered the final stage of its stabilization.
3) The practice of treaty parties to the multilateral instruments concerning protection of refugees as well as the practice of international bodies acting in this field should be directed towards the enhancement of the continuity principle.

---

[16] Schachter, O., "State Succession: The Once and Future Law", 33 *Virg. JIL* (1993), p. 258.
[17] *Ibidem*, pp. 257 and 259.

It accords with the conclusion of O.Schachter, according to whom "As a matter of policy, the case for presuming continuity makes sense today when the State system is increasingly fluid."[18]

The Office of the UN High Commissioner for Refugees has an important role to play in this respect. In taking a progressive attitude in enhancing the continuity principle, the Office will not contravene the requirements of its non-political character. The contribution to the stabilization of the treaty-based legal regime elaborated with the wide participation of the international community is a laudable effort fully compatible with the noble humanitarian mission of the High Commissioner.

II. The Problem of State Nationality in Relation to Refugees

State nationality is another issue which has special importance in the context of the dissolution of States in Eastern Europe.

The dismemberment of the Soviet Union gave rise to a number of problems as far as the nationality laws of the different new States are concerned.[19] The refusal of certain new republics, which re-established their independence after 1990, to grant nationality to the ethnic Russian population that settled there during several decades of a large-scale migration of population between different republics of the former Union has created uncertainty about the legal status of hundreds of thousands of individuals.

In Czechoslovakia, which dissolved on 31 December 1992, the problem has been easier to solve due to the existence, since 1969, of separate Czech and Slovak citizenships linking each Czechoslovak national to one of the two constituent republics, and thanks to a quite liberal policy allowing the change of this citizenship together with the change of the habitual residence.

In contrast, the situation is very critical in some new States born on former Yugoslav territory, in particular in Bosnia-Herzegovina, where the population is ethnically mixed and the armed conflict is accompanied by "ethnic cleansing".

The dissolution or separation of States has had major consequences on changes in State nationality affecting the population on a massive scale. The loss of State nationality of the predecessor State and the difficulties in relation to the acquisition of a new nationality may lead to many human tragedies. Persecution by reason of nationality, or a well-founded fear of such persecution, is recognized to be one of the causes of the flow of refugees.[20] Thus, the manner in which problems related to State nationality are resolved by

[18] *Ibidem*, pp. 258–259.
[19] For more see Ginsburgs, G., "From the 1990 Law on the Citizenship of the USSR to the Citizenship Laws of the Successor Republics (1)", 18 *Review of Central and East European Law*, (1) (1992), pp. 1–55.
[20] See *Statute of the Office of the UN High Commissioner for Refugees*, Chapter II, B.

successor States becomes a matter of concern to the international community.

The solution to the problems concerning nationality also has a direct impact on the application of multilateral treaties concerning the protection of refugees. The effective use of these treaties in many respects presupposes that the nationality or the stateless status of persons falling under their terms can be established. As an example, provisions of section C of Article 1 of the 1951 Convention Relating to the Status of Refugees defining conditions under which the convention shall cease to apply, can be mentioned. Practically in each indent a reference is made to the nationality criterion.

The determination of State nationality is not an academic problem but a practical difficulty, in particular in relation to refugees from former Yugoslavia. Many of them are unable to prove or even presume their State nationality.[21]

A. *Nationality Laws of Successor States*

The effect of a change of sovereignty upon the nationality of the inhabitants of the territory concerned is one of the most difficult problems in the law of State succession.[22]

There is considerable disagreement as to the manner in which a change of nationality of inhabitants may be brought about and it is not at all certain which categories of persons are susceptible of having their nationality affected by a change of sovereignty. While one theory asserts that the nationality of inhabitants of the territory concerned is automatically changed at the moment of State succession,[23] the other contends that the inhabitants acquire the nationality of the successor State only by an express or a tacit submission to the new sovereign.[24]

---

[21]   Thus, for example, the official report of the Czech Republic, reflecting the situation in refugee facilities at the end of 1993, states that: "The Government of the Czech Republic has granted temporary asylum on the territory of the Czech republic to 1,739 persons from former Yugoslavia who are in refugee camps and humanitarian facilities administered by the Ministry of the Interior of the Czech republic and about 700 persons **from former Yugoslavia** accommodated outside these facilities." See *Data Report of the Czech Republic for the Seventh Session of the CEI Working Group on Migration (Rome, February 21–22, 1994)*. No doubt, many other governments confronted with the problem of refugees from former Yugoslavia face similar difficulties.

[22]   See O'Connell, D.P., *The Law of State Succession*, Cambridge 1956, p. 245. For doctrine on State nationality in relation to State succession see: Graupner, R., *Nationality and State Succession, Transactions*, 1946; Kelsen, H., "Théorie générale du droit international public", *RCADI* 1932, IV, pp. 314 and 325–327; Castrén, E., "La succession d'Etats", *RCADI* 1951, I, p. 487; Weis, P., *Nationality and Statelessness in International Law*, 2nd ed., Sijthoff-Noordhoff 1979, p. 242.

[23]   See e.g. Kunz, J., "L'option de nationalité", *RCADI* 1930, I, p. 117. In the British practice inhabitants of the territory acquired by the Crown have ordinarily been held automatically to have acquired British nationality. See examples cited by D.P. O'Connell, *op. cit.* (note 22), p. 247, note 4.

[24]   For cases in which this theory was expressed see O'Connell, *op. cit.* (note 22), p. 250.

According to the prevailing, third, school of thought which regards nationality primarily as a matter of domestic jurisdiction,[25] it is the prerogative of a successor State to determine on its own whom it claims as its nationals, and to indicate the methods through which its nationality can be acquired. Conversely, it is the domestic law of the predecessor State which determines which persons have lost their nationality as a result of the loss of territory.[26]

The Hague Convention on Certain Questions Relating to the Conflict of Nationality Laws of 1930, in its Article 1 provides that:

> It is for each State to determine under its own laws who are its nationals. This law shall be recognised by other States in so far as it is consistent with international conventions, international custom, and the principles of law generally recognised with regard to nationality.[27]

Article 13 of the Code Bustamante stipulates:

> In collective naturalizations, in case of the independence of a State, the law of the acquiring or new State shall apply, if it has established in the territory an effective sovereignty which has been recognized by the State trying the issue, and in the absence thereof that of the old State, all without prejudice to the contractual stipulations between the two interested States, which shall always have preference.[28]

As this matter primarily belongs to the sphere of internal law, no serious attempt has ever been made to set up a universal instrument providing for the uniform solution of this problem. (Indeed it would be a mistake to undertake such an exercise even today had conventional form been envisaged). This also explains why the International Law Commission was not anxious

---

[25]   In this sense the Permanent Court of International Justice advised in 1923 that questions of nationality are within the 'reserved domain' of the State. See Advisory Opinion on the *Nationality Decrees Issued in Tunis and Morocco*, PCIJ, Ser. B, No. 4, p. 24.

[26]   After the Second World War, as regards the practice of States becoming independent and remaining within the British Commonwealth, the automatic acquisition of nationality was based on the technique of combining the *jus soli* and *jus sanguinis* criteria, supplemented in a few instances by the residence criterion. For the persons affected by the automatic acquisition of nationality, no option was provided. This practice had the advantage of avoiding disputes over the nationality of a particular person by reducing the possibilities of dual nationality and, at the same time, minimizing the possibility of persons becoming stateless.

The French system of acquisition of nationality did not have the same effect. The new States drew largely on the techniques of the French Code de la nationalité of 1945 which did not always fit the situation of a newly independent State. Moreover, as each State chose the test for "genuine links" according to its own particular inclinations, various nationality laws overlapped or left lacunae, thus favouring dual nationality or statelessness. For more see Zemanek, K., "State Succession after Decolonization", *RCADI* 1965, III, pp. 272–277.

[27]   See *Law Concerning Nationality*, UN Legislative Series, doc. ST/LEG/SER.B/4.

[28]   See "Code of Private International Law" (Code Bustamente) 1928, Book I, Title I, Chapter I, *LNTS*, 86, p. 111.

to deal with the problem of nationality in relation with the State succession topic, which it discussed for nearly 20 years.[29]

This does not, however, mean that international law does not have any relevance for the problem of State nationality in the event of State succession. To the contrary, the legislative competence of the successor State must be exercised within the limitations imposed by general international law as well as international treaties.[30]

These limitations have different characteristics and are derived, in particular, from:
- **the principle of effective nationality,** and
- **the protection of human rights.**

The principle of effective nationality was stated by the ICJ in the Nottebohm case. According to it, for nationality to have an effect vis-à-vis other States, there must be a real and effective link, a genuine connection, between the State and the individual concerned.[31] Thus, for example, the incompetence of the successor State to claim as its nationals persons born in the territory affected by the substitution of sovereignty but not resident there would appear to be widely admitted, while the predecessor State would seem to lose its competence to claim as its nationals the inhabitants of the territory it had lost when the bond uniting it with them is dissolved.[32]

The obligations of States in the field of protection of human rights make questionable the techniques leading to statelessness or any kind of

---

[29] The problem of the nationality of natural and juridical persons was originally part of the second heading of the topic of State succession included in a long-term program of the ILC in 1949. In 1963 the topic was divided into three headings:
a) succession in respect of treaties;
b) succession in respect of matters other than treaties;
c) succession in respect of membership of international organizations.

The second heading was studied by the ILC from 1968 to 1981. Some preliminary comments on nationality were made in the ILC during the debate on the first report by the Special Rapporteur at the twentieth session of the Commission. This heading, in view of its breadth and complexity, was later narrowed to the economic aspects of succession and led to the adoption of the Vienna Convention on Succession of States in Respect of State Property, Archives and Debts of 7 April 1983. Nationality was not included among the issues coming under the narrowed heading.

See First Report by M. Bedjaoui, Special Rapporteur, Doc. A/CN.4/202, *YBILC* (1968), vol. II, pp. 114–115; *Report of the International Law Commission*, Doc.A/7209/Rev.1, paras 73 and 78; *ibidem*, pp. 220–221.

[30] The commentary to Article 2 of the Draft Convention on Nationality of 1929 prepared by the Harvard Law School's Research On International Law asserts that the power of a State to confer its nationality is not unlimited.

[31] See Nottebohm case, ICJ Rep. 1955. For a quite different approach see Flegenheimer case (1958), *Recueil des Sentences Arbitrales*, vol. XIV, p. 327. See also the debates in the International Law Commission on elimination and reduction of statelessness, *YBILC* (1953), I, pp. 180–181, 184, 186, 218, 237, 239.

[32] Compare O'Connell, *op. cit.* (note 22), pp. 248 and 253.

discrimination. As Article 15 of the Universal Declaration of Human Rights provides:
1. Everyone has the right to a nationality.
2. No one shall be arbitrarily deprived of his nationality nor denied the right to change his nationality.

In light of this it is no longer possible to maintain the traditional opinion according to which:

> [I]t can not be asserted with any measure of confidence that international law, at least in its present stage of development, imposes any duty on the successor State to grant nationality.[33]

Furthermore, Article 9 of the UN Convention on Reduction of Statelessness (1961) prohibits the deprivation of nationality on racial, ethnic, religious, or political grounds. Should not this be understood, in the event of State succession, as a prohibition of a selective policy by the successor State, when granting nationality to the inhabitants of the territory concerned?

According to the Estonian Citizenship Law of 1938, restored in January 1992, only citizens of 1940 Estonia and their direct descendants can automatically become Estonian citizens. All other residents must go through the process of naturalization, notwithstanding how long they have lived in Estonia and whether or not they were born in Estonia. R. Mullerson, when analyzing the situation, finds such an approach "politically doubtful and legally unsound" and concludes that:

> [I]t is apparent that a desire to obtain (or at least approximate) ethnic purity, and not considerations of legal consistency, led to the approach toward citizenship questions in Estonia. [. . .] This approach led to the deprivation of the political rights of almost forty percent of the population of the Republic, many of whom were born in Estonia or had lived there for decades. It seems [. . .] that such a division of the permanent residents of Estonia into two categories is not based on objective and reasonable criteria and therefore constitutes discrimination.[34]

The recent tendency of emphasizing ethnic origin when determining the criterion for granting the new State's nationality to the inhabitants is an alarming sign. This approach not only favours statelessness but in many respects is questionable on the basis of fundamental human rights standards. The international community should, through the relevant multilateral fora, make an effort to orient State practice to such concepts which are fully compatible with contemporary international law.

---

[33]   *Ibidem*, p. 249.
[34]   Mullerson, R.," New Developments in the Former USSR and Yugoslavia", 33 *Virg. JIL* (1993), p. 312.

B. *International Treaties Concerning Nationality in Cases of*
State Succession

1) *Criteria for the* Ipso Facto *Acquisition of Nationality*
In the past, there were many cases in which the problem of the criteria and
other conditions for the acquisition of nationality of a successor State was
solved by an international treaty. The most frequently used criterion was that
of domicile or habitual residence.

Examples of such treaty provisions include Articles 4 and 6 of the Versailles
Treaty of 28 June 1919 between the Allied Powers and Poland. Furthermore,
all peace treaties after the First World War contained similar provisions.[35]

2) *The Loss of the Predecessor's Nationality*
The peace treaties following the First World War provided, at the same time,
for the recognition by the conquered States of a new nationality acquired
ipso facto by their former nationals under the laws of the successor State
and for the consequent loss of the allegiance of these persons to their country
of origin.[36]

3) *The Right of Option*
There is substantial support in the doctrine for the conclusion that the
successor State is entitled to extend its nationality to those rendered susceptible by the change of sovereignty, irrespective of their wishes. Nevertheless
an important number of international treaties, including several of those
mentioned above or instruments related thereto, provided for the right of option.
In exceptional cases, this right was granted for a considerable period of time
during which the affected individuals enjoyed a kind of dual nationality.[37]

For the majority of authors the right of option can be deduced only from
a treaty, although some authors tend to assert the existence of an independent right of option as an attribute of the principle of self-determination.[38]

The right of option was envisaged also by the Arbitration Commission of
the International Conference on the Former Yugoslavia. It recalled that, by
virtue of the right to self-determination:

. . . every individual may choose to belong to whatever ethnic, religious
or language community he or she wishes. In the Commission's view, one
possible consequence of this principle might be for the members of Serbian
population in Bosnia-Herzegovina and Croatia to be recognised under

---

[35] See *Law Concerning Nationality*, UN Legislative Series, ST/LEG/SER.B/4, pp. 90 *et seq.*
[36] *Ibidem*, pp. 586–589.
[37] See e.g. The Evian Declaration (Algeria-France) of 19 March 1962, *UNTS* 507, pp. 35
and 37.
[38] For more see Kunz, J., *loc. cit.* (note 23), p. 109 *et seq.*; "Nationality and Option Clauses
in the Italian Peace Treaty", 41 *AJIL* (1947), pp. 622 *et seq.*; Rousseau, Ch., *Droit interna-*
tional public, vol. III, Les compétences, Paris 1977, pp. 366–372.

agreements between the Republics as having the nationality of their choice, with all the rights and obligations which that entails with respect to the States concerned.[39]

In his comments on this opinion of the Arbitration Commission A.Pellet says:

L'intention est ici très nette: s'il n'est pas question de dépecer la Yougoslavie davantage que les faits l'imposent [. . .] il convient, dans cette situation nouvelle, que les droits des minorités soient entièrement sauvegardés, y compris par le maintien de liens étroits entre les populations minoritaires au sein des nouveaux Etats et les Républiques dont ces minorités se sentent les plus proches.

[. . .]

[L']on peut penser à une articulation entre la "nationalité" et la "citoyenneté" s'inspirant de celle qui est prévue par la deuxième partie de l'Accord de Maastricht du 8 février 1992 sur 'la citoyenneté de l'Union'. Grâce à cela les membres des 'populations serbes' de Bosnie-Herzégovine et de Croatie pourraient jouir de droits civiques étendues dans leurs Etats de résidence et bénéficier d'une large protection internationale tout en demeurant 'nationaux' de la Serbie [. . .]. Bien d'autres statuts sont possibles.

En orientant la réflexion dans cette direction, la Commission suggère une dissociation très remarquable entre la nationalité et la territorialité, certainement féconde pour l'avenir et d'autant plus indispensable que l'imbrication des éthnies est telle, dans certaines Républiques – surtout en Bosnie-Herzégovine –, que de nouveaux découpages territoriaux semblent totalement irréalistes.[40]

One could, however, ask how this concept would be reconciled with the principle of effective nationality, given that in the majority of cases persons of the Serbian ethnic group in Bosnia-Herzegovina or in Croatia were neither born in Serbia nor ever had their domicil there. What would then be the substance of the "genuine link" between them and Serbia to which the International Court of Justice refers? Would not this concept add further emphasis to the ethnic feeling which is one of the underlying causes of the conflict ? Is it appropriate to transplant the concept of European Union citizenship from a region where integration is progressing quickly to a region where just the opposite is true ? These questions are worth careful examination.

[39]   Opinion No. 2, 11 January 1992, 31 *ILM* (1992), p. 1498.
[40]   A. Pellet, "Note sur la Commission d'arbitrage de la Conference européenne pour la paix en Yougoslavie", 37 *AFDI* (1991), pp. 329–348, note on pp. 340–341.

C. *The Work on the Topic Envisaged by the International Law Commission*

As D.P.O'Connell stressed as early as in 1956, "Upon [the subject of State nationality], perhaps more than any other in the law of State succession, codification, or international legislation, is urgently demanded."[41]

At its 45th session, in 1993, the International Law Commission decided to add to its agenda as a new topic the question of State succession and its impact on the nationality of natural and juridical persons. The UN General Assembly, in the light of the situation in Eastern Europe, endorsed this proposal by its Resolution 48/31 of 9 December 1994.

In the Commission's view, the comprehensive examination of State practice should reveal whether a set of principles concerning nationality in cases of State succession can be identified.

The clear statement of a minimum standard criteria for *ex lege* acquisition of nationality could provide useful guidelines to legislators of new States that are in the process of drafting laws in this matter.

It could also facilitate the role of third States as far as the application of international treaties between them and a successor State is concerned. The application of many such treaties directly concerns individuals, or more precisely "nationals" of the treaty parties. Sometimes there is a need for the application of these treaties even before the law on nationality is adopted by the successor State. Thus a "preliminary" determination of the nationality of individuals residing in the territory where the change of the sovereignty occurred becomes the pre-condition for the continued application of the mentioned treaties.

The possible outcome of the work of the International Law Commission on this subject could be a study in the form of a report or a draft declaration to be adopted by the General Assembly. The Commission recognized that the elaboration of a draft convention, the traditional form it has given to the majority of its drafts, might be subject to the risk of facing the same kind of problems that the International Law Commission faced during the work on the previous State succession topics, for example, the length of the codification work, or the problem of application of the convention in respect of the new States as non-parties to it.

[41]　O'Connell, *op. cit.* (note 22), p. 258.

ALAIN PELLET

Commentaires sur:
les problèmes découlant de la création et de la
dissolution des Etats et les flux de réfugiés[1]

1. Indépendamment de mon ignorance – très réelle –, le sujet qui nous a été imparti m'a plongé dans une certaine perplexité. Il me semble en effet qu'au plan juridique, le rapprochement des deux thèmes qui le composent: création et dissolution d'Etats d'une part, flux de réfugiés d'autre part, est passablement artificiel.

Certes, dans les faits, la création ou la dissolution d'un Etat peut être à l'origine d'un flux migratoire mais il n'y a aucune relation juridique de cause à effet entre ceci et cela, tout au plus une certaine fréquence statistique. Il est du reste significatif qu'aucun index des matières des principaux ouvrages récents consacrés aux réfugiés ne mentionne le mot "succession".[2]

2. Je crois comprendre que cette perplexité est partagée par Václav MIKULKA et il me semble qu'elle transparaît dans son exposé.

Il retient une interprétation stricte du premier élément de notre sujet puisque, sans aborder le problème général de la création d'Etats, il s'est interrogé exclusivement sur la seule création d'Etats résultant de la dissolution d'un Etat pré-existant et, sans remonter dans le temps, il a concentré son attention sur les trois cas les plus récents de dissolution: celle de l'URSS, celle de la Yougoslavie et celle de la Tchécoslovaquie. Sans méconnaître le fait que le passé est souvent utile pour éclairer le présent, je crois qu'il a eu raison: les précédents des Empires austro-hongrois et ottoman sont trop spécifiques pour fournir des guides utiles permettant de dégager des situations juridiques applicables aux situations contemporaines. Ceci a du reste été rappelé à

---

[1] La présente contribution ne constitue pas une étude autonome. Il s'agit de réactions spontanées et sans prétentions scientifiques au rapport de Václav MIKULKA, reproduit ci-dessus.

[2] V. par exemples: Goodwin-Gill, Guy S., *The Refugee in International Law,* Oxford 1983 XXVI-318p.; Hathaway, James C., *The Law of Refugee Status,* Toronto 1991, XXVIII-252p.; Joly, Danièle, *Refugees and Asylum in Europe,* San Francisco 1992, X-166p.; Loescher, Gil et Monahan, Leila (eds.), *Refugees in International Relations,* Oxford 1989, XII-430p.; Nanda, V.P., *Refugee Law and Policy,* New York 1989, X-228p. ou Plender, Richard, *International Migration Law,* Dordrecht 1988, XXVII-587p.

V. Gowlland-Debbas (ed.), The Problem of Refugees in the Light of Contemporary International Law Issues,
51–57.
© 1996 *Kluwer Academic Publishers. Printed in the Netherlands.*

plusieurs reprises durant les débats de la CDI préalables à l'adoption de la Convention de 1978 sur la succession d'Etats en matière de traités. Václav MIKULKA en a fait une analyse fouillée et je n'y reviendrai pas sinon pour dire que je partage globalement ses vues sur ce point et rappeler qu'en tout état de cause, le problème ne se pose pas en ce qui concerne l'ancienne Yougoslavie puisque tous les nouveaux Etats ont notifié leur intention de succéder aux conventions universelles concernant les réfugiés.

3. En ce qui concerne le second élément de notre sujet, Václav MIKULKA a, au contraire, retenu une conception assez extensive puisqu'il a passé en revue les problèmes concernant l'acquisition de la nationalité dans les nouveaux Etats issus de la dissolution. Toutefois, ici encore, nous buttons sur un problème d'interprétation du thème traité; les règles relatives à la nationalité ne concernent pas, en elles-mêmes, directement les réfugiés; les notions juridiques de réfugié d'une part et d'apatride d'autre part, sont clairement distinctes:[3] un réfugié est un étranger placé dans une situation spéciale vis-à-vis de l'Etat d'accueil qui lui accorde sa protection du fait de la persécution dont il est ou risque d'être victime dans son Etat d'origine; l'apatride est, conformément à la définition qu'en donne la Convention de 1954, une personne "qu'aucun Etat ne considère comme son ressortissant par application de la législation".[4]

Toutefois, et c'est je crois ce qui justifie le choix de Václav MIKULKA, ces notions distinctes ont fréquemment une cause unique: bien souvent, l'apatride est un réfugié qui fuit un régime politique oppresseur et la privation de nationalité est, pour ce régime, un moyen de persécution[5] aussi incompatible que cela soit avec le principe posé à l'article 15, paragraphe 2, de la Déclaration universelle des droits de l'homme.

4. En outre, la détermination de la nationalité a des incidences précises sur le statut juridique des réfugiés qui tiennent à la définition même qu'en donne l'article 1.A.2 de la Convention de 1951 modifié par le protocole de 1977:

> Le terme 'réfugié' s'applique à toute personne: 2) qui craignant avec raison d'être persécutée du fait de sa race, de sa religion, *de sa nationalité,* de son appartenance à un certain groupe social ou de ses opinions politiques, se trouve hors du pays *dont elle à la nationalité* et qui ne peut ou, du fait de cette crainte, ne veut se réclamer de la protection de ce pays . . .[6]

La seule lecture de ce texte montre combien la nationalité joue un rôle central dans la définition même du réfugié:[7] une personne ne peut être

---

[3] En ce sens, v. Goodwin-Gill, *op. cit.* (note 2), p. 26.
[4] Article 1er, par. 1.
[5] En ce sens, Goodwin-Gill, *op. cit.* (note 2), p. 26.
[6] Souligné par moi.
[7] Je laisse de côté le cas des apatrides envisagé dans la phrase suivante de l'article 1.A.2.

considérée comme telle que si elle peut craindre des persécutions dans le pays dont elle a la nationalité. Et ceci soulève quantité de questions dont les Commissions de recours des réfugiés existant dans les Etats parties à la Convention de 1951 ont eu à connaître depuis longtemps, mais qui présentent un caractère particulièrement aigu à l'heure actuelle s'agissant des personnes originaires de l'ex-Yougoslavie. On peut au moins songer aux questions suivantes:

1° le demandeur d'asile territorial a-t-il une nationalité?
2° selon quel(s) critère(s) ou en fonction de quelle loi convient-il de déterminer sa nationalité?
3° si l'application de ce ou de ces critères conduit à constater que l'on est en présence d'un double (ou d'un multiple) national, les persécutions doivent-elles venir ou risquer de venir de chacun des Etats de rattachements ou suffit-il qu'elles soient à redouter de la part de n'importe lequel ou d'un Etat déterminé? et, si tel est le cas, selon quel(s) critère(s) procéder à cette détermination?

Cette problématique est, je crois, tout à fait banale, même si les réponses des Commissions nationales de recours des réfugiés sont assez diversifiées. Je n'ai ni l'ambition ni la capacité d'analyser cette jurisprudence, mais il peut être intéressant de voir comment, concrètement, ces problèmes se posent à la lumière du rapport de Václav MIKULKA.

5. En effet, la dissolution d'un Etat vient encore compliquer les réponses à ces questions comme le montre l'exemple particulièrement douloureux, mais qui est aussi celui que je connais le moins mal, de la Yougoslavie.

Par hypothèse, l'Etat prédécesseur, "dissout", n'existe plus: nous sommes uniquement en présence d'Etats successeurs; cinq dans notre exemple. En conséquence, les ressortissants de l'ancienne République socialiste fédérative de Yougoslavie (RSFY) ne peuvent plus se prévaloir de cette nationalité. A l'inverse, chacun ayant droit à une nationalité,[8] je partage l'opinion de Václav MIKULKA selon laquelle toutes ces personnes ont le droit à la nationalité de l'un au moins[9] des Etats successeurs.

6. Ici, plusieurs considérations, en partie contradictoires, interfèrent et s'entrechoquent. Le principe de souveraineté peut s'opposer au droit de chaque être humain à une nationalité. Les Etats successeurs sont tous des Etats nouveaux (même si la terminologie, sinon confuse, du moins extrêmement compliquée, des Conventions de Vienne de 1978 et 1983 occulte quelque peu cette évidence); et, tant la Convention de La Haye de 1930 que la jurisprudence traditionnelle font de l'octroi et de la réglementation de la nationalité une compétence souveraine de l'Etat.

---

[8] Cf. l'article 15, para. 1 de la Déclaration universelle des droits de l'homme.
[9] Sur la question de la combinaison éventuelle de plusieurs "nationalités", v. *infra* n°. 9, 12, 13.

Autant il est certain que les principes posés à l'article 15 de la Déclaration universelle de 1948 excluaient que l'ancienne Yougoslavie puisse priver ses nationaux de leur nationalité; autant le droit souverain de chaque Etat de déterminer les règles applicables en matière de nationalité paraît exclure, *prima facie,* que les nouveaux Etats issus de sa dissolution puissent avoir des obligations juridiques strictes d'octroyer leur nationalité à toutes les personnes qui le demandent: il ne s'agit nullement de "priver" des personnes de leur nationalité mais de déterminer celle-ci.

7. Il ne me paraît pourtant pas certain que l'on ne puisse pas trouver, dans le droit international positif, de directives dans ce domaine – car, même si les Etats bénéficient à cet égard de compétences souveraines, celles-ci ne peuvent s'exercer que dans le cadre des règles générales qui les réglementent.[10] Après tout, de l'affaire *Nottebohm*[11] à l'affaire *Florence Mergé,*[12] de l'affaire *Flegenheimer,*[13] à la sentence A/18[14] du Tribunal des différends irano-américains, les juridictions et les tribunaux arbitraux internationaux ont dû et pu, en cas de contestation, déterminer aux fins du règlement des affaires qui leur étaient soumises, la nationalité des requérants ou des bénéficiaires de la protection diplomatique.

On peut déduire de cette jurisprudence au moins un principe dans ce domaine: les Etats bénéficient de compétences souveraines; mais cela ne signifie pas qu'ils puissent "faire n'importe quoi". Au delà des divergences de jurisprudence que ces arrêts et sentences arbitrales révèlent, un principe au moins surnage, celui du lien de rattachement effectif sur lequel la CIJ s'est fondée en 1955[15] et que les autres affaires citées ne démentent pas; et, sans entrer dans une discussion fort technique qui nous éloignerait trop de notre sujet, il convient de noter que, dans ce rattachement effectif, le "lieu de vie", les centres d'intérêt et d'activité jouent, dans tous les cas, un rôle fondamental. Je crois que l'on peut tirer de ceci la conclusion suivante: les Etats issus de la dissolution d'un Etat pré-existant, ne peuvent y refuser leur nationalité aux personnes établies sur leur territoire et y ayant leur principal centre d'activités (c'est le principe de rattachement effectif), si du moins elles n'ont pas, par ailleurs, une autre nationalité (c'est la conséquence du principe du droit de tout être humain à une nationalité).

8. Ce raisonnement me paraît être renforcé par un autre principe, lui "négatif" si l'on peut dire: celui de l'interdiction de toute discrimination fondée sur la

---

[10]   V. Plender, R., *op. cit.* (note 2), p. 48, ou Iovanovic, Stovan, *Restriction des compétences discrétionnaires des Etats en droit international*, Paris 1988, pp. 78–80.

[11]   CIJ, Arrêt du 6 avril 1955, *Rec.* 1955, p. 4.

[12]   Commission de conciliation Etats-Unis-Italie, sentence du 10 juin 1953, *RSANU*, vol. XIV, p. 236.

[13]   *Id.* sentence du 20 septembre 1958, *ibidem* p. 327.

[14]   Sentence du 6 avril 1986, *CTR.* 1985, p. 251.

[15]   *Rec.* 1955, p. 23.

race ou les croyances religieuses ou politiques.[16] En d'autres termes, les Etats nouveaux issus de la dissolution de la RSFY – mais ceci vaut également pour l'URSS et la Tchécoslovaquie – doivent, me semble-t-il, en vertu du droit international, reconnaître comme leurs nationaux toutes les personnes établies sur leur territoire qui avaient auparavant la nationalité yougoslave sans que les considérations ethniques aient le moindre rôle à jouer à cet égard.

Ceci a-t-il une incidence sur le statut des réfugiés? Je pense que oui; en tout cas sur son octroi.

Si fuyant la Yougoslavie (Serbie et Monténégro) un Musulman auquel cet Etat refuserait sa nationalité (et ce serait vrai d'un Serbe fuyant la Bosnie-Herzégovine), demandait le statut de réfugié en Suisse ou en France, il me semble que ces pays devraient se fonder sur sa nationalité "yougoslave", les décisions des autorités serbo-monténégrines ne pouvant être opposées ni au demandeur d'asile, ni aux Etats tiers.

9. Pour ce qui concerne les doubles ou multiples nationaux, je suis, en tout cas en règle générale, plus réservé que Václav MIKULKA sur la pertinence de l'effectivité pour en limiter la survenance, car l'effectivité peut être "plurale". On peut imaginer, par exemple, qu'une personne soit née et travaille en Croatie, mais aie toute sa famille en Yougoslavie (Serbie et Monténégro). Dans ce cas, les deux Etats peuvent légitimement le revendiquer comme un national, ne serait-ce que parce que *jus sanguinis* et *jus soli* constituent, au même titre l'un que l'autre, des principes juridiques traduisant l'effectivité du rattachement.

Et une telle situation me paraît également susceptible d'avoir des incidences sur le droit des réfugiés: si notre demandeur d'asile est menacé aussi bien en Croatie qu'en Yougoslavie (Serbie et Monténégro) – et cette éventualité ne peut malheureusement être totalement exlue –, le statut de réfugié pourra lui être octroyé. Mais si, *dans l'un* au moins de ces pays, aucune menace particulière ne pèse sur lui, il me semble qu'il n'est pas inhumain de lui refuser ce droit: les pays d'accueil aussi ont des droits. Telle a du reste été la position récente de la Commission française de recours des réfugiés, qui a pris une position ferme en ce sens, confirmant la jurisprudence antérieure adoptée dans d'autres pays.[17]

10. J'ajoute cependant que le cas des pays baltes dont a parlé Václav MIKULKA en citant Rein MULLERSON[18] me paraît être un peu différent, au moins en droit strict: incorporés de force dans l'ancienne URSS, ces Etats, en tout cas l'Estonie, ont dit à juste titre, rétablir le *statu quo ante* et ont imposé un droit de la nationalité reposant strictement sur le *jus sanguinis*. Ceci était

---

[16] V. les articles 1er et 7 de la Déclaration de 1948 et 2, para.1, du Pacte relatif aux droits civils et politiques.

[17] En ce sens, v. Goodwin-Gill, *op. cit.* (note 2), p. 26.

[18] V. à ce sujet Mullerson, Rein, *International Law, Rights and Politics*, Londres-New York 1994, pp. 92–116.

techniquement possible et l'on peut comprendre, en droit, le raisonnement sur lequel cette décision est fondée: il s'agit de "gommer" les conséquences de l'occupation soviètique.

Comme Václav MIKULKA et Rein MULLERSON, je pense cependant que cette position est fort discutable humainement et qu'à défaut de constituer une discrimination juridiquement interdite, ce genre de politique risque d'aboutir à la multiplication des cas d'apatridies, que le droit international s'efforce de limiter; car à l'inverse, les principes que j'ai évoqués tout à l'heure[19] n'obligent nullement la Russie à reconnaître ces personnes comme étant ses ressortissants. Les choses étant ce qu'elles sont, il m'apparaît que, en ce qui concerne le statut des réfugiés, l'Etat d'accueil devrait, dans ce cas, considérer le demandeur d'asile comme un apatride et, en prévision d'hypothèses de ce genre qui tendent à se multiplier, il serait sans doute bon de réfléchir à une coordination plus étroite entre le droit des réfugiés et celui de l'apatridie.

11. On pourrait penser qu'après tout, le cas de l'ancienne Yougoslavie n'est pas tellement différent puisque, au sein même de la RSFY, les nationaux de cet Etat pouvaient déclarer la "nationalité" à laquelle ils appartenaient. Dés lors, pourrait-on prétendre, le principe de continuité serait, là aussi, applicable. Je ne le crois pas.

En premier lieu, à côté des nationalités reconnues (serbe, slovène, croate, etc.), il y avait aussi des "Yougoslaves" sans rattachement "national", c'est à dire sans appartenance ethnique déclarée. En second lieu et surtout, le critère de ces "nationalités" n'avait rien à voir avec ceux en vigueur pour la détermination de la nationalité au plan international; admettre un tel raisonnement, ce serait consacrer "l'ethnicité" en droit des gens, c'est à dire, pour user d'un mot plus cru: le racisme. Dire qu'un "Croate" dont la famille est établie au Montenegro où il travaille a, après la dissolution de la Fédération, la nationalité du nouvel Etat croate, c'est le "classer" selon un inacceptable critère ethnique au mépris du principe de non discrimination.

12. Ce problème est très différent de celui qu'évoque Václav MIKULKA à la fin de son intervention lorsqu'il parle de l'avis n° 2 de la Commission d'Arbitrage de la Conférence pour l'ex-Yougoslavie, en date du 11 Janvier 1992.[20]

Dans cet avis la "Commission Badinter" a affirmé le droit pour chaque être humain de voir reconnue son appartenance à la communauté ethnique, religieuse ou linguistique de son choix. Mais ceci n'a rien à voir avec le lien de nationalité au sens du droit international qui est un lien de rattachement *à un Etat* déterminé. En l'espèce, la Commission visait simplement le droit des personnes appartenant à une minorité d'être traitée en tant que telle *à*

---

[19]   *Supra*, n° 7 et 8.
[20]   Cet avis est reproduit in *RGDIP* (1992), p. 266; pour le texte anglais, v. 31 *ILM* (1992), p. 1494.

l'intérieur de l'Etat. La première question posée par Václav MIKULKA ne me paraît donc pas se poser; le problème de la "nationalité effective" n'est pas pertinent à cet égard: il ne s'agit tout simplement pas de "nationalité" dans l'acception que le droit international donne à ce mot.

Notre rapporteur semble en second lieu reprocher à la solution préconisée par la Commission d'arbitrage[21] d'encourager le sentiment d'appartenance ethnique et donc de pérenniser les causes de conflit. Ceci me paraît être une vue très abstraite des choses: le sentiment d'appartenance ethnique existe; on ne le crée pas en le reconnaissant et je ne suis pas sûr que le nier ou l'empêcher de s'exprimer soit le meilleur moyen de résoudre les problémes en résultant. Au demeurant je ne suis pas convaincu non plus que cela soit compatible avec le niveau minimum de protection découlant de l'article 27 du Pacte relatif aux droits civils et politiques de 1966.

13. Enfin, et c'est plus à mon commentaire paru dans l'*Annuaire français de droit international*[22] qu'à la position de la Commission d'arbitrage elle-même que s'oppose Václav MIKULKA, celui-ci me reproche d'avoir suggéré qu'une solution possible, à peine esquissée par l'avis n°2, serait d'opérer une dissociation entre nationalité et citoyenneté, la première étant fondée sur le "rattachement effectif", le *locus*, le centre de vie, la seconde sur les aspirations des personnes concernées, étant entendu que pourraient résulter de cette citoyenneté certains droits (de vote par exemple) dans un Etat autre que celui de la nationalité.

Il n'est évidemment pas question de considérer l'Europe de Maastricht comme un modèle idéal à exporter; il me semble simplement que la crise yougoslave (comme d'ailleurs les problèmes qui se posent dans certaines "marches" de la Fédération de Russie) est trop complexe pour que l'on puisse s'en tenir aux vieilles recettes jacobines classiques et qu'il serait bon d'expérimenter des solutions plus neuves, plus imaginatives et mieux adaptées.

Mais ceci, finalement, nous entraîne bien loin du thème initial de ce débat – sauf à considérer que c'est l'attachement rigide au vieil Etat-nation, qui est la cause, en tout cas l'une des causes de l'instabilité que connaît l'Est de notre continent et que c'est ce manque d'imagination et de projet neuf qui est à l'origine de l'hideuse épuration ethnique et des flux de réfugiés qu'elle crée·. . .

---

[21] Le passage le plus directement pertinent de l'avis N° 2 du 11 janvier 1992 se lit ainsi: "En outre, l'article 1er de chacun des deux Pactes internationaux relatifs aux droits de l'homme de 1966 établit que le droit d'autodétermination est un principe protecteur des droits de l'homme. En vertu de ce droit,chaque être humain peut revendiquer son appartenance à la communauté ethnique, religieuse ou linguistique de son choix. Selon la Commission, l'une des conséquences de ce principe pourrait être que, sur la base d'accords entre les Républiques, les membres des populations serbes de Bosnie-Herzégovine et de Croatie puissent, s'ils le désirent, se voir reconnaître la nationalité de leur choix avec tous les droits et toutes les obligations en découlant à l'égard de tous les Etats concernés" (*RGDIP* (1992) p. 267).

[22] "Note sur la Commission d'arbitrage de la Conférence européenne pour la paix en Yougoslavie", 37 *AFDI* (1991), pp. 329–348, not. pp. 340–341.

CHRISTIAN TOMUSCHAT

State Responsibility and the Country of Origin

Since its origins back in the 1920s refugee law has invariably been understood as a special branch of international law addressed almost exclusively
to potential asylum countries. In particular, the Geneva Convention of 1951
on the Status of Refugees[1] sets forth an elaborate regime of legal rules that
create duties for States Parties having received refugees or being faced with
demands for admission. Pursuant to the principle of non-refoulement (Article
33), which may also have acquired the legal force of international customary
law,[2] these obligations go even so far as to prohibit States from expelling or
returning ("refouler") a refugee to a country where his life or freedom would
be threatened on account of his race, religion, nationality, membership in a
particular social group or political opinion.

Yet, flows of refugees have their causes in human conduct outside the
destinations to which the persons involved are heading. Under the Geneva
Convention, a refugee is a person who, because of well-founded fear of
political persecution, finds himself outside his State of nationality, unable to
obtain the protection of that State. Thus, the country of origin, which has
set in motion the tragic sequence of events, is an essential – and even the
most important – actor in the complex triangular relationship whose other
elements are the refugee and the receiving State. If it behaved in consonance
with current human rights standards, the whole problem would simply dis-
appear. Therefore, why should the burden be entirely on other States? Should
it not in the last analysis fall back on the country of origin?[3] This is the issue
which the present paper will attempt to explore.

---

[1] *UNTS* 189, p. 150.
[2] For a full discussion see Kälin, W., *Das Prinzip des Non-Refoulement*, Bern/Frankfurt 1982,
pp. 59–82, 352–353. The recent judgment of the US Supreme Court in *Sale v. Haitian Centers
Council* of 21 June 1993, 88 *AJIL* (1994), p. 114, interpreting Article 33 (1) of the Geneva
Convention, held that even *bona fide* refugees may be returned outside the territory of the US.
For a complete documentation concerning that case see 6 *IJRL* (1994), pp. 69 et seq.
[3] See, in particular, Coles, G. J. L., *State Responsibility in Relation to the Refugee Problem,
with Particular Reference to the State of Origin*, Geneva 1993, pp. 4–8; Garvey, J. I., "Toward
a Reformulation of International Refugee Law", 26 *Harv.ILJ* (1985), p. 483, at 483–484;

V. Gowlland-Debbas (ed.), The Problem of Refugees in the Light of Contemporary International Law Issues,
59–79.
© 1996 *Kluwer Academic Publishers. Printed in the Netherlands.*

I. STATE RESPONSIBILITY

A. *Responsibility Towards Individuals*

1) *Refugee – Term Used in a Non-Technical, Broad Sense*

An examination of possible rights of individuals against a State of origin cannot take as its starting point the refugee as defined by the 1951 Geneva Convention. Article 1 of that instrument has created an extremely artful construct which, on the one hand, includes persons who may not have suffered any actual injury – because fear of persecution is sufficient to claim refugee status – and which, on the other hand, excludes persons whose human rights may have been seriously violated, for instance in a civil war. It would be extremely difficult for the purposes of the enquiry undertaken here to follow strictly the borderlines of that definition. In order to simplify matters, we shall confine ourselves to considering whether an individual who has been coerced into leaving his or her country may have a claim against that country under general rules on State responsibility.[4] Most refugees will fall within this category.

2) *Action Attributable to the State*

According to the draft articles on State responsibility, Part I, adopted by the International Law Commission (ILC) in 1980,[6] an internationally wrongful act presupposes first and foremost that an act or omission has occurred which is attributable to the State concerned (Article 3 (a)). This requirement excludes many scenarios from the scope of possible claims under the law of State responsibility.[6] Natural disasters, famine and epidemics are not phenomena that can be directly imputed to human activity, although in many cases it might

---

Martin, D. A., "Interdiction, Intervention, and the New Frontiers of Refugee Law and Policy", 33 *Virg.JIL* (1993), p. 473, at 477; Takkenberg, A., "Mass Migration of Asylum Seekers and State Responsibility", XIII *Thesaurus Acroasium* (1987), p. 787, at 788. In political documents, the issue is raised with an infinite amount of caution, as exemplified by the Report of Special Rapporteur Sadruddin Aga Khan, "Questions of the Violation of Human Rights and Fundamental Freedoms in any Part of the World, with Particular Reference to Colonial and other Dependent Countries and Territories", UN Doc. E/CN.4/1503 (31 December 1981), whose only relevant recommendation suggests that an "early-warning system" be established. Only slightly more courageous is the Report of the Group of Governmental Experts on International Co-operation to Avert New Flows of Refugees, UN Doc. A/41/324 (13 May 1986), paras. 8, 9, 66 c) and d), which was endorsed by UN General Assembly Resolution 41/70 of 3 December 1986. For a comment on that report see Lee, L. T., "Toward a World without Refugees: The United Nations Group of Governmental Experts on International Co-operation to Avert New Flows of Refugees", 57 *BYIL* (1986), pp. 317 *et seq.*

[4]   This was also the point of departure of the Group of Governmental Experts, see their Report, *op. cit.* (note 3), para. 26.

[5]   *YBILC* (1980), Vol. II, Part 2, p. 30.

[6]   Rightly stressed by Hofmann, R., "Refugee-Generating Policies and the Law of State Responsibility", 45 *ZaöRV* (1986), p. 694, at 700. See also Akhavan, P./Bergsmo, M., "The Application of the Doctrine of State Responsibility to Refugee Creating States", 58 *Nordic Journal of International Law* (1989), p. 243, at 252.

be found that preventive measures could have avoided the fatal consequences. Nor does civil war as such constitute a complex of occurrences wholly under the responsibility of a national government: it can only be made accountable for actions carried out by its own troops.[7] Lastly, it stands to reason that a State cannot be answerable if its citizens flee the country because it has become the victim of foreign aggression. However, what essentially remains as a pattern of actions susceptible of entailing responsibility is a policy that flagrantly violates human rights to the detriment of (almost) all citizens or a specific group of the population of the State of origin.

3) *Breach of an International Obligation*

An internationally wrongful act presupposes, second, a breach of an international obligation.[8] On the reverse side, all international human rights constitute obligations for the State to which they are addressed. The most pertinent right in this connection is the right of every person to live without disturbance in his or her country. Today, there is no longer a need to rely in this respect solely on Article 13 of the Universal Declaration of Human Rights.[9] The International Covenant on Civil and Political Rights, which guarantees the right of everyone not to be deprived of the right to enter his own country and thereby implicitly recognizes a right of abode (Article 12 (4)), has by now (31 March 1994) been ratified by not less than 126 States. Through that wide acceptance from countries all across the globe, it has become the relevant yardstick for State conduct in the field of human rights. In any event, one can safely assume that the right of a person to stay and live in his or her country constitutes, today, customary international law, all the more so since it reflects the traditional position that the "natural" place for an individual is the territory of the State of nationality.

If an individual is not directly expelled, but is subjected instead to pressure and harassment affecting his other rights under the Covenant or customary law – his life and physical integrity, freedom from arbitrary arrest, freedom of expression, etc.[10] – so that eventually no other option remains open than to leave the country of residence in order to be able to lead a life in human dignity, there is still no escaping the conclusion that the right under Article 12 of

---

[7] For a full discussion see von Sternberg, M. R., "Political Asylum and the Law of Armed Conflict: Refugee Status, Human Rights and Humanitarian Law Concerns", 5 *IJRL* (1993), pp. 153 et seq.

[8] *YBILC, op. cit.* (note 5), Article 3 (b).

[9] Notwithstanding many voices to the contrary, the Declaration has not yet as such, in its entirety, crystallized as customary law; for a recent discussion see, for instance, Carrillo Salcedo, J., entry "Human Rights, Universal Declaration (1948)", in *Encyclopedia of Public International Law*, Vol. 8, Amsterdam *et al.* 1985, pp. 303–307; Kamminga, M. T., *Inter-State Accountability for Violations of Human Rights*, Philadelphia 1992, pp. 133–134; Meron, Th., *Human Rights and Humanitarian Norms as Customary Law*, Oxford 1989, pp. 82–85.

[10] For an examination of the possible human rights violations connected with generating flows of refugees see the report by Sadruddin Aga Khan, *op. cit.* (note 3), pp. 17–29.

the Covenant – or the corresponding right under general international law – has been violated. To be sure, Article 12 (4) is a right that may be restricted. Restrictions are permitted to the extent that they are not "arbitrary". In order to interpret this term, a possible option is to have indirect recourse to the limitation clause of paragraph 3, which as such does not apply to paragraph 4.[11] However, although the scope of the notions set forth in paragraph 3 (in particular: "public order (*ordre public*)") is fairly wide, governments cannot possibly rely thereon to expel on a mass scale their own citizens. In an individual case, to pronounce a banishment against a person may be a more humane solution than to confine him or her to a place of detention. The tradition of ancient Greece in this respect should not be lightly discarded.[12] But State power, which is always governmental power, lacks the legitimacy to push entire parts of a population out of their ancestral homes.[13] A government that sees no other solution than to have recourse to this extreme remedy, or which puts is citizens under such unbearable pressure that they "voluntarily" choose to flee, acts contrary to the basic interests of its people and thereby breaches the covenant of trust from which it has received its authority. As Berthold Brecht sarcastically noted: If the government is dissatisfied with its people, why does it not dissolve it and elect another one?[14]

[11]   The drafting history points to a more restrictive interpretation, see Nowak, M., *UNO-Pakt über bürgerliche und politische Rechte und Fakultativprotokoll. CCPR-Kommentar*, Kehl/ Straßburg/Arlington 1989, commentary on Article 12, notes 45–47, pp. 229–230. Almost irrationally, St. Jagerskiold, "The Freedom of Movement", in Henkin, L. (ed.), *The International Bill of Rights*, New York 1981, p. 180, contends that "there was no intention here to address the claims of masses of people who have been displaced as a byproduct of war or by political transfers of territory or population".

[12]   This is what the drafters considered lawful, if determined under a procedure according to law, see Nowak, *op. cit.* (note 11), *idem.*

[13]   The Cairo Declaration of the ILA of Principles of International Law on Compensation to Refugees, April 1992, reprinted in 87 *AJIL* (1993), p. 157, provides somewhat lightly (principle 2) that "the State that turns a person into a refugee commits an internationally wrongful act". Individual cases are no sufficient basis for a conclusive legal assessment.

[14]   "Die Lösung", *Buckower Elegien*, 1953, Edition Suhrkamp 1397, Frankfurt 1986, p. 11:

"Nach dem Aufstand des 17. Juni
Ließ der Sekretär des Schriftstellerverbands
In der Stalinallee Flugblätter verteilen
Auf denen zu lesen war, daß das Volk
Das Vertrauen der Regierung verscherzt habe
Und es nur durch doppelte Arbeit
Zurückerobern könne. Wäre es da
Nicht doch einfacher, die Regierung
Löste das Volk auf und
Wählte ein anderes?"

4) *The Legal Consequences Flowing from a Breach of Human Rights Obligations*

The question is what legal consequences flow from a breach of human rights obligations? Does a person having suffered the fate of expulsion from his or her home country acquire an individual right of reparation?

a) *Human Rights – Individual Entitlements Under International Law?* As a general premise of this question, it would be helpful to know whether human rights establish in general a juridical relationship at the level of international law between States and individuals under their jurisdiction. In spite of many general writings on the position of the individual in international law,[15] to date this issue has not been sufficiently clarified. As far as treaties for the protection of human rights are concerned, they are generally implemented by and through national authorities and become applicable to the individual by virtue of acts of domestic legal systems, which can either make those treaties part and parcel of the internal legal order by a national law of approval (continental system) or attempt to implement them on the basis of municipal legislation (British system).[16] However that may be, as long as a human rights treaty is confined to substantive provisions, the individual lacks a right of action of his own within a juridical context outside the domestic legal order. It is only when such a treaty additionally provides for a remedy to be submitted to an international body that the legal relationship grows beyond the confines of national law.[17] This is true of the European Convention of Human Rights, where the substantive guarantees and the individual application under Article 25 now form an integrated whole since acceptance of that remedy, although formally a distinct and separate act, is considered by the community of States

---

[15] In the more recent literature, an essentially affirmative answer is given by Barberis, J. A., "Nouvelles questions concernant la personnalité juridique internationale", 179 *RdC* (1983-I), p. 145, at 181–189; Dominicé, C., "L'émergence de l'individu en droit international public", 16 *Annales d'études internationales* (1987–1988), pp. 1–16; Dormenval, A., *Procédures onusiennes de mise en oeuvre des droits de l'homme: limites ou défauts?*, Graduate institute of international studies, Paris 1991, pp. 100–102; Fourlanos, G., "Subjectivity in International Law and the Position of the Individual", 53 *Nordisk Tidsskrift for International Ret* (1984), pp. 9 *et seq.*; Janis, M. W., "Individuals as Subjects of International Law", 17 *Cornell International Law Journal* (1984), pp. 61 *et seq.*; and Sunga, S. L., *Individual Responsibility in International Law for Serious Human Rights Violations*, Dordrecht *et al.* 1992, pp. 139–156, in particular p. 155; more skeptical are Partsch, K. J., entry "Individuals in International Law", in *Encyclopedia of Public International Law*, Vol. 8, Amsterdam *et al.* 1985, pp. 316–321; and Perrin, G., "La défense de l'individu en droit international public", 36 *Revue juridique et politique indépendance et coopération* (1982), pp. 701–710. Generally, all authors recognize the decisive importance of remedies enabling an individual to enforce his or her rights before an international forum.

[16] See our study "National Implementation of International Standards on Human Rights", *Canadian Human Rights Yearbook* (1984/85), pp. 31 *et seq.*, and generally Jacobs, F. G./Roberts, St., *The Effect of Treaties in Domestic Law*, London 1987.

[17] This is also the test applied by the ICJ in the *Reparation for Injuries* case, ICJ Rep. 1949, p. 174, at 179.

associated in the Council of Europe a political obligation inextricably bound up with the ratification of the Convention itself. Under the International Covenant on Civil and Political Rights, too, the relationship has become a very close one in as much as States parties have submitted to the Optional Protocol providing for the remedy of individual communication; indeed, out of the 126 States parties, not less than 76 are at the same time bound by the Optional Protocol.

Furthermore, a relationship under international law comes into being whenever a State, through its agents, executes a policy of grave human rights violations, characterized by the international community as crimes which in no instance can be justified by domestic law and for which the authors involved incur penal liability under international law. Under such circumstances, as a necessary corollary of the absolute outlawing of the criminal action concerned, the potential victims must be deemed to enjoy a right of resistance, directly conferred upon them by the international legal order.[18] With regard to genocide, this logic is particularly obvious. Nobody can be required by law passively to endure his or her assassination by a government that has turned into a murderous machine.

b) *An Individual Right to Reparation?* However, even if one proceeds from the assumption that human rights constitute individual entitlements under international law, at least to the extent that they are supported by an international mechanism of individual complaint or that core entitlements of the individual are arbitrarily impaired, it is by no means sure what consequences are entailed by the violation of such a right. The general proposition that a breach of an international engagement involves an obligation to make reparation, as it was formulated by the Permanent Court of International Justice in the *Chorzow* case,[19] is well known and need not be repeated here. Similarly, it should be noted that under Article 6 *bis* of the draft articles elaborated by the ILC on the form and contents of State responsibility "the injured State is entitled to obtain from the State which has committed an internationally wrongful act full reparation".[20] However, the relevant rule has always been formulated as inter-State law governing legal relationships between States as subjects of international law. Indeed, it has never occurred to any of the Special Rapporteurs of the ILC on the topic of State responsibility that a State could incur responsibility vis-à-vis the individuals injured in case of a breach of a human rights obligation.[21] This finding carries all the more weight since

---

[18]   For more details see Tomuschat, C., "The Right of Resistance and Human Rights", in UNESCO (ed.), *Violations of Human Rights. Possible Rights of Recourse and Forms of Resistance*, Paris 1984, pp. 13 *et seq.*

[19]   Of 13 September 1928, *Collection of Judgments*, Series A No. 17, at 29, 47.

[20]   Report of the ILC on the work of its forty-fifth session, 48 GAOR Suppl. No. 10, UN Doc. A/48/10 (1993), p. 130.

[21]   This neglect of the specific aspects of State responsibility has been rightly criticized by Kamminga, *op. cit.* (note 9), p. 128; Van Boven, Th., *Study concerning the right to restitution,*

violation of human rights is specifically mentioned in the available drafts. Article 19 of Part I,[22] which deals with "international crimes", devotes an entire sub-paragraph (para. 3 (c)) to "serious" breaches "on a widespread scale of an international obligation of essential importance for safeguarding the human being, such as those prohibiting slavery, genocide and *apartheid*", and Article 5 of Part II,[23] which defines the "injured State", refers explicitly to human rights treaties (para. 2 (e) (iii)). Thus, the existence of human rights law has by no means been overlooked. But seemingly the legal position was assessed as not conferring any right of reparation directly on an individual victim of a violation.

It is significant, in this connection, that the relevant human rights treaties remain largely silent on the issue of the consequences deriving from non-compliance with its obligations by a State. The premise is always that a State must fulfill what it has formally pledged to do. Thus, to the extent that one may assume the existence of an individual entitlement under international law, there exists a right to specific performance. The individual has the right to claim that the governmental machinery he or she is confronted with behave as set forth in the relevant provisions. As far as violations of a continuing character are concerned, one may therefore speak of a right to cessation. Yet, it is less clear – or even totally obscure – whether a right to reparation proper comes into being, a right that would be designed to "wipe out" the consequences of the commission of the unlawful act.

The relevant stipulations of the European Convention of Human Rights are remarkably cautious. According to Article 50, the European Court of Human Rights (Court) shall, "if necessary, afford just satisfaction to the injured party", if the internal law of the author State "allows only partial reparation to be made for the consequences" of the unlawful conduct complained of and found to exist.[24] First of all, the phrase "if necessary" grants the Court a wide margin of discretion. Second, domestic law, which ordinarily is considered from the viewpoint of international law as a pure factual element, is recognized as an obstacle justifying the wrong-doing State to abstain from restitution in kind. Thirdly, one may note that the individual is not openly recognized as the holder of a right to "just satisfaction" in lieu of reparation in kind; what Article 50 does, instead, is authorize the Court to grant satis-

---

compensation and rehabilitation for victims of gross violations of human rights and fundamental freedoms, UN Doc. E/CN.4/Sub.2/1993/8 (2 July 1993), p. 19 para. 47.

[22]   *YBILC, loc. cit.* (note 5).

[23]   *YBILC* (1986), Vol. II, Part 2, p. 38.

[24]   For a detailed study of the importance of Article 50 see Dannemann, G., *Schadensersatz bei Verletzung der Europäischen Menschenrechtskonvention*, Köln *et al.* 1984; Polakiewicz, J., *Die Verpflichtungen der Staaten aus den Urteilen des Europäischen Gerichtshofs für Menschenrechte*, Berlin *et al.* 1993; Traßl, M., *Die Wiedergutmachung von Menschenrechtsverletzungen im Völkerrecht*, Berlin 1994, pp. 18 *et seq.*, as well as Frowein, J. A., "Entschädigung für Verletzung von Grundrechten", in *Des Menschen Recht zwischen Freiheit und Verantwortung. Festschrift für Karl Josef Partsch*, Berlin 1989, pp. 317 *et seq.*

faction as required under the circumstances. Lastly, in its jurisprudence the Court has constantly interpreted "just satisfaction" as being tantamount to financial compensation. Attempts by applicants to obtain a pronouncement requiring the defendant State to make good in kind the consequences of its unlawful conduct have always been in vain. Thus, in the *Bozano* case, the applicant had insisted on *restitutio in integrum*, namely re-surrender to French territory from which he had been removed in disregard of applicable French extradition procedures and therefore also in disregard of Article 5 of the Convention (right of individual freedom). But the Court did not accede to this demand; by avoiding to give a clear-cut answer, it implicitly made clear that its competence was confined to granting financial compensation.[25]

The legal position under the American Convention on Human Rights can be described in terms slightly more favourable to the individual. Article 63 (1) enjoins the Inter-American Court of Human Rights (Court) to rule, if it has made a finding of a violation, "that the injured party be ensured the enjoyment of his right or freedom that was violated". Thus, the Court is required to bring about cessation of the wrongful conduct complained of and found to exist. Additionally, however, it is incumbent on the Court (it "shall") to rule, "if appropriate, that the consequences of the measure or situation that constituted the breach of such right or freedom be remedied and that fair compensation be paid to the injured party". Judgments which fix compensatory damages are enforceable under the laws of the country concerned (Article 68 (2)). Some language in the first judgment on the merits of a case, the decision of the Court in *Velásquez Rodríguez* of 29 July 1988,[26] and in the subsequent judgment on compensatory damages in that case of 27 July 1989,[27] could be interpreted as conveying the message that the individual victim of a violation holds a true right to financial compensation. But nowhere do the judgments openly say so. Each time, they speak of a duty to make reparation[28] which was incumbent on the defendant, the State of Honduras. In fact, one may harbor serious doubts as to whether the "if-appropriate" clause permits to affirm the existence of an individual right proper – which could hardly be committed to the discretion of the Court. It is significant, in this regard, that the compensation due in the *Velásquez Rodríguez* case was to be negotiated and agreed upon between the Inter-American Commission and the Government of Honduras, not by the beneficiaries themselves.[29]

The body that has consistently shown a bold approach to the issue of

---

[25]   Judgment of 18 December 1986, *Publications of the European Court of Human Rights (PECHR)*, Series A, Vol. 111, p. 28 para. 65.

[26]   Inter-American Court of Human Rights, Series C: *Decisions and Judgments*, No. 4, p. 91 (English version).

[27]   Inter-American Court of Human Rights, Series C: *Decisions and Judgments*, No. 7, p. 33 (English version).

[28]   In particular: Judgment of 21 July 1989, paras. 25, 54.

[29]   Judgment of 29 July 1988, para. 194, subpara. 6. No agreement was reached, see judgment of 21 July 1989, para. 22.

reparation is the Human Rights Committee under the International Covenant on Civil and Political Rights. The Covenant itself mentions a right to compensation in two places, each time in relation to personal freedom. Article 9 (5) specifies that an individual who has been the victim of unlawful arrest or detention "shall have an enforceable right to compensation". Similarly, Article 14 (6) sets forth that a person who has been the victim of a miscarriage of justice "shall be compensated according to law". Although these two provisions are primarily intended to enjoin States to establish individual rights under domestic law by enacting the requisite legislation, they shed nonetheless some light on the stand of the authors of the Covenant as to when a situation must be considered so serious as to warrant being remedied by some compensation in money – an assessment that would seem to permit appropriate conclusions *e contrario*.

Notwithstanding the restrictive conception enshrined in the Covenant itself, the Human Rights Committee has not felt prevented from expressing in its final views under Article 5 (4) of the Optional Protocol fairly far-reaching suggestions as to the way in which a wrong committed is to be corrected. Already in its first views on the merits of a case, brought against Uruguay, it held that the defendant State was under an obligation "to provide effective remedies to the victims".[30] In many instances, it has held that the victim of a violation was entitled to a remedy, including appropriate compensation.[31] A culmination point of its jurisprudence was reached in a series of views addressing trials resulting in the imposition of the death penalty that had not been conducted in conformity with the procedural standards laid down in Article 14 of the Covenant. In view of the gravity of some of the procedural defects found by it, the Human Rights Committee pronounced itself for the immediate release of the convicted persons.[32] These rulings are not understood by the Committee as the exercise of some jurisdiction *ex aequo et bono*. Rather, the Committee views its appeals for the liberation of the victims as a logical consequence of the breach of the obligations in issue. Indeed, one is confronted here with an ineluctable choice where questions concerning the true meaning of international human rights cannot be papered over anymore

---

[30]   Case of *Bazzano/Massera*, 15 August 1979, in UN (ed.), *Human Rights Committee. Selected Decisions under the Optional Protocol*, Doc. CCPR/C/OP/1 (1985), p. 40, at 43.

[31]   See, for instance, from the 1993 Report (48 GAOR, Suppl. No. 40, UN Doc. A/48/40) the following cases (all contained in Part II): *Linton v. Jamaica*, 22 October 1992, p. 12, at 16 para. 10; *Orihuela Valenzuela v. Peru*, 14 July 1993, p. 48, at 51 para. 8; *Chiiko Bwalya v. Zambia*, 14 July 1993, p. 52, at 55 para. 8; *Francis v. Jamaica*, 24 March 1993, p. 62, at 67 para. 14; *Kalinga v. Zambia*, 27 July 1993, p. 68, at 71 para. 8; *Bailey v. Jamaica*, 31 March 1993, p. 72, at 76 para. 11.1; *Balkissoon Soogrim v. Trinidad and Tobago*, 8 April 1993, p. 110, at 115 para. 15.

[32]   The following cases from the 1993 Report (*Ibidem*) may be referred to: *Smith v. Jamaica*, 31 March 1993, p. 28, at 36 para. 12; *Campbell v. Jamaica*, 24 March 1993, p. 41, at 45 para. 8; *Francis v. Jamaica*, 22 March 1993, p. 62, at 67 para. 14; *Simmonds v. Jamaica*, 23 October 1992, p. 78, at 83 para. 10 (with dissenting opinion by Prado Vallejo, Sadi, Wennergren, p. 84); *Collins v. Jamaica*, 25 March 1993, p. 85, at 90 para. 10.

by some vague formulae. If an individual injured by a human rights obligation cannot obtain any redress for the loss suffered, the "right" at stake becomes almost meaningless. To buttress its line of reasoning, the Committee has taken to invoking Article 2 (3) of the Covenant, which provides that an individual claiming that his or her rights under the Covenant have been violated must be given an effective remedy. This argument is hardly persuasive, however. As is shown by a perusal of the other language versions, which speak of "recours" in French and "recurso" in Spanish, Article 2 (3) refers to a remedy of a kind which permits an individual to challenge in some formalized procedure State conduct adversely affecting his or her rights. The reading of the Committee, according to which "remedy" is equated with remedial action for the reparation of the wrong done, cannot be maintained in the light of the French and the Spanish texts, whose words do not have the same double connotation as the English word "remedy". Thus, the only remaining explanation is an application of the general rules of State responsibility.[33]

A leap forward in legal thinking was made by the Security Council when it determined in resolution 687 (1991) that Iraq "is liable under international law for any direct loss, damage . . . or injury to foreign Governments, nationals and corporations as a result of its unlawful invasion and occupation of Kuwait" (para. 16). Here, for the first time, it was unequivocally recognized that grave breaches of international law may entail direct responsibility towards the individuals injured.[34] However, resolution 687 (1991) remains an isolated precedent as yet. In no event could it be extended to any kind of human rights violation. It should also be observed that its philosophy is based on traditional concepts of the law of aliens. Only foreign nationals are mentioned as being entitled to claim reparation, whereas Iraqi citizens are not taken into account.

5) *The Refugee Problem – A Mass-Scale Problem*

The ideas just developed rest on an analysis of configurations characterized by their individuality. Generally, however, refugees are not isolated individuals. When a tense political situation in a given country develops to the point of making departure an advisable option, many people will start leaving their homes at the same time. Mass migration sets in. The question is whether the

---

[33]   Same assessment by Ramcharan, B.G., "State Responsibility for Violations of Human Rights Treaties", in *Contemporary Problems of International Law: Essays in Honor of Georg Schwarzenberger*, London 1988, p. 242, at 254.

[34]   It is significant, however, that according to the Secretary-General's recommendation made in the relevant report (S/22559, 2 May 1991, para. 21) "only consolidated claims filed by individual Governments on their own behalf or on behalf of their own nationals and corporations" will in general be entertained by the Compensation Commission. It is only if a government fails to submit a private claim that the corporation or entity concerned may itself make a claim to the Compensation Commission. A trustee will act on behalf of persons "who are not in a position to have their claims submitted by a Government", UN Compensation Commission, Provisional Rules for Claims Procedure, doc. S/AC.26/1992/INF.1, Article 5.

large-scale dimension of the phenomenon changes the terms under which it should be addressed.

For the refugee himself, the best solution is normally to be able to return to his country, provided of course that the circumstances prompting his or her departure have fundamentally changed. The right to return is nothing other than the original right guaranteed under Article 12 of the Covenant and at the same time anchored in customary law. It is not a "new" right brought into being by the wrongful measures taken by the State concerned. No valid legal defence can be perceived that might be adduced to justify restrictions aimed at preventing masses of people from regaining their country of origin. In fact, the General Assembly has often asserted a right of refugees to return back home.[35] This was done for the first time in the famous Resolution 194 (III) of 11 December 1948 on Palestine. In that resolution, the General Assembly

> "*Resolve(d)* that the refugees wishing to return to their homes and live at peace with their neighbours should be permitted to do so at the earliest practicable date, and that compensation should be paid for the property of those choosing not to return and for loss of or damage to property which, under principles of international law or in equity, should be made good by the Governments or authorities responsible".

Similar wording can be found in the relevant resolutions on Afghanistan and Cambodia. Recently, addressing the situation of human rights in the territory of the former Yugoslavia, the General Assembly reaffirmed

> "the right of all persons to return to their homes in safety and dignity",[36]

and likewise the Human Rights Commission stressed a few months ago

> "the right of any victims [scil. of ethnic cleansing] to return to their homes".[37]

In all of these instances, apparently the right to return was highlighted precisely because a mass phenomenon was in issue. The General Assembly would not have pronounced itself on individual cases, and the same is true of the Human Rights Commission.

Compensation for the losses suffered, by analogy to what would be regarded as the applicable rule in an inter-State relationship, may be a different matter. It should first be noted that the resolutions referred to refrain generally – with the exception of the resolutions on Palestine – from dealing with this theme, confining themselves to claiming that refugees should be able to return to their homes, which implies that they have a right to recover the proper-

---

[35] See our Study "Das Recht auf die Heimat. Neue rechtliche Aspekte", in *Festschrift Partsch, op. cit.* (note 24), at 187, pp. 195–199.
[36] Resolution 48/153, 20 December 1993, op. para. 13.
[37] Resolution 1994/72, 9 March 1994, op. para. 8.

ties owned by them at the time of their departure.[38] To go further than that and claim a right of compensation for the benefit of those who are forced to stay abroad transcends the original logic of an inter-State system where entities that are essentially alien to one another maintain between themselves "foreign relations". Refugees having left their country of origin and demanding compensation lay a claim against the remainder of the population which still lives under the regime responsible for giving rise to the mass departure for other countries. However, those staying back home may be exposed to even greater suffering. More often than not, refugees eventually enjoy much better opportunities for personal development than those choosing or involuntarily having to endure the mismanagement of public affairs by a government not in compliance with its human rights obligations. The complexity of this situation cannot be dealt with in accordance with relatively simple recipes of international law which seem to require full reparation for any injury caused to another nation.[39] Within a national community, one would first have to establish a comprehensive balance sheet of all the damage resulting from the activity of a criminal regime; thereafter, one would have to make a determination on the extent to which reparation may seem feasible in light of the potential of the national economy. Lastly, it would also have to be determined how the financial burden for the damage caused should be distributed among all of the members of the national community, taking into account basic principles of just taxation.

We are not going to develop these arguments any further. Our aim is simply to recall that compensation for massive human rights violations raises a delicate problem of distributive justice. If one would grant a right of compensation to everyone having lived under an arbitrary system of governance, everyone would become debtor and creditor at the same time. Here, the model of international responsibility must yield to more subtle regimes which many countries have conceived of when trying to cope with a past that made victims of large numbers of the population.[40] A good case in point is the situation in South Africa. During the last decades, many black South Africans were forced to leave their country because of the brutal strategies of repression resorted to by the white minority government. On the other hand, those who stayed

---

[38]   See, in particular, the resolutions on Cyprus: General Assembly Resolutions 3212 (XXXIX), 1 November 1974, op. para. 5; 34/30, 20 November 1979, op. para 7; Security Council Resolution 361 (1974), 30 August 1974, op. para. 4.

[39]   This is the thrust of draft article 6 *bis* on State responsibility adopted by the ILC (note 20). It should be noted, however, that during the many decades that the GATT or the European (Economic) Community have existed, there has not been a single instance where one State has requested financial compensation for the consequences of a breach of an international obligation of another State.

[40]   The Federal Republic of Germany, for instance, has enacted two complex laws for the settlement of unlawful measures taken by the communist regime in the former German Democratic Republic, Law of 29 October 1992, *Bundesgesetzblatt* (*Federal Gazette*) 1992 I, p. 1814; Law of 23 June 1994, *Bundesgesetzblatt* 1994 I, p. 1311.

behind lived under the daily harassment of blatant racial discrimination. Thus, both groups of the black population were victims of measures gravely violating universally accepted human rights standards. Yet, now to make the new democratic body politic accountable for the violations committed in the past would lead to an absurd result, since the victims would have to pay their own compensations.[41]

The case of Palestine was different. Here, a national community, the Jewish people, took possession of the properties and other assets of the Arab population that had fled to neighbouring countries. Consequently, the issue of reparation could be stated in the classical terms by analogy with inter-State law, where the simple maxim applies that a population organized as a State may not unjustly enrich itself to the detriment of another similar group so that harm done must be repaired. A similar assessment is justified in cases of "ethnic cleansing", when a specific ethnic group is the target of persecution intended to bring about a definitive expulsion from the former community of residents.[42]

B. *Responsibility Towards Receiving States*

When looking into the issue of responsibility of a State of origin towards receiving States, one should from the very outset draw a distinction between States that have suffered tangible injury by being burdened with having to take care of a substantial group of people from the relevant country of origin, and other countries that are not directly affected but may make representations and raise claims as guardians of international legality.

1) *States Directly Injured*
a) *Breach of an International Obligation.* As already pointed out, claims under the legal heading of State responsibility presuppose in the first place that a breach of an international obligation has occurred at the hands of the State. Three different sets of rules may be relevant here.

aa) *Territorial Integrity.* Pursuant to the fundamental principle of sovereign equality, each State must respect the sovereign equality of its neighbours. If it pushes large groups of its own citizens out of its territory, fully knowing that

---

[41]   It is a different situation altogether when only some persons become individual targets of human rights violations. This fundamental difference has not been taken into account by the "Principles Concerning Treatment of Refugees", Article V (1) ("A refugee shall have the right to receive compensation from the State or the Country which he left or to which he was unable to return"), adopted by the Asian-African Legal Consultative Committee in 1966, *Report of the Eighth Session Held in Bangkok*, p. 211, at 215, nor by the 1992 Cairo Declaration of the ILA, *loc. cit.*, which later also posits a comprehensive duty of compensation in favor of refugees (Principle 4).

[42]   General Assembly Resolution 48/153, 20 December 1993, op. para. 13, is therefore fully justified.

the victims of such arbitrariness have no right of entry to another country but will eventually have to be admitted somewhere else on purely humanitarian grounds, it deliberately affects the sovereign rights of its neighbours to decide whom they choose to admit to their territories.[43]

bb) *Human Rights Obligations.* Things are less clear when a government conducts a human rights policy contrary to generally recognized standards, not acting, however, with the avowed or hidden purpose of coercing the victims to flee. It may then be asked whether it in fact violates its obligations vis-à-vis another State so that it may become liable to make reparation towards any such other State. It can be demonstrated, though, that human rights obligations have manifold objectives. They are not only designed to protect their immediate beneficiaries, but have from the very outset been conceived of as important elements of a state of peace in the world. In the preambles of the UN Charter and the Universal Declaration of Human Rights, as well as the two International Covenants of 1966,[44] the close relationship between peace and human rights is formally acknowledged. Thus, without distorting the finality of human rights, one may conclude in very general terms that respect for, and full observance of, human rights are also designed to prevent any spillover effects resulting for States from unrest and turmoil in another State.

cc) *Prohibitions Regarding a Population in General.* Lastly, reference may be made to rules which prohibit specific conduct. According to the Charter of the Nürnberg International Military Tribunal,[45] "deportation" was considered a crime against humanity (Article 6 (2) (c)), and this rule was confirmed by the ILC in its codification project under the title "Principles of International Law Recognized in the Charter of the Nürnberg Tribunal and in the Judgment of the Tribunal".[46] However, deportation is the deliberate act of transferring human beings to a specific destination, generally to the territory of an occupying power, whereas a State generating a flow of refugees confines itself to driving people out of its territory, either coercing them to leave the country or putting them under such pressure that they "voluntarily" choose to go away, if possible. Thus, a prohibition of deportation does not squarely address the issue of a refugee-generating policy.

The Fourth Geneva Convention of 1949 relative to the Protection of Civilian

[43] This is generally recognized, see, for instance, Coles, *op. cit.* (note 3), p. 146; Garvey, *loc. cit.* (note 3), p. 494; Hofmann, *loc. cit.* (note 6), p. 708; Lee, L.T., "The Right to Compensation: Refugees and Countries of Asylum", 80 *AJIL* (1986), p. 532, at 535–554.

[44] The Universal Declaration proclaims in particularly emphatic terms: "*Whereas* recognition of the inherent dignity and of the equal and inalienable rights of all members of the human family is the foundation of freedom, justice and peace in the world".

[45] Annex to the Agreement for the Prosecution and Punishment of the Major War Criminals of the European Axis, of 8 August 1945, *UNTS* 82, p. 280; also reprinted in: Schindler, D./Toman, H. (eds.), *The Law of Armed Conflict,* 3rd ed., Geneva 1988, p. 913.

[46] Reprinted in: UN (ed.), *The Work of the International Law Commission,* 4th ed., New York 1988, p. 140.

Persons in Time of War[47] goes one important step further in mentioning alongside with deportation unlawful "transfer" of a protected person (Articles 45, 49, 147). Transfer may be understood as being synonymous with removal, the connotation being that governmental authorities forcibly displace a person from his or her place of residence.[48] Again, therefore, this definition of an unlawful act does not fully meet the specific characteristics of actions resulting in a flow of refugees. Mostly, refugees leave the country of persecution on their own initiative, although prompted to do so by strong pressure brought to bear upon them. Generally, they are neither deported nor transferred to a foreign country. In addition, the Convention only applies to armed conflict. This is also the weakness of Additional Protocol I to the Geneva Conventions (Article 84 (4) (a)).

Not even the draft Code of Crimes against the Peace and Security of Mankind,[49] currently under active consideration by the ILC for its second reading, has established a clear rule enjoining States from pushing their citizens out of the national territory. Following the logic of Article 85 (4) (a) of Additional Protocol I to the Geneva Conventions, it characterizes as an unlawful systematic or mass violation of human rights "deportation or forcible transfer of population", irrespective of the context of such measures, be it an armed conflict of an internal or international character or another situation of anarchy or disorder (Article 21). Even here, however, the causing of a refugee problem as such is not addressed.

Thus, each situation requires careful consideration on its own merits. There exists no international legal rule which in explicit terms puts States under an obligation not to turn themselves into a source of refugee flows. On the other hand, receiving States can rely on non-observance by a State of origin of its basic human rights obligations; they can claim, additionally, that such conduct necessarily affects their sovereign right of territorial integrity.

b) *Causality.* It might be argued that, as far as States as injured parties are concerned, a causal link was missing since every State had the sovereign right to close its borders to persons requesting admission. However, such objection would have to be dismissed. As far as refugees under the 1951 Geneva Convention are concerned, the prohibition of refoulement applies. With

---

[47]   *UNTS* 75, p. 287; also reprinted in: Schindler/Toman, *op. cit.* (note 45), p. 495.

[48]   See Pictet, J. (ed.), *The Geneva Conventions of 12 August 1949. Commentary. IV Geneva Convention relative to the Protection of Civilian Persons in Time of War*, Geneva 1958, p. 266. For the recent discussion see de Zayas, A., " The Illegality of Population Transfers and the Application of Emerging International Norms in the Palestinian Context", VI *The Palestine Yearbook of International Law* (1990/91), pp. 17 *et seq.*; Meindersma, C., "Legal Issues Surrounding Population Transfers in Conflict Situations", 41 *Netherlands International Law Review* (1994), pp. 31 *et seq.*; Palley, C., "Population Transfer", in Gomien, D. (ed.), *Broadening the Frontiers of International Law. Essays in Honour of Asbjørn Eide*, Oslo 1993, pp. 219 *et seq.*

[49]   Adopted on first reading in 1991, Report of the ILC on the work of its 43rd session, 46 GAOR Suppl. No. 10, UN doc. A/46/10 (1991), p. 238.

regard to *de facto* refugees, on the other hand, who attempt to escape from the horrors of civil war, in particular, States are at least under a moral obligation to demonstrate human solidarity vis-à-vis the victims. Within a civilized community, it is only natural that even those who cannot invoke an international legal instrument to their benefit should find refuge in some other country. If the dignity of the human being is proclaimed time and again as the supreme element in a hierarchy of values to be protected, a policy of shutting all doors to undesired arrivals would mean a deadly blow to the very idea of international protection of human rights. Therefore, a State refusing to bear the costs incurred by other States as a consequence of its refugee-generating policies must be deemed to be estopped from claiming that to receive its citizens was an independent decision that interrupted the original chain of events.[50]

c) *Injury.* In order to set the record straight, it should be made absolutely clear that the arrival of human beings cannot as such be considered to constitute injury. It is the expenditure incurred in taking care of the refugees that is susceptible of being taken into account as a financial loss relevant under the rules on State responsibility.

d) *Cessation and Reparation.* Many consequences may derive from the commission of an internationally wrongful act. Here, the main consequences would be twofold. First of all, there is a general obligation to cease unlawful conduct.[51] Second, however, to the extent that restitution in kind is impossible because the refugees concerned cannot be expected to return to conditions as bad as those prevailing when they left, a right to financial compensation comes into being.[52] Here, the complexities of the internal situation in the State of origin are without any legal relevance. The burden of internal unrest and strife cannot legally be shifted to other nations.

e) *Theory and Practice.* Although the legal reasoning may be developed to this point without any apparent flaws, one cannot ignore the fact that there is little practice confirming the existence of a duty to pay financial compensation.[53] The international community has established the office of the UNHCR

[50]   See Garvey *loc. cit.* (note 3), pp. 494–495; Hofmann, *loc. cit.* (note 6), p. 708; Lee, *loc. cit.* (note 43), pp. 554–555.

[51]   Article 6 of Part II of the ILC's draft articles on State responsibility, *loc. cit.* (note 20).

[52]   Article 8 of Part II of the ILC's draft articles on State responsibility, *loc. cit.* (note 20). Such a right to compensation was suggested for the first time back in 1939 by Jennings, R.Y., "Some International Law Aspects of the Refugee Question", 20 *BYBIL* (1939), p. 98, at 112. Today, this seems to be the prevailing opinion in legal doctrine, see, in particular, Coles, *op. cit.* (note 3), pp. 164–165; Lee, *loc. cit.* (note 43), pp. 552 *et seq.*; Sohn, L.B./Buergenthal, Th., *The Movement of Persons Across Borders*, Washington 1992, p. 88.

[53]   Rightly stressed by Hathaway, J.C., Reconceiving Refugee Law as Human Rights Protection", 4 *Journal of Refugee Studies* (1991), p. 113, at 119.

precisely because of its experience that source States are normally in such dire condition that any effort to squeeze the least amount of money out of them would be doomed beforehand. Germany is the one great exception to this lesson of the past,[54] but it should not be overlooked that payments were made only by the new democratic regime after the fall of the Hitler dictatorship.

The same holds true with regard to the duty of cessation. It is logically most satisfactory to conclude that a government which submits its people to such abuses of power that large groups start leaving the country is under a duty to modify its conduct, returning to the path of legality. In a realistic perspective, however, one must acknowledge that to enforce such a duty belongs to the most challenging tasks ever imaginable. In a chaotic situation like the one currently prevailing in Rwanda all legal considerations have lost any real impact on the motivation of the feuding political leaders. Nothing can stop the murderous fighting other than sheer military might. In one instance only has the international community intervened with some success to stop merciless persecution of a minority. As is well known, in order to allay the plight of the Kurds in Northern Iraq the Security Council established a security zone (Resolution 688 of 5 April 1991).[55] Given the many doubts concerning the role it can and should play within a new world order, the Security Council will certainly not repeat this experimental strategy in the near future. In any event, a hard look at realities shows again that there exists a wide discrepancy between theory and practice. It is precisely in recognition of the powerlessness of the international community vis-à-vis the collapse of civilized standards of conduct in a given society that refugee law has emerged. Because of the obvious lack of effectiveness of the ordinary rules of international law in such a situation, other States step in, motivated by considerations of human solidarity for the benefit of the victims. Still, the basic parameters have changed. While 55 years ago R. Y. Jennings had to rely, in a somewhat strained fashion, on the doctrine of abuse of rights to show that States did not enjoy sovereign freedom to shove parts of their population out of their territories,[56] well-established principles of human rights law now restrict the powers inherent in sovereign Statehood.

The lack of trust in the effectiveness of the traditional rules of international law is most conspicuously reflected in the relevant resolutions of the competent political bodies, the General Assembly and the Human Rights Commission. Regarding the situation in Bosnia-Herzegovina, in particular, although "ethnic cleansing" and other human rights violations are constantly deplored and unambiguously condemned, one does not find a single line that

---

[54] For references see the commentaries on the ILA's Draft Declaration of Principles of International Law on Compensation to Refugees and Countries of Asylum, in ILA (ed.), *Report of the 64th Conference*, Sydney 1991, pp. 339 *et seq.*

[55] For the legal intricacies see Stopford, M., "Humanitarian Assistance in the Wake of the Persian Gulf War", 33 *Virg.JIL* (1993), p. 491, at 496.

[56] Jennings, *loc. cit.* (note 52), p. 112.

would suggest that the aggressor country involved could be under an obligation to defray at least part of the costs entailed by providing adequate care to the refugees expelled from their native towns and villages.[57]

2) *States Acting as Guardians of International Legality*

Even States that have not directly been affected by a flow of refugees may have legal claims against the State of origin. The jurisprudence of the ICJ on obligations *erga omnes* is too well known to have to be described here in any detail. What matters is the fact that according to the authoritative pronouncement in the *Barcelona Traction* case[58] every State has legal standing to act – in some form – for the protection of basic human rights that have been breached. Generation of refugees is of course not an element of the indicative list given by the ICJ, and it would not fit therein. The criterion chosen by the ICJ is that of particular gravity. Hence, everything depends on the specific circumstances. If, for instance, a government engages in a policy of genocide, thereby terrorizing the members of the persecuted group and inducing them to flee abroad, every member of the international community may be considered affected. The same is true with regard to a policy of *apartheid*, as explicitly emphasized by the ICJ in its advisory opinion on *Namibia*.[59] In the case of more subtle harassment, however, the threshold of gravity may not have been crossed.

The dictum of the ICJ has not remained an isolated incident. According to Article 5 of Part II of the draft articles of the ILC on State responsibility, in case of a violation of a human rights obligation under customary international law or if the breach attains by its seriousness the quality of an international crime, all other States are to be considered injured; in case of a human rights obligation based on treaty law, all other States parties. This gives them legal standing to participate in the enforcement process.[60]

Unfortunately, the precise legal meaning of that position as *defensor legis* recognized for every State has not been fully clarified as yet. The articles adopted by the ILC grant most generously all the rights to which an internationally wrongful act may give rise to the "injured State" *tout court*, without drawing any distinction as to whether the State concerned has suffered tangible injury itself or whether its standing is solely justified *dans l'intérêt de la loi*. It is in this sense also that the special rapporteur on the topic, Gaetano Arangio-

---

[57]   General Assembly Resolution 48/153 of 20 December 1993 recognizes "the right of victims of 'ethnic cleansing' to receive just reparation for their losses" (op. para. 13).

[58]   ICJ Rep. 1970, p. 3, at 32.

[59]   Of 21 June 1971, ICJ Rep. 1971, p. 16, at 57.

[60]   The main instrument for that purpose is diplomatic representations, see Kamminga, *op. cit.* (note 9), pp. 6 *et seq.* For a description of the relevant practice of the French Government, see 38 *AFDI* (1992), pp. 1128–1132. The European Union, in particular, makes public statements on the human rights situation in given countries on a regular basis; recently, the situation in Haiti and Malawi was addressed, see *Bulletin des Presse-und Informationsamts der Bundesregierung* 1994, p. 504 and p. 516.

Ruiz, has suggested a new article 5 *bis*[61] intended to do away with any legal differentiation between the two groups of States. However, while nobody would have any doubt that the minimum content of a right of response to injury caused must include the right to make representations, it is a different matter altogether to acknowledge for any injured State a right to obtain compensation, as suggested by draft article 8, already adopted by the ILC.[62] In the view of the present writer, this enlargement of the circle of right-holders is simply wrong and would necessarily lead to utter confusion.[63]

C. *Responsibility Towards the International Community*

On more than one occasion the General Assembly has stressed that flows of refugees unleashed by one country affect the entire international community.[64] Indeed, this simple truth finds confirmation in the fact that persons having lost the protection of their home State must be given a place to stay, food, shelter and medical care. To assist national governments in performing this task, the UN has created the office of the UNHCR, which for its part requires to be financed by the members of the international community.

In order to implement the responsibility of the State of origin, the international community can make use of the powers of the Security Council, provided that the requirements for action in accordance with Article 39 of the UN Charter – a threat to or a breach of the peace or an act of aggression – are met. Intervention by the Security Council can serve in particular to stop the actions that have set in motion a mass exodus. Almost unchallengeable in theory, this conclusion is hard to translate into concrete practice. Except in the case of the Kurds of Iraq, the Security Council has never taken the view that to generate a flow of refugees may constitute a threat to international peace and security.[65] The guarded language of Resolution 918 (1994) of 17 May 1994 on Rwanda is most revealing. It is certainly not by sheer oversight that the Security Council confines itself to pointing out that "the massive exodus of refugees to neighbouring countries constitutes a humanitarian crisis of enormous proportions".

It goes without saying that the international community has additionally a vivid interest in recovering from a State of origin the costs it has defrayed for taking the requisite measures of protection. First of all, recovery would

---

[61] UN Doc. A/CN.4/444/Add.2 (1 June 1992), para. 153.

[62] ILC, *loc. cit.* (note 20).

[63] It should be noted, though, that the ILC has not yet completed its examination of "international crimes" under Article 19 of Part I of its draft articles on State responsibility; for a panorama of the opinions in that regard see the report of Special Rapporteur G. Arangio-Ruiz, UN Docs. A/CN.4/453/Add.2, 3 (8 and 24 June 1993).

[64] Latest statements to that effect: Resolution 48/139 of 20 December 1993, preamb. para. 5 (general); 48/152, 20 December 1993, op. para. 13 (Afghanistan); 48/118, 20 December 1993, op. para. 6 (Africa).

[65] Resolution 688 (1991), preamb. para. 3.

help replenish the budget of UNHCR which is constantly under threat in as much as it rests totally on voluntary contributions by interested States. On the other hand, if governments had to realize that monies spent for the benefit of refugees were recoverable from them, this might act as a deterrent in critical situations where fundamental policy determinations are being made. In law, a good case can be made for a claim to reimbursement. If, in accordance with the judgment of the ICJ in *Barcelona Traction*, generation of large-scale flows of refugees in a given situation can be evaluated as a violation of an obligation *erga omnes*, then the international community as such must first and foremost be considered as the injured party. Indeed, the ICJ introduced the *omnes* only as a subsidiary construction to fill in the gap caused by the international community's lack of operative institutions. The office of the UNHCR, however, is a fully effective institution. It has been entrusted by all States with discharging the charitable functions which in a civilized world are owed to those having lost their homes. Thus, the international community is not a hollow word precisely in this connection. It has established appropriate mechanisms, and it continually spends important financial sums to counterbalance the wrongs inflicted on it by States that violate basic human rights of their citizens. Therefore, one is on safe ground in concluding that the UN, as the legal person to which UNHCR belongs, has a right to recover the costs disbursed by it from a State of origin that has willfully caused massive departures of its citizens through a policy of systematic human rights violations.[66]

The same result may also be obtained through a different line of reasoning. It is arguable that the international community, by taking care of the elementary vital needs of the citizens of a given country, engages in *negotiorum gestio*, an institution found in all major systems of law and whose rules can therefore be characterized as general principles of law. Normally, whoever supplies necessities to an indigent person who should have been taken care of by the principal, has a right to be compensated for his expenditure.[67] This is precisely the situation at issue here where the international community through UNHCR provides shelter, food and medical care to refugees in order to save their lives and protect their physical integrity.

II. LIABILITY

State responsibility is not the only possible basis for a legal claim to compensation. One could also resort to objective liability in the sense that a

---

[66]   Lee, *loc. cit.* (note 43), p. 551, is right in suggesting that the advisory opinion of the ICJ in the *Bernadotte* case is a directly relevant precedent in this connection, see ICJ Rep. 1949, p. 174, at 186. For a negative stance see Kamminga, *op. cit.* (note 9), p. 164.

[67]   See Stoljar, S.J., entry "Negotiorum Gestio" in *International Encyclopedia of Comparative Law*, Vol. X, Chapter 17, Tübingen *et al.* 1984, sections 134–166, 301.

State of origin, whatever its human rights record, is duty-bound to repair the damage caused to other States by a massive influx of its nationals into their territories. Some authors have suggested that the *Trail Smelter* case could be used as the starting point for this approach.[68] The famous dictum by the arbitration tribunal to the effect that:

> no State has the right to use or permit the use of its territory in such a manner as to cause injury by fumes in or to the territory of another or the properties or persons therein, when the case is of serious consequence and the injury is established by clear and convincing evidence,[69]

could with some hesitation be applied to refugees as well. Quite obviously, it is rather embarassing to compare refugees with toxic fumes, and the authors concerned have not failed to notice the qualitative difference, presenting their apologies for the equation. But even if one accepts that, viewed from the angle of the receiving State, the effect may have some similarity, one must note that to date the notion of objective liability, which does not require as one of its constitutive elements a breach of an international obligation, has not yet been generally accepted in international law. There is not a consistent practice, nor does the observer succeed in identifying a clear and unambiguous *opinio juris*. Ample proof for this lack of general consensus is provided by the ILC's inability to agree on a set of principles to deal with the issue of liability. The topic was put on the ILC's agenda back in 1978.[70] To date, after 16 years, no more has been produced than a set of fairly innocuous principles of prevention with regard to activities involving risk.[71] The general feeling of uneasiness with the topic results precisely from the fact that the ILC, instead of codifying time-honored rules, would engage in progressive development in a highly sensitive field, the available practice of State failing to furnish any consolidated guiding criteria. It would be more than hazardous, therefore, to try to derive any rule concerning refugees from the *Trial Smelter* precedent.

[68]   Coles, *op. cit.* (note 3), p. 148; Goodwin-Gill, G.S., *The Refugee in International Law*, Oxford 1983, p. 228 (relying more specifically on the *Corfu Channel* case, ICJ Rep. 1949, p. 4, at 22, as well as Principle 21 of the Stockholm Declaration); Lee, *loc. cit.* (note 43), Takkenberg, *loc. cit.* (note 3), p. 799.

[69]   Arbitral award of 11 March 1941, *RIAA* III, p. 1905, at 1965.

[70]   For a review of the work done until 1989 see our study "International Liability for Injurious Consequences Arising out of Acts not Prohibited by International Law – The Work of the International Law Commission", in Francioni, F./Scovazzi, T. (eds.), *International Responsibility for Environmental Harm*, London/Dordrecht/ Boston 1991, pp. 37–72.

[71]   In 1993, these principles had not even reached the level of the plenary. They were finally adopted by the ILC plenary in 1994, see UN Doc. A/CN.4/L.498/Add.2 (15 July 1994).

BRIGITTE STERN

Commentaires sur:
la responsabilité de l'Etat d'origine des réfugiés

Partant de la relation triangulaire complexe entre l'Etat d'origine du réfugié, le réfugié et l'Etat d'accueil du réfugié, M. Christian Tomuschat a centré ses réflexions sur la responsabilité de l'Etat d'origine du réfugié; il a également retenu une conception large et non technique du terme de réfugié. Je m'en tiendrai donc dans mes commentaires au cadre ainsi défini, tout en m'interrogeant sur le choix de la définition large du réfugié.

M. Tomuschat a abordé deux aspects de la question pour laquelle le français ne possède qu'un vocable, "la responsabilité", deux aspects que la langue anglaise qualifie respectivement de "*responsibility*" et "*liability*". Mais en réalité il n'a traité que très rapidement, à la fin de son intervention, de la "*liability*", c'est-à-dire de la responsabilité pour activités licites, que l'on appelle aussi aujourd'hui responsabilité pour activités non interdites par le droit international ou encore responsabilité pour activités ni illicites, ni licites. L'essentiel de son propos s'est centré sur la "*responsibility*", c'est-à-dire la responsabilité pour faits illicites. L'essentiel du mien se rapportera donc également à ce thème.

Poser la question de la responsabilité d'un Etat d'origine de réfugiés face à un problème de réfugiés, c'est d'abord se demander à l'égard de qui l'Etat d'origine pourrait éventuellement voir sa responsabilité engagée. M. Tomuschat a répondu:

– les réfugiés
– les Etats, parmi lesquels il a regroupé, d'une part les Etats d'accueil, d'autre part les Etats pouvant mettre en cause l'Etat d'origine dans le cadre d'une *actio popularis*
– la communauté internationale, incarnée dans les organisations internationales.

Je présenterai mes commentaires selon une typologie légèrement différente, qui me semble permettre de mieux visualiser les *différentes fonctions de la responsabilité internationale*. Il est ainsi possible d'étudier successivement la responsabilité de l'Etat d'origine à l'égard:

81

V. Gowlland-Debbas (ed.), The Problem of Refugees in the Light of Contemporary International Law Issues,
81–92.
© 1996 *Kluwer Academic Publishers. Printed in the Netherlands.*

– des réfugiés, c'est-à-dire des individus
– des Etats d'accueil et des organisations internationales humanitaires, c'est-à-dire des sujets de droit international
– de la communauté internationale par le biais de la mise en cause politique et de l'*actio popularis*.

* La responsabilité de l'Etat à l'égard des réfugiés **met en cause la protection des individus par le droit international** et se pose à deux niveaux:
– La responsabilité pour violation du droit international dans le cadre du droit interne.
– La responsabilité pour violation du droit international sur le plan international.

Ce qui amène à examiner deux questions classiques: l'application du droit international par le juge interne; et l'existence d'un droit d'action de l'individu à l'égard de son propre Etat sur le plan international. Cette question a été très largement abordée.

* La responsabilité de l'Etat d'origine des réfugiés à l'égard des Etats d'accueil et des organisations internationales est une responsabilité dont la fonction principale est **la protection des intérêts, notamment matériels, des Etats ou des organisations internationales.**

* Au contraire la responsabilité de l'Etat d'origine des réfugiés à l'égard de la communauté internationale, responsabilité pouvant être mise en oeuvre soit au niveau politique par des organes politiques tels que le Conseil de sécurité, soit au niveau juridique par tout Etat même en dehors d'un dommage propre, a pour fonction principale **le respect de la légalité internationale.**

Apparaissent ainsi ce que l'on pourrait appeler trois strates dans les fonctions de la responsabilité internationale:
– La protection de l'individu par le droit international avec toutes les limitations auxquelles elle est encore soumise.
– La protection des intérêts des Etats et des organisations internationales.
– La protection de l'ordre juridique international.

I. LA RESPONSABILITE DE L'ETAT D'ORIGINE A L'EGARD DES REFUGIES

En réalité, l'existence d'une véritable responsabilité de l'Etat d'origine à l'égard des réfugiés suppose la réunion de plusieurs conditions:
– Premièrement, que l'Etat d'origine assume certaines obligations internationales à l'égard de ses nationaux, avant qu'ils ne deviennent réfugiés.
– Deuxièmement, que les conditions classiques d'apparition de la responsabilité internationale soient remplies.
– Troisièmement, que les réfugiés aient des moyens juridiques – nationaux ou internationaux – pour mettre en cause la responsabilité de leur Etat, en cas de violation de ses obligations à leur égard.

A. *Quelles sont les obligations internationales pertinentes assumées par un Etat à l'égard de ses nationaux?*

Deux types principaux d'obligations paraissent pertinents au regard du problème des réfugiés: i) d'abord, l'Etat doit autoriser juridiquement la résidence sur le territoire; ii) ensuite, l'Etat ne doit pas interdire en fait, par son comportement, la résidence sur le territoire.

1) *L'obligation d'autoriser les nationaux à résider sur le territoire*
M. Tomuschat a largement présenté cette question, indiquant que les textes pertinents sont l'article 13 de la **Déclaration universelle des droits de l'homme,** et surtout l'article 12 du **Pacte des droits civils et politiques,** qui dans son paragraphe 4 dispose que "Nul ne peut être arbitrairement privé du droit d'entrer dans son propre pays".

A cela on peut ajouter l'article 3 §2 du **Protocole n° 4 à la Convention européenne des droits de l'homme** (signé le 16 septembre 1963, entré en vigueur le 2 mai 1968, ratifié par la France le 3 mai 1974), qui est encore plus protecteur des nationaux puisque le mot "arbitrairement" a disparu. L'article 3 §2 du Protocole n° 4 énonce: "Nul ne peut être privé du droit d'entrer sur le territoire de l'Etat dont il est le ressortissant". M. Tomuschat a fort justement indiqué qu'une disposition de ce genre implique nécessairement le droit de résider sur le territoire de son Etat, et donc à titre de corollaire, le droit de ne pas être contraint de le quitter.

Sur l'analyse détaillée que M. Tomuschat a faite de l'article 12 du Pacte, j'aurais quelques réserves mais qui sont relativement mineures. Il indique en effet que le droit d'entrer peut être restreint pour protéger la sécurité nationale, l'ordre public etc. . . . Je n'en suis pas aussi sûre que lui, compte tenu de la structure de l'article 12 ; ces restrictions, en effet, prévues au paragraphe 3 concernent les "droits mentionnés ci-dessus", c'est-à-dire les droits énoncés aux paragraphes 1 et 2. Pour ce qui est du droit d'entrer sur le territoire – et donc d'y rester – prévu au paragraphe 4, la seule obligation qui pèse sur l'Etat, c'est de ne pas le restreindre arbitrairement. Que cette obligation soit plus ou moins contraignante que celle qui résulte du paragraphe 3, on pourrait sans doute en discuter, mais elle nous semble en tous cas différente.

Malgré les nuances et les degrés que l'on peut constater entre le Pacte des droits civils et politiques et la Convention européenne et ses Protocoles, je suis d'accord avec M. Tomuschat pour dire que "le droit de toute personne de vivre dans son pays est aujourd'hui une règle de droit international coutumier".

2) *Une obligation de ne pas violer les droits fondamentaux des nationaux au point qu'ils soient contraints de quitter le territoire*
Ainsi, une politique générale de violation flagrante des droits de l'homme, ou une politique de violation des droits d'un groupe particulier de la popula-

tion, défini par la race ou la religion ou tout autre critère, peut mettre en cause la responsabilité de l'Etat.

Pour savoir quels droits des nationaux sont protégés, il convient de se référer aux textes déjà mentionnés: Pacte, Convention européenne. Mais il nous semble qu'il faudrait faire aussi ici une référence à d'autres textes internationaux importants: je pense en particulier à la Convention de 1951 pour la prévention et la répression du crime de génocide.

On peut peut-être aussi indiquer – et il me semble que M. Tomuschat n'a pas mentionné ce point – qu'en cas de violation des droits de l'homme ou de génocide, l'Etat engage sa responsabilité à l'égard de ses nationaux, que ceux-ci restent sur son territoire, ou qu'ils cherchent refuge à l'étranger.

Aux deux types principaux d'obligations assumées par un Etat à l'égard de ses nationaux, doit être ajoutée une catégorie d'obligations moins importante, mais qu'il convient de mentionner pour mémoire.

3) *Les obligations spécifiques concernant ses nationaux réfugiés dans une ambassade étrangère*
En réalité ces obligations concernent aussi bien les nationaux, que d'éventuels étrangers, réfugiés dans une ambassade située sur le territoire d'un Etat, mais elles ne nous intéressent vraiment que pour ce qui est des nationaux, compte tenu du thème traité. Ces obligations consistent essentiellement à accorder des sauf-conduits pour permettre aux nationaux réfugiés dans une ambassade, de quitter le territoire de leur Etat, pour obtenir l'asile dans le territoire de l'Etat de l'ambassade.

B. *A quelles conditions, une responsabilité internationale de l'Etat d'origine peut-elle naître à l'égard de ses nationaux réfugiés à l'étranger?*

La responsabilité internationale à l'égard d'un particulier naît lorsqu'un acte contraire au droit international peut être imputé à un Etat et qu'il en résulte un dommage subi par un particulier.

1) *Les problèmes d'imputabilité*
Je suis parfaitement en accord avec l'analyse de l'imputabilité présentée par mon collègue:
– pas d'imputabilité à l'Etat pour les catastrophes naturelles, les famines, les épidémies qui sont souvent à l'origine de flux de réfugiés, sauf, – et ce point que M. Tomuschat a mentionné est important, – si l'Etat n'a pas rempli son obligation de prévention.
– pas d'imputabilité en cas de guerre allant au-delà de l'imputabilité des actes des troupes gouvernementales. J'ajouterai cependant à cela, l'imputabilité des actes des rebelles si ceux-ci sont victorieux. Une telle précision pourrait par exemple un jour ne pas être sans conséquences au Rwanda.
– imputabilité au contraire de tous les actes des organes étatiques violant les droits de l'homme.

Pour que le tableau soit complet, on doit sans doute ajouter:
– imputabilité des actes d'individus ou de groupes: on pense à des bandes armées, aux forces irrégulières en Bosnie-Herzégovine, forces paramilitaires serbes bosniaques notamment, si le gouvernement les prend à son compte; on pense aussi à l'action des militants islamistes, que la Cour internationale de Justice a considéré imputable au gouvernement iranien, non pas dès le moment de la prise d'otages à l'ambassade américaine à Téhéran, mais quelques jours plus tard, quand l'Iman Khomenei a pris à son compte cette action.

Il ne suffit pas cependant, pour que naisse une responsabilité internationale, qu'un acte contraire au droit international ait été commis par un Etat, il faut encore que le préjudice dont se plaint le particulier soit lié à cet acte par un lien de causalité.

2) *Les problèmes de lien de causalité*

Prenons comme hypothèse que l'acte illicite est une grave violation des droits d'un individu, il n'aura pas de mal à prouver le lien de causalité qui est inhérent, immédiat.

Par contre, si le réfugié se plaint également d'avoir été contraint de quitter son pays – et je pense que c'est surtout cette hypothèse qu'il faut envisager, car elle constitue la spécificité de notre sujet – les choses à mon avis sont assez délicates. Et je ne suis pas sûre de pouvoir suivre facilement mon collègue qui semble ne pas considérer qu'il y ait là un problème: en tout cas, il ne l'a pas soulevé, sinon de façon tout à fait allusive. Dans sa communication, M. Tomuschat a en effet parlé d'un Etat qui met ses nationaux *"under such unbearable pressure that they 'voluntarily' choose to flee"* et il a mis des guillemets à *"voluntarily"*. Et bien justement tout le problème est là: c'est celui de la liberté de la victime lorsqu'elle réagit à un acte illicite. C'est une question que j'ai posée, – il y a un quart de siècle! – dans ma thèse, où j'écrivais la chose suivante:

> Supposons qu'à la suite d'un acte illicite, un individu réagisse d'une manière dommageable pour autrui ou pour lui-même. Cet acte de la victime de l'acte illicite ou d'un tiers sera-t-il considéré comme "produit" par l'acte illicite initial? Il est très rare que dans une hypothèse de ce genre la jurisprudence internationale admette qu'une activité humaine puisse être entièrement déterminée par un acte illicite antérieur. L'intervention de la volonté de l'individu crée – à son détriment – une présomption de liberté. Aussi le lien de causalité sera-t-il en général considéré comme rompu: c'est la rançon de la liberté sur le déterminisme![1]

Il conviendra donc dans chaque cas de vérifier que l'acte illicite était absolument contraignant et que la victime n'avait absolument aucun autre choix

---

[1] *Le préjudice dans la théorie de la responsabilité internationale*, Paris, Pedone, 1973, pp. 194–195.

que de s'expatrier. Il ne suffit pas par exemple d'un état général d'insécurité poussant certains à aller se réfugier à l'étranger, il faut vraiment des actes du gouvernement créant une pression irrésistible. Tout sera donc une question d'espèce, une question de preuve.

Il est clair que lorsque l'Iran lance une *fatwa* contre Salman Rushdie, celui-ci, s'il avait été en Iran, n'aurait pas eu d'autre choix que de se réfugier à l'étranger, et étant à l'étranger n'avait pas d'autre choix que d'y rester, et même de s'y cacher.

Il est clair que dans certains cas, le national n'a pas d'autre option – *"no other option remains open"*, selon les termes de mon collègue – que de quitter son pays. Je songe ici au cas de l'Algérie, et de la menace de mort lancée contre tous les étrangers par le FIS. Un Algérien marié avec une Française n'a d'autre choix que de partir. Si le FIS prenait le pouvoir, l'Algérie pourrait être tenue responsable par ce réfugié algérien; mais, en l'état actuel des choses, le gouvernement algérien ne peut se voir imputer les actes d'un mouvement qu'il combat.

C. *Quels sont les moyens juridiques dont disposent les réfugiés pour mettre en oeuvre la responsabilité de l'Etat d'origine?*

M. Tomuschat a fort justement évoqué à la fois les tribunaux internes et les instances internationales.

1) *Le recours du réfugié devant les tribunaux internes*

Le recours du réfugié devant les tribunaux internes de l'Etat d'origine. J'ajouterai simplement ici une information relative à la France, qui n'est d'ailleurs pas très surprenante. Elle est tirée d'un ouvrage collectif intitulé "Droits de l'homme en France. Dix ans d'application de la Convention européenne des droits de l'homme devant les juridictions françaises".[2] D'après ce livre, entre 1975 et 1985, jamais l'article 3 du Protocole 4 n'a été invoqué. L'article 2 relatif au droit pour un national de quitter le territoire a été invoqué, mais pas l'article 3.

Le recours du réfugié devant les tribunaux internes de l'Etat d'accueil. Je voudrais ouvrir ici une parenthèse, en étant tout à fait consciente que ce que je vais dire est un peu hors sujet, mais je pense que c'est tout de même intéressant, car cela concerne la protection du réfugié par des conventions internationales, même si cette protection ne se fait pas par la mise en cause de l'Etat d'origine, mais par la mise en cause d'individus restés dans l'Etat d'origine.

Le cas dont je veux parler concerne des réfugiés bosniaques en France: ceux-ci ont déposé plainte contre X avec constitution de partie civile, pour tortures, génocide, crimes de guerre et crimes contre l'humanité. Ils ont invoqué:
– la convention sur l'imprescriptibilité des crimes de guerre et des crimes contre l'humanité de 1968

---

[2]   Strasbourg 1985.

- la convention sur le génocide de 1951
- la Charte du Tribunal de Nüremberg ainsi que la résolution des Nations-Unies du 13 février 1946 qui reprend ses principes
- la convention de New-York du 10 décembre 1984 contre la torture et autres peines ou traitements cruels, inhumains ou dégradants
- les conventions de Genève du 12 août 1949.

Une ordonnance a été rendue le 6 mai 1994 par le Tribunal de grande instance de Paris, qui examinait la constitution de parties civiles. Les trois premiers instruments ont été écartés par le juge, mais le juge s'est déclaré compétent sur la base de la convention sur la torture et des conventions de Genève. Le ministère public a fait appel de cette décision, estimant que les tribunaux français étaient incompétents.

Que penser de la solution adoptée? Sur l'interprétation de la convention de New-York, je crains avoir du mal à suivre le juge Getti. Cette convention met en application effectivement ce que l'on appelle la compétence universelle: mais cette compétence signifie simplement, selon l'interprétation coutumière, que tout Etat sur le territoire duquel se trouve un auteur présumé des faits punis par la convention a compétence pour le juger.

Qu'est ce que cela implique? Cela signifie simplement que du point de vue des règles internationales de répartition des compétences entre Etats, il a le droit d'exercer sa compétence; cela ne signifie pas qu'il y soit obligé (d'où d'éventuelles interprétations divergentes, dans les systèmes juridiques internes, de la compétence universelle telle qu'affirmée sur le plan international).

En ce qui concerne les conventions de Genève de 1949, je pense par contre qu'il était effectivement possible de fonder la compétence du juge français sur ses dispositions. Je ne pense cependant pas que l'on puisse arriver à cette conclusion par le même raisonnement que celui qui a été fait pour la convention sur la torture.

Je crois que c'est la *combinaison* de la *compétence universelle* et de "*l'obligation de rechercher* les personnes prévenues d'avoir commis, ou d'avoir ordonné de commettre l'une ou l'autre de ces infractions graves" qui fonde juridiquement la compétence des juridictions françaises.

Il y a en effet d'une part, compétence universelle, c'est à dire compétence virtuelle des tribunaux français à juger de toute violation grave aux conventions de Genève. D'autre part, une obligation de rechercher les coupables: comment mieux remplir cette obligation qu'en mettant en marche la compétence virtuelle? Autrement dit, cette compétence virtuelle se transforme en compétence réelle du fait de l'obligation de rechercher les coupables.

Ceci me parait clairement exprimé dans le passage suivant de l'ordonnance qui est extrêmement pertinent:

> Si les articles précités desdites conventions édictent deux obligations, celle de rechercher et déférer aux tribunaux nationaux les prévenus, elles sont bien distinctes l'une de l'autre, mais néanmoins indissociables.

Voici donc un développement qui n'est pas sans intérêt. Je crois qu'il y a d'ailleurs eu un cas analogue en Allemagne mais que je ne connais pas en détail.

2) *Le recours du réfugié devant les instances internationales*

Les instances ouvertes aux réfugiés. Ce point a été largement abordé par M. Tomuschat, mais j'aimerais apporter ici quelques compléments. Mon collègue a évoqué principalement:

- le Pacte des droits civils et politiques et le protocole optionnel qui permet le recours du réfugié devant le *Comité des droits de l'homme.*
- la Convention européenne bien sûr et son article 25 qui permet le recours du réfugié devant la *Commission européenne des droits de l'homme.*
- la Convention interaméricaine des droits de l'homme.

A cela, il convient d'ajouter:

- *la Commission des droits de l'homme* crée dès 1946 par ECOSOC en vertu de l'article 68 de la Charte pour assurer le progrès des droits de l'homme (on sait qu'elle a élaboré la Déclaration universelle des droits de l'homme) et devant laquelle est possible depuis 1970 un recours individuel: c'est la procédure 1503 (Résol. d'ECOSOC du 27 mai 1970). Mention doit également être faite de la *Sous-commission des droits de l'homme,* dite Sous-commission de la lutte contre la discrimination raciale et la protection des minorités.
- Le Protocole n° 9 à la Convention européenne, adopté le 6 novembre 1990, qui prévoit une saisine directe de la *Cour européenne* par l'individu.

Enfin, je pense qu'on ne peut pas totalement passer sous silence:

- *le tribunal pénal international pour l'ex-Yougoslavie,*[3] crée par le Conseil de sécurité. Ce tribunal est ouvert aux individus et est chargé de juger "les personnes présumées responsables de violations graves du droit humanitaire". On ne juge certes pas des Etats, mais des personnes, comme toujours dans le cadre du droit pénal international. Mais il faut mentionner ici l'article 7 §2 du Statut qui déclare que "La qualité officielle d'un accusé, soit comme chef d'Etat ou de gouvernement, soit comme haut fonctionnaire, ne l'exonère pas de sa responsabilité pénale et n'est pas un motif de diminution de sa peine".

Que peut obtenir le réfugié? Cette question a fait l'objet d'un examen très exhaustif de la part de M. Tomuschat. L'existence d'une responsabilité internationale implique en principe que soit rétablie la situation qui aurait existé, n'eut été l'acte illicite, soit par exécution en nature, soit par réparation par équivalent. Rétablir la situation implique aussi, comme l'a souligné mon collègue, en cas de violation continue, de mettre fin à la violation, c'est-à-dire implique une cessation de la violation.

Devant *la Commission des droits de l'homme,* la question de la réparation ne se pose pas. Le seul résultat peut être une condamnation de l'action passée

---

[3] Depuis la rédaction de cet article, le Conseil de sécurité a egalement crée un tribunal pénal pour le Rwanda.

de l'Etat, et une demande de cessation des violations pour l'avenir, par une résolution en termes plus ou moins sévères. Par exemple, la Commission des droits de l'homme a récemment réaffirmé le droit au retour dans leur pays de tous les réfugiés de l'ex-Yougoslavie.

En ce qui concerne le *Comité des droits de l'homme*, M. Tomuschat nous a indiqué qu'il avait eu *"a bold approach to the issue of reparation"*, et je partage sur ce point sa critique selon laquelle le Comité a confondu l'existence d'un recours et l'existence d'une compensation, en se basant sur l'ambiguïté du terme anglais *"remedy"*.

Il n'est pas question non plus de réparation devant le *tribunal pénal international pour l'ex-Yougoslavie*. Le seul but du tribunal est de punir les coupables. Aucun droit à réparation n'a été prévu pour les victimes, si ce n'est la restitution aux victimes des biens qui leur avaient été enlevés.

Pour la *Cour européenne* et la *Cour américaine* des droits de l'homme, M. Tomuschat a bien montré qu'il pouvait y avoir, – plus dans le cadre de la seconde que dans le cadre de la première – un droit à indemnité et je n'y reviendrai donc pas ; sauf à dire que je ne vois pas une aussi grande différence que mon collègue entre la disposition européenne prévoyant une indemnité *"if necessary"* et la disposition américaine prévoyant une indemnité *"if appropriate"*.

II. La responsabilite de l'Etat d'origine a l'egard de l'Etat d'accueil
et des organisations internationales

A. *La responsabilité à l'égard de l'Etat d'accueil*

On se trouve là dans un cadre classique de responsabilité interétatique. L'Etat, on le sait, peut mettre en cause la responsabilité internationale d'un autre Etat, s'il est atteint dans l'un de ses droits propres, ou s'il est atteint dans la personne de l'un de ses ressortissants.

1) *L'existence des réfugiés peut-elle être analysée comme une atteinte à certains intérêts juridiquement protégés de l'Etat d'accueil?*
Nous sommes ici dans l'hypothèse présentée par mon collègue où un Etat engage des frais pour accueillir de nombreux réfugiés, *"a State being burdened with having to take care of a substantial group of people"*. Pour qu'il puisse réclamer réparation, il faut que l'Etat d'origine puisse se voir reprocher une violation du droit international, et que cette violation soit la cause du dommage.

M. Tomuschat examine trois règles internationales dont on pourrait invoquer la violation:
– le principe de l'intégrité territoriale
– les droits de l'homme et les règles relatives au maintien de la paix
– les règles relatives à sa propre population.
Ne trouvant aucune règle pertinente pour notre étude dans cette dernière

catégorie, il pense que l'Etat d'accueil peut invoquer des violations des deux premières règles.

Certes, il y a une objection que mon collègue a bien vue à la reconnaissance d'une violation de l'intégrité territoriale: c'est que le réfugié n'a aucun droit à entrer sur un territoire, et qu'il ne pourra donc le faire qu'avec l'accord de l'Etat. M. Tomuschat avance deux arguments pour écarter cette objection, dont l'un au moins ne me paraît pas convaincant.

Premièrement, selon lui, l'Etat est dans l'obligation morale d'accueillir les réfugiés. Peut-être, mais une obligation morale ne peut être source de droits et d'obligations internationales.

Deuxièmement, selon lui, l'Etat peut être considéré comme ayant été contraint d'accepter les réfugiés. Cet argument est peut-être utilisable, si l'on imagine de véritables hordes de réfugiés déferlant vers un Etat, en fuyant des massacres. L'actualité, évidemment, fournit des exemples tragiques d'une telle situation.

Mais il me semble qu'il y a une autre objection plus sérieuse: c'est que l'intégrité territoriale d'un Etat ne peut être violée que par un autre Etat. Or en l'espèce ce sont des individus qui quittent le territoire d'un Etat pour aller dans un autre Etat. Il me paraît vraiment difficile d'analyser cela comme une atteinte à la souveraineté territoriale.

M. Tomuschat souligne qu'il y a de toute façon peu d'exemples de mise en oeuvre d'une responsabilité de l'Etat d'origine à l'égard de l'Etat d'accueil, à l'exception notoire de ce qui s'est passé après la première guerre mondiale. La RFA a effectivement signé avec Israël l'accord de Luxembourg, le 10 septembre 1952, dans lequel il était mentionné qu'

> Israël avait assumé la lourde charge de réinsérer un grand nombre de juifs, déracinés et dépourvus de tout, réfugiés d'Allemagne ou de territoires antérieurement sous l'autorité allemande et, sur cette base, avait émis une revendication à l'égard de la République fédérale allemande visant au dédommagement du coût de l'intégration de ces réfugiés.

En supposant cependant qu'une violation soit établie, qu'un lien de causalité existe entre cette violation et la présence de réfugiés sur le territoire, de quel dommage peut se plaindre l'Etat d'accueil?

M. Tomuschat rappelle fort opportunément que "*the arrival of human beings cannot as such be considered to constitute injury*". Cela me fait penser à un arrêt rendu, il y a quelque temps, par la Cour de Cassation en France: une femme demandait une indemnisation à un médecin qui avait raté une interruption de grossesse, parce qu'elle avait eu un enfant alors qu'elle n'en voulait pas: et la Cour de Cassation a refusé toute indemnité, en considérant qu'"un bébé n'est pas un préjudice".

Peut-être plus encore qu'une responsabilité de l'Etat d'origine, faudrait-il songer à une sorte de responsabilité collective de la communauté internationale pour supporter les charges financières occasionnées par l'accueil de réfugiés par un Etat? Cette idée d'une responsabilité collective a été énoncée, par exemple, dans la conclusion No. 19 (XXXI) sur l'asile temporaire, énoncée en 1980 par le Comité exécutif du HCR qui suggère "qu'en cas d'afflux massifs, les personnes qui cherchent un asile devraient toujours se voir accorder au moins l'asile temporaire et que les Etats qui, en raison de leur situation géographique ou pour d'autres raisons, font face à un afflux massif, devraient si nécessaire, à la demande de l'Etat intéressé, recevoir une aide immédiate d'autres Etats conformément au principe du partage équitable des charges".

2) *L'Etat d'accueil peut-il exercer la protection diplomatique du réfugié si celui-ci a la double nationalité?*

Je reprends ici un exemple qui pourrait avoir, malheureusement, une certaine actualité. Prenons une Algérienne qui a épousé un Français et qui a obtenu à la suite de son mariage la nationalité française. A la suite des menaces pesant sur eux, le couple fuit l'Algérie et se réfugie en France. En vertu des règles du droit international classique, on pouvait penser que c'est la règle de l'irresponsabilité internationale de l'Etat à l'égard d'un de ses nationaux qui devait prévaloir. Cette règle est énoncée à l'article 4 de la Convention de la Haye sur les conflits de nationalités: selon cet article, "un Etat ne peut exercer la protection diplomatique au profit de ses nationaux à l'encontre d'un Etat dont celui-ci est aussi le national".

En réalité, une importante évolution s'est produite sur cette question, du fait de la jurisprudence du tribunal irano-américain des différends sur les doubles nationaux. Dans un litige entre un double national, ayant à la fois la nationalité américaine et iranienne, et réclamant une indemnisation pour dommages à l'Iran, le tribunal arbitral a appliqué le principe de la nationalité dominante. Ce principe est énoncé à l'article 5 de la Convention de la Haye précitée:

Dans un Etat tiers, l'individu possédant plusieurs nationalités devra être traité comme s'il n'en avait qu'une. Sans préjudice des règles de droit appliquées dans l'Etat tiers en matière de statut personnel et sous réserve des conventions en vigueur, cet Etat pourra sur son territoire reconnaître exclusivement, parmi les nationalités que possède un tel individu, soit la nationalité du pays dans lequel il a sa résidence habituelle soit la nationalité de celui auquel, d'après les circonstances, il apparaît comme se rattachant le plus en fait.

En application d'une telle jurisprudence, il pourrait donc y avoir des cas où un réfugié pourrait bénéficier de la protection diplomatique de son Etat d'accueil à l'encontre de son Etat d'origine.

B. *La responsabilité à l'égard des organisations internationales humanitaires*

Peu de choses sont ici à ajouter à ce qu'a dit M. Tomuschat sur ce point. La question est celle de savoir si les organisations internationales humanitaires peuvent exiger un financement des camps de réfugiés par l'Etat d'origine de ceux-ci, si une responsabilité peut lui être imputé dans leur fuite du territoire national. Aucune pratique n'existe, à ce jour, en ce sens.

III.   LA RESPONSABILITE DE L'ETAT D'ORIGINE A L'EGARD DE LA COMMUNAUTE INTERNATIONALE

La responsabilité de l'Etat d'origine à l'égard de la communauté internationale peut être mise en jeu sur le plan politique ou sur le plan juridique.

A. *La mise en jeu de la responsabilité de l'Etat d'origine sur le plan politique, devant l'ONU*

Mon collègue a évoqué la résolution 194 (III) du 11 décembre 1948 sur les réfugiés palestiniens, ainsi que les résolutions plus récentes de l'Assemblée générale sur les réfugiés de l'ex-Yougoslavie victimes du nettoyage ethnique.

Il examine, à ce propos, la question d'une éventuelle compensation, au moment du retour, et ne semble pas la considérer comme souhaitable pour des raisons d'équilibre social, si j'ai bien compris. Ce qui est juste dans son propos est que tout va dépendre des circonstances et je crois que la comparaison entre le cas de l'Afrique du Sud et celui d'Israël et de la Palestine est assez éclairant.

Mais il n'y a pas que l'Assemblée générale qui est concernée, le Conseil de sécurité peut l'être aussi. Il suffit de songer à la fameuse résolution 688: c'est justement parce qu'il y avait un flux de réfugiés vers les frontières que le Conseil de sécurité a considéré qu'il constituait une menace à la paix.

B. *La mise en jeu de la responsabilité de l'Etat d'origine sur le plan juridique par l'actio popularis*

M. Tomuschat rappelle ce qu'a dit la Cour internationale de Justice sur les obligations *erga omnes*; ainsi que l'article 5 du Projet de la CDI qui élargit le champ des Etats qui peuvent mettre en cause la responsabilité d'un autre Etat, en cas de violation de normes fondamentales. Mon collègue se dit hostile à cette évolution: *"this enlargement of the circle of right-holders is simply wrong and would necessarily lead to utter confusion"*.

Il me semble au contraire que le fait de donner à tous les Etats le droit de se prévaloir de ce que j'appelle un "préjudice juridique" pour réclamer une réparation, c'est à dire le rétablissement de l'ordre juridique violé, lorsque sont en jeu des règles fondamentales, est un progrès considérable du droit: l'*actio popularis* est justement destinée à permettre un meilleur respect de la légalité internationale, en dehors de l'existence d'un préjudice matériel ou moral distinct de la violation du droit.

GUY S. GOODWIN-GILL

The Right to Leave, the Right to Return and the Question of a Right to Remain

Introductory Remarks

The subject of this paper and of the present session is potentially vast, with great opportunities for ambiguity and confusion awaiting anyone, practitioner, academic, national or international official, who might venture in. It is as confusing and contradictory, perhaps, as much of the discourse and most of the literature so far surrounding the issue.

Who are we talking about when we speak of the right to leave, the right to return and the right to remain? Nationals, non-nationals, permanent residents, temporary visitors, refugees, asylum seekers, migrant workers, clandestine migrants? Why one group, and not the next? What distinctions of principle separate one from another? When do the rights "apply"? Why at these times and not at others? Do the rights have an international dimension? And who is responsible for implementation?

This Colloquium is about the problem of refugees in light of contemporary international law issues, and these opening questions are not intended to be superficial or without merit, for there are real problems involved. Any examination of these rights ought therefore to take account of the protection and solutions needs of refugees, considered as those who have already fled, who are seeking to take flight, or are otherwise in search of a solution, such as return home. But there is also another purpose in asking the questions, which is to allow some preliminary definition of scope and terms.

The first premise is that the present analysis is limited in principle to the rights of *nationals*. Who is a national (or a citizen, and I shall use the words as synonyms) is a closely related question, and the rights to leave and to return are normally and rightly, if not exclusively, regarded as incidents of citizenship, somewhat imperfectly matched by correlative duties on the part of the State. The right to a nationality is outside the scope of the present paper, but the issue of citizenship does raise other dimensions often ignored in current discourse, namely, the inherent linkage to statehood and the responsibilities of States; so far as a State has authority over territory and population, it also has responsibilities towards the inhabitants that include freedom of movement

93

V. Gowlland-Debbas (ed.), The Problem of Refugees in the Light of Contemporary International Law Issues, 93–108.

and entitlement to remain. A sense of these implications can be found in the judgment of the International Court of Justice in the *Nottebohm* case, with its reference to the necessity, from the point of view of international law, for nationality to be based upon "a social fact of attachment, a genuine connection of existence, interests and sentiments, together with the existence of reciprocal rights and duties".[1]

Secondly, this paper will not deal, except indirectly, with the rights of permanent or long-term residents, or with the refugee's right or claim to remain in a country of refuge or asylum, or with the right or claim of the "diaspora" to return to the motherland. Each of these is important and will become more so in the future; each is also an issue on which international law already has something to say, but the rules and principles in question are likely to face challenge as a result of increasing State activity.

Finally, this paper is premised on a certain doubt about the *positive* nature of some of the rights in question, or at least some of the claims made for those rights, not all of which stand on the same level. To take a simple illustration: both the right to leave any country, including one's own, and the right to return to one's country can be found in one form or another in any number of universal and regional human rights instruments. The "right to remain", however, figures nowhere–in Philip Alston's words, it is "conjured up"; and even to a positivist international lawyer with occasional natural law leanings, that is rather worrying. Perhaps the best that can be said is that the "right to remain" stands in fact for something else, and beginning to identify that "something else" is one objective of what follows.

In this sense, then, the right to remain can be understood as a *concept*, deduced from a variety of other, not necessarily related premises – an umbrella term whose penumbra is sufficiently wide to include not just the sorts of basic life rights whose effective protection is essential to the practical dimension of actually remaining anywhere (personal security, livelihood, economic activity, self-sufficiency, to mention but a few); but also the broader, social, cultural and political rights that are part and parcel of community building, stability and community development, including political rights, (the right to vote, to stand for election, to participate in government), and perhaps also the entitlement, actual, potential or putative, of peoples within nation States to a measure of recognition, autonomy or self-government. In short, we may end up talking about all that is necessary to realize the full potential of the link between people and territory.

If this is a working sense of the right to remain, then the other rights, the right to leave or to return to one's own country, may well occupy a rela-

[1]   ICJ Rep.1955, p. 23. See also *Namibia* (Advisory Opinion), ICJ Rep.1971, pp. 16, 54, 56; *Western Sahara* (Advisory Opinion), pp. 12, 59 (paras. 13 and 70), p. 64 (para. 152); Ammoun, sep. op., pp. 85–86; and for discussion, Goodwin-Gill, G.S., 'Voluntary Repatriation: Legal and Policy Issues,' in Loescher, G./Monahan, L. (eds.)., *Refugees and International Relations*, Oxford 1989, pp. 255, 258–263.

tively minor though not inessential place in the overall picture: they do not express sufficiently the totality of what is required in the name of freedom from persecution or solution, but they are nevertheless essential elements in the realization of the right to remain.

The present paper looks at the right to leave and tries to show what it means in practical terms, both generally and specifically in relation to the right to seek asylum; secondly, the comparatively uncontroversial right to return to one's own country is considered, and finally a few only of the possible senses of a "right to remain" are examined. Admittedly, however, the recent actions of States and international organizations give some cause for concern about the future, and put in question many of the assumptions that have traditionally accompanied discussion of these human rights.

I. THE RIGHT TO LEAVE ONE'S OWN COUNTRY

The right to leave any country, including one's own, has featured regularly in international human rights instruments,[2] beginning with the Universal Declaration of Human Rights. Article 13 (2) declares the right, immediately after the right to freedom of movement and residence within the borders of each State, set out in the first paragraph.

Article 5 of the 1965 Convention on the Elimination of all Forms of Racial Discrimination uses the same contextual approach, requiring equality and no impermissible distinctions in the enjoyment of the right in question. Article 12 (2) of the 1966 Covenant on Civil and Political Rights provides similarly, as does Article 10 (2) of the 1989 Convention on the Rights of the Child, which speaks both to family reunion and to the right of the child and his or her parents to leave any country, including their own.

Regional instruments recognize the right almost without exception. It can be found in Article 12 (2) of the 1981 African Charter of Human and People's Rights, Article 22 (2) of the 1969 American Convention on Human Rights, and Article 2 (2) of the Fourth Protocol to the European Convention on Human Rights.

Treaties and instruments with more specific purposes also support the basic principle: Article 5 (2) of the 1985 UN Declaration on the Rights of Non-Nationals confirms the right to leave the country. Article 4 (1) of the 1977 European Convention on the Status of Migrant Workers requires each Contracting State to guarantee to migrant workers the right to leave the State Party of which they are nationals. Article 2 of the 1973 Convention on the Suppression of the Crime of Apartheid defines the crime to include legislative and other restrictions on freedom of movement, including the right to leave and return to the country, so far as they may be calculated to "prevent a

---

[2] See below, *The Right to Enter, Leave and Remain – Selected Texts.*

racial group or groups from participation in the political, social, economic and cultural life of the country".

In each case the context is instructive, for the right to leave one's country clearly shares in the greater or more general *value* attributed to freedom of movement.[3] At the same time, however, freedom of movement is not quite the same as other fundamental rights. As with free speech, how much value is placed on the freedom to move will likely reflect a particularly personal scale. And like speech and a number of other rights, the conditional and limited nature of freedom of movement has long been recognized, so far as the State is recognized as having the right, in circumstances described more fully below, to limit its exercise.

A.1. *Permissible Restrictions*

The "right to leave" has never been considered an absolute right. Common sense says that it does not apply to convicted criminals, that it should be restricted in the case of some minor children, and that it may also be limited with respect to those seeking to evade prosecution or certain civil obligations. State practice reveals further limitations applicable, for example, to those in possession of military secrets, who do not possess a visa for entry to another State, who are intending to travel to restricted territories, who have attained or are about to attain military age, or whose education has been paid for or subsidized by the State.[4] Not all of these manifestations of the "national interest" are necessarily accepted by even a majority of States, but the very breadth of actual practice is strong evidence against the emergence of a general principle of free movement.

The Covenant on Civil and Political Rights, Protocol 4 to the European Convention on Human Rights, the American Convention on Human Rights and the African Charter of Human and People's Rights all allow restrictions on the right to leave a State. The terminology varies slightly. The restriction must be provided by or according to law and, in the case of the American and European Conventions, also be "necessary in a democratic society". The

---

[3]   Sieghart identifies six aspects to freedom of movement: freedom to choose a residence within the territory of a State; freedom to move about within the borders of a State; freedom to leave a State; freedom to enter/return to a State; freedom from expulsion from a State; and freedom from exile: *The International Law of Human Rights*, Oxford 1983, pp. 178–179.

[4]   For a recent example of restrictions, see UN Doc. E/CN.4/1993/43 (Report on human rights in Albania), para. 43: 'Albanian law guarantees freedom of movement. Any Albanian national, irrespective of race, national origin, colour, sex, language, social status and so on, enjoys the right to travel abroad, whether for official, health or personal reasons. This right does not apply to persons who have not yet reached the age of 16 (except when they are accompanied by their parents), persons physically unable to travel, persons convicted of a criminal offence or against whom proceedings have been instituted, persons with financial obligations towards the State or towards other individuals, or persons who have not done military service. To travel abroad, persons must have a passport and a visa for the country they are visiting . . .'

permissible objectives of such restrictions nevertheless include national security and public order, the rights and freedoms of others, public health, public safety and public morals.

Notwithstanding almost universal formal support for the principle of freedom of movement, including the right to leave one's country, the scope of permissible restrictions and the nature and extent of State practice show clearly why the right in question has scarcely emerged from the context of domestic, constitutional norms to the level of internationally enforceable claim. Freedom to leave any country is a good in itself, but not to the point that it may be considered to impose either obligations or expectations on other States. Is that perhaps a little too cynical, or just pragmatic?

A.2. *Drafters and Intentions*

Sixty years ago, Reale wrote that the passport regime was characterized by control and discretion.[5] Not quite so long ago, I also concluded with respect to passports and the "right to travel", that,

> . . . State practice in the municipal sphere tends to reflect a claim of absolute discretion, rather than any restrictive rule of general international law . . . The general rule remains that the issue of passports is a matter within the reserved domain of domestic jurisdiction, and an aspect of executive control over foreign affairs. States feel themselves free . . . to impose those conditions and restrictions which they deem fit, and . . . the majority of States accept that the passport may be used to control the movement of their nationals.[6]

What *were* the intentions of those who proposed recognition of the right to leave in the 1948 Universal Declaration, given their then and subsequent practice? What did they mean?

Is it unreasonable to infer that little more than a political gesture was involved, aimed at the perceived constitutional deficiencies of totalitarian regimes at a time when cold war battle lines were consolidating? Many commentators and reasonable people at large see freedom of movement as an essential part of personal liberty,[7] on the assumption that it is fundamental to the integrity and development of individual personality. A statement of value was certainly put on the table in 1948, but not one that was considered to

---

[5] Reale, E., 'Le problème des passeports,' 50 *RCADI* (1934-IV), pp. 89, 114: 'Etant un acte administratif qui ressortit au domain réservé et à la souverainété nationale, elle est soustraite à tout contrôle et à tout appréciation.'

[6] Goodwin-Gill, G.S., *International Law and the Movement of Persons between States*, Oxford 1978, p. 29.

[7] See, for example, Dowty, A., *Closed Borders: The Contemporary Assault on Freedom of Movement*, 1987 (linking the 'right to personal self-determination' to the right to freedom of movement); Lillich, R., 'Civil Rights,' in Meron, T. (ed.), *Human Rights in International Law–Legal and Policy Issues*, Oxford 1984, p. 115.

require any international "implementation" or any correlative obligations beyond the particular nation-State.

The Soviet Union's proposal that the right, both in its internal and external aspects, should be recognized as exercisable *only* in accordance with the laws of the State was rejected as a matter of principle,[8] and yet State practice, then and now, seems indeed to support that interpretation, or one close to it.[9]

Leaving aside the rhetoric, whose rights and responsibilities were involved? Only those of the "national" government. That is, the right to leave was not a "right" which other States needed to complete; freedom of movement was something each government should guarantee to its own citizens, as a matter of constitutional principle, but not something in respect of which other States had any obligation.

State practice since then hardly provides convincing support for any alternative conclusion. During the 1970s and early 1980s, the United States attempted to use trade sanctions and political pressure to secure compliance by other States with the "right to leave", but with little overall success.[10] The work in the late 1980s on a draft declaration on freedom and non-discrimination with respect to the right to leave and return was remarkable more for its confusion and lack of focus, than for any concrete results.[11] As this effort drew to an end in 1989, the USSR was on the point of breaking up, democratization was beginning to course through most of the old "eastern bloc", and *domestic* recognition of the "right to travel" had arrived, but with the usual national controls and in a form leaving relatively unscathed the sovereign rights of other States to maintain control over entry.

Today, the question is whether we have moved at all from the national constitutional dimension to the human rights dimension, at least in the context of flight from persecution and danger. Or is free or "freer" movement of

---

[8] Cited in Lillich, *op. cit.* (note 7), at 150.

[9] The International Organization for Migration (IOM), set up in 1951 outside the United Nations but in the same political context, is founded on one human right in particular – freedom of movement. The Organization's Constitution, however, recognizes that "control of standards of admission and the number of immigrants to be admitted are matters within the domestic jurisdiction of States": Art. 1(3), IOM Constitution (text in 1 *IJRL* (1989), p. 597).

[10] See Lillich, *op. cit.* (note 7), pp. 115, 151–152. So far as the USSR did allow more of its citizens to leave, this may reflect more the results of a bilateral, contractual engagement than recognition of any universal principle. In that context, the right to leave one's country, in the absence of another State's formal undertaking to admit, was meaningless, and in the presence of such undertaking, it was redundant.

[11] See, among others, UN Docs. E/CN.4/Sub.2/1989/44 (with a draft declaration by Special Rapporteur Mubanga-Chipoya annexed at p. 20), E/CN.4/Sub.2/1989/47 (containing a summary of general observations and specific comments and alternative drafts and suggestions on the proposed declaration), and E/CN.4/Sub.2/1989/54 (working paper prepared by Mr. Diaconu). See also the 1986 and 1989 Declarations adopted by the International Institute of Human Rights, Strasbourg; Hannum, H., *The Right to Leave and Return in International Law and Practice,* Dordrecht 1987.

persons between States only likely to be realized at the juridical level within regional, political and economic arrangements, such as the European Union, in which national concerns are ultimately assuaged in reciprocal reassurances among like-minded States?

A.3. *The Right to Leave and the Right to Seek Asylum*

Is the relatively slow or non-existent progress in consolidating the "right to leave" in general or customary international law explicable perhaps by the fact that it is *only* essential or fundamental in one dimension, that is, as "the right to seek and to enjoy asylum" from persecution, where it is backed and made effective by the principle of *non-refoulement?* How does the right to leave to seek and to enjoy asylum mesh with the sovereign rights of the State to control admission to its territory?

Given the protection orientation and objectives of refugee and human rights law, this limited notion of the right to leave to seek and to enjoy asylum may be the only aspect in international law that is recognized as imposing any duty on States. It might be argued that the (nearly) correlative duty on States is *not to frustrate the exercise of that right* in such a way as to leave individuals exposed to persecution or other violation of their human rights, and that correspondingly intentional policies and practices of containment *without protection* will constitute an abuse of rights.

To paraphrase Judge Roberto Ago in his former persona as ILC Rapporteur on State Responsibility, a "primary" rule of international law, perhaps, forbids the "abusive" exercise of rights of control over the movement of persons, rights which will be violated if certain limits are exceeded in the course of their exercise, or if they are exercised with the (sole) intention of harming others.[12]

Essentially, this argument boils down to the proposition that, in a refugee-type situation (one in which nationals are at risk of persecution or other serious violation of human rights in their own country), other States are obliged to recognize the "right to leave to seek and to enjoy asylum". To an as yet undefined extent, they ought not to exercise their own rights to control the movement of persons, including the admission of individuals to their territory,[13] in an "abusive" manner, that is, solely with a view to ensuring that potential refugees remain in their own country and do not find protection.

This limited notion of an internationally recognized and meaningful "right to leave" is at least indirectly supported by the principle of non-rejection at the frontier and by the prohibition on torture and cruel, inhuman and degrading treatment or punishment, both of which are widely recognized as imposing

---

[12]   Ago, Roberto, *Second Report on State Responsibility*, UN Doc. A/CN.4/233: *YBILC* (1970-II) pp. 191, 193.

[13]   The conditions attaching to admission must remain open at this juncture; given the potential variety of circumstances, the objective of protection may not necessarily require asylum, residence or any permanent status.

100   *Guy S. Goodwin-Gill*

specific limitations on State rights with respect to the admission and removal of non-nationals.

It still leaves open the possibility, however, of a valid, non-abusive policy and program of restriction, for example, where other protection opportunities exist, such as an "internal flight alternative" or internationally guaranteed safety zone, where the quality of the protection will nevertheless determine their acceptability. Whatever the intrinsic merits of this thesis, it carries significant implications for other manifestations of State authority, for example, with respect to the grant or refusal of visas to applicants in danger in their own country, that are far from being accepted in the practice of States. For this reason, it may be inadvisable to advance the argument in isolation, apart from a general context that integrates principles of cooperation and solidarity with due regard to causes.

II. THE RIGHT TO RETURN TO ONE'S OWN COUNTRY

By contrast to the right to leave as understood in the practice of States, the right to return has a clear *international* dimension. At the traditional level of State to State relations, the State's obligation to admit its nationals is the correlative to other States' right of expulsion. Considered from another perspective, the State's right of protection over its citizens abroad is matched by its duty to receive those of its citizens who are not allowed to remain on the territory of other States.[14]

To this reciprocal relationship of rights and duties that comes about when one State admits the nationals of another may now be added a human rights dimension: the individual's right to return to the State of which he or she is a national.[15] As an incident of nationality, the duty to admit thus encompasses both the rights of other States (who themselves have no general duty to accommodate foreign citizens), and the right of the individual to access his or her own country.

The existence of the right to return and the duty to admit are beyond dispute.[16] Instances in which return has been denied or heavily qualified[17]

[14] See Goodwin-Gill, *op. cit.* (note 6), pp. 136–137 and sources cited.
[15] The word "return" is used for convenience, but should also be interpreted sufficiently broadly to include the admission of a national who, for whatever reason, may be making a first-time entry.
[16] In *Van Duyn v. Home Office* [1975] 1 CMLR 1, 18, the European Court of Justice considered that it was "a principle of international law, which the EEC Treaty cannot be assumed to disregard in the relations between Member States, that a State is precluded from refusing to its own nationals the right of entry or residence".
[17] In 1975, for example, the Provisional Revolutionary Government of Vietnam stated that it would only consider repatriation on a case-by-case basis, stating that decisions on the readmission of its citizens were a matter falling within its sovereign rights: Goodwin-Gill, G.S., *The Refugee in International Law*, Oxford 1983, pp. 10–11.

are generally part of broader contexts involving persecution, other violations of human rights, or situations in which political issues dominate legal entitlements.[18]

The human right to return to one's own country is implied in Article 9 of the Universal Declaration of Human Rights, prohibiting "arbitrary arrest, detention or exile", and in the prohibitions on the expulsion of nationals. It is expressly recognized also in Article 13 (2).

The only restriction or limitation with respect to the right to return is that the beneficiaries must be *citizens*.[19] Both the American and European Conventions provide that citizens shall not be deprived of the right to enter their own country.[20] Article 12 (4) of the 1966 Covenant on Civil and Political Rights seems to qualify the absolute entitlement by providing that "no one shall be *arbitrarily* deprived of the right to enter their country", but general principles, State practice, and the obligations of States to each other require a limited interpretation of this provision.[21] A similar approach is called for with regard to Article 12 of the African Charter, which declares the citizen's right to return to be subject to the same restrictions as apply to the right to leave.

The relevance and importance of the human rights dimension for refugees is obvious, for the primary solution of voluntary repatriation is premised upon their basic human right to return to their own country in conditions of security. The State of origin may seek to "write off" those who have fled, and to ignore the link of nationality, but this potentially involves a breach of obligation to the State of refuge, even though in the prevailing conditions the actual return of refugees may be prohibited by the principle of *non-refoulement*. How those competing responsibilities may be resolved in the best interests of the refugees is a frequently repeating challenge in the political context linking State of origin, State of refuge and the international community.[22]

---

[18] Successive UN General Assembly resolutions on the situation of Palestinian refugees, for example, recognized both the inherently political dimension of the problem, and the inalienable "right to return".

[19] This does *not* exclude the possibility that re-admission obligations may also be owed to permanent residents, refugees and stateless persons.

[20] Art. 3, Protocol 4, European Convention on Human Rights; Art. 22 (5), American Convention on Human Rights.

[21] On occasion, it may be difficult to determine which is "one's country", for example, in the case of persons having dual nationality. The factual criteria described by the International Court of Justice in the *Nottebohm* case (the idea of genuine and close connection) may therefore be necessary to show what is or is not arbitrary, and to identify a "dominant" nationality. In addition, State practice recognizes that nationality conferred by naturalization can be withdrawn in certain circumstances, and therefore presumably also the right to enter the country. See Goodwin-Gill, *op. cit.* (note 6) pp. 7–8, 202–203.

[22] See Goodwin-Gill, in Loescher/Monahan, *op. cit.* (note 1), pp. 255, 258–263.

III. The "Right to Remain"

A large number of displaced persons would not have to seek refuge abroad if their security could be guaranteed and if they could be provided with both sufficient food supplies and adequate medical care. In this context the concept of security zones within the territory of Bosnia-Herzegovina should be actively pursued.[23]

This conclusion of the Special Rapporteur on former Yugoslavia in 1992 contains a somewhat narrow idea of what is meant by the right to remain, namely, the provision of security and the basic necessities of life. The context belies the suggestion that this alone will make the search for asylum unnecessary, but it does open up the field for inquiry.

The United Nations High Commissioner for Refugees herself has also spoken of the "right to remain" in order to,

underline the basic right of the individual not to be forced into exile . . . The right to remain is implicit in the right to leave one's country and to return. In its simplest form it . . . include(s) the right to freedom of movement and residence within one's own country. It is linked also to other fundamental human rights because when people are forced to leave . . . a whole range of other rights are threatened, including the right to life, liberty and security of person, non-discrimination, the right not to be subjected to torture or degrading treatment, the right to privacy and family life.[24]

If the right to leave still is essentially a domestic matter, and the right to return an essentially non-controversial yet absolute incident of nationality, where does that place the right to remain?

The emerging question of the right to remain, I suggest, invites close attention to what exactly is meant by all our references to the right to leave, in its relation to the search for protection and refuge, and also to the implications of State actions to contain, restrict or prevent persons from leaving their own country, for whatever good or bad reason. The "right to remain" is not as such a recognized human right; the up-side to this is that simply invoking the right in defence of actions obliging populations at risk to stay where they are is not enough; that is, we cannot pretend to be in the business of protecting human rights when we "enforce" the right to remain. The downside is that we still do not have an adequate repository of principle and practice by which to judge the *quality* of so-called preventive measures.

In his 1992 report on the situation in former Yugoslavia, the Special Rapporteur further concluded that,

---

[23]   *Report on human rights in former Yugoslavia*, UN Doc. E/CN.4/1992/S-1/10, (1992), para. 25 (b).

[24]   Sadako Ogata, UN High Commissioner for Refugees, Statement to the Commission on Human Rights, Geneva, 3 March 1993.

The argument that providing refuge . . . is to conform to the policy of ethnic cleansing cannot override the imperative of saving their lives . . . Thus far, European countries have agreed to provide refuge to only a small percentage of those whose lives are at stake. In order to ensure that providing refuge will not contribute to ethnic cleansing, it is essential to reaffirm and provide lasting protection for the right to return.[25]

What is important here is the symbiotic relationship between protection, refuge and return.

The "prevention of refugee movements", in particular where the emphasis is on stopping flight rather than removing causes, is no solution and, so far as it follows from the actions of other States, will often amount to an abuse of rights. State objectives in this context, which will tend to limit directly the human right to leave and seek asylum, will therefore only be valid[26] if *effective protection* of human rights is provided to those who would otherwise flee.

The right to leave a country to seek asylum, considered as the right of individuals or groups, is now in question. In part, this is due to increasing acceptance of the *internal, constitutional* dimensions of freedom of movement, which itself has occurred simultaneously with a hardening of views with respect to the movement and admission of asylum seekers generally. This seems to have begun with States' concerns over the so-called irregular movements of refugees, moving on through the notions of internal flight alternative, safe third country, safe country of origin, and so to the idea of safe havens and "preventive protection". Experience with novel international exercises to provide protection on site and somehow or other to address the causes for flight has also contributed to diminish the perception in some quarters that the right to leave in search of asylum is fundamental.

Turkey's decision to close its border to Kurdish refugees, and the support or non-objection of a substantial number of members of the international community, clearly violated the principle of *non-refoulement*, understood in the single sense of a general principle of international law that includes the dimension of non-rejection at the frontier.[27] In that particular case, the international response was part of the problem, so far as the creation of a safe zone for Kurds in Iraq arguably removed the factual/legal basis for departure in search of asylum.

While no one would deny the importance of removing the causes for flight, in many cases international measures have been inadequate to the purpose; the right to remain has not been protected to such a degree as to avoid the necessity to flee in search of asylum. Until we have international, open and

---

[25] See *Report on human rights in former Yugoslavia, loc. cit.* (note 23), para. 25 (a).

[26] Which is *not* the same as "legal", and more legal work is needed on this issue.

[27] Turkey maintains the geographical limitation to its obligations under the 1951 Convention, and is thus not bound by treaty towards non-European refugees arriving on its territory or at its borders.

verifiable means for monitoring results and determining the success or failure of such activities, the right to leave to seek asylum itself will require active protection.

In short, the "right to remain" comprises the common or garden sense of not having to become a refugee, not having to flee, not being displaced by force or want, together with the felt security that comes with being protected. It is another way of expressing, in concrete terms, the connection between individual, community and territory, but its effective realization depends upon human rights and development considerations that are staggering in their breadth. Perhaps this is the sort of challenge that we need for the next century.

IV. The Right to Enter, Leave and Remain – Selected Texts

A. *Universal Treaties and Other Instruments*

1948 Universal Declaration of Human Rights

Article 13
(1) Everyone has the right to freedom of movement and residence within the borders of each state.
(2) Everyone has the right to leave any country, including his own, and to return to his country.

1965 Convention on the Elimination of All Forms of Racial Discrimination

Article 5
In compliance with the fundamental obligations laid down in Article 2 of this Convention, States Parties undertake to prohibit and to eliminate racial discrimination in all its forms and to guarantee the right of everyone, without distinction as to race, colour, or national or ethnic origin, to equality before the law, notably in the enjoyment of the following rights:
. . .
(d) Other civil rights, in particular:
   (i) The right to freedom of movement and residence within the border of the State;
   (ii) The right to leave any country, including one's own, and to return to one's country . . .]

1966 International Covenant on Civil and Political Rights

Article 12
1. Everyone lawfully within the territory of a State shall, within that territory, have the right to liberty of movement and freedom to choose his residence.

2. Everyone shall be free to leave any country, including his own.
3. The above-mentioned rights shall not be subject to any restrictions except those which are provided by law, are necessary to protect national security, public order (*ordre public*), public health or morals or the rights and freedoms of others, and are consistent with the other rights recognized in the present Covenant.
4. No one shall be arbitrarily deprived of the right to enter his own country.

1973 Convention on Suppression of Crime of Apartheid

Article 2
For the purpose of the present Convention, the term "the crime of apartheid", . . . shall apply to the following inhuman acts committed for the purpose of establishing and maintaining domination by one racial group of persons over any other racial group of persons and systematically oppressing them:
. . .
(c) Any legislative measures and other measures calculated to prevent a racial group or groups from participation in the political, social, economic and cultural life of the country and the deliberate creation of conditions preventing the full development of such a group or groups, in particular by denying to members of a racial group or groups basic human rights and freedoms, including . . . the right to leave and to return to their country, the right to a nationality, the right to freedom of movement and residence . . .

1985 UN Declaration on Rights of Non-Nationals

Article 5
. . .
2. Subject to such restrictions as are prescribed by law and which are necessary in a democratic society to protect national security, public safety, public order, public health or morals or the rights and freedoms of others, and which are consistent with the other rights recognized in the relevant international instruments and those set forth in this Declaration, aliens shall enjoy the following rights:
   (a) The right to leave the country . . .
3. Subject to the provisions referred to in paragraph 2, aliens lawfully in the territory of a State shall enjoy the right to liberty of movement and freedom to choose their residence within the borders of the State.

1989 Convention on the Rights of the Child

Article 10
1. In accordance with the obligation of States Parties under article 9, paragraph 1, applications by a child or his or her parents to enter or leave a

State Party for the purpose of family reunification shall be dealt with by States Parties in a positive, humane and expeditious manner. States Parties shall further ensure that the submission of such a request shall entail no adverse consequences for the applicants and for the members of their family.

2. A child whose parents reside in different States shall have the right to maintain on a regular basis, save in exceptional circumstances personal relations and direct contacts with both parents. Towards that end and in accordance with the obligation of States Parties under article 9, paragraph 2, States Parties shall respect the right of the child and his or her parents to leave any country, including their own, and to enter their own country. The right to leave any country shall be subject only to such restrictions as are prescribed by law and which are necessary to protect the national security, public order (*ordre public*), public health or morals or the rights and freedoms of others and are consistent with the other rights recognized in the present Convention.

B. *Regional Treaties and other Instruments*

1948 American Declaration of the Rights and Duties of Man

Article VIII
Every person has the right to fix his residence within the territory of the state of which he is a national, to move about freely within such territory, and not to leave it except by his own free will.

1950 European Human Rights Convention, Protocol No. 4

Article 2
1. Everyone lawfully within the territory of a State shall, within that territory, have the right to liberty of movement and freedom to choose his residence.
2. Everyone shall be free to leave any country, including his own.
3. No restrictions shall be placed on the exercise of these rights other than such as are in accordance with law and are necessary in a democratic society in the interests of national security or public safety, for the maintenance of *ordre public*, for the prevention of crime, for the protection of health or morals, or for the protection of the rights and freedoms of others.
4. The rights set forth in paragraph 1 may also be subject, in particular areas, to restrictions imposed in accordance with law and justified by the public interest in a democratic society.

Article 3
1. No one shall be expelled, by means either of an individual or of a collective measure, from the territory of the State of which he is a national.
2. No one shall be deprived of the right to enter the territory of the State of which he is a national.

Article 4
Collective expulsion of aliens is prohibited.

1969 American Convention on Human Rights

Article 22
Freedom of Movement and Residence
1. Every person lawfully in the territory of a State Party has the right to move about in it and to reside in it subject to the provisions of the law.
2. Every person has the right to leave any country freely, including his own.
3. The exercise of the foregoing rights may be restricted only pursuant to a law to the extent necessary in a democratic society to prevent crime or to protect national security, public safety, public order, public morals, public health, or the rights or freedoms of others.
4. The exercise of the rights recognized in paragraph 1 may also be restricted by law in designated zones for reasons of public interest.
5. No one can be expelled from the territory of the state of which he is a national or be deprived of the right to enter it.
6. An alien lawfully in the territory of a State Party to this Convention may be expelled from it only pursuant to a decision reached in accordance with law.
7. Every person has the right to seek and be granted asylum in a foreign territory, in accordance with the legislation of the state and international conventions, in the event he is being pursued for political offences or related common crimes.
8. In no case may an alien be deported or returned to a country, regardless of whether or not it is his country of origin, if in that country his right to life or personal freedom is in danger of being violated because of his race, nationality, religion, social status, or political opinions.
9. The collective expulsion of aliens is prohibited.

1977 European Convention on Legal Status of Migrant Workers

Article 4
Right of exit–Right to admission–Administrative formalities
1. Each Contracting Party shall guarantee the following rights to migrant workers: – the right to leave the territory of the Contracting Party of which they are nationals; – the right to admission to the territory of a

Contracting Party in order to take up paid employment after being authorised to do so and obtaining the necessary papers.

2. These rights shall be subject to such limitations as are prescribed by legislation and are necessary for the protection of national security, public order, public health or morals.

3. The papers required of the migrant worker for emigration and immigration shall be issued as expeditiously as possible free of charge or on payment of an amount not exceeding their administrative cost.

1981 African Charter on Human and People's Rights

Article 12

1. Every individual shall have the right to freedom of movement and residence within the borders of a State provided he abides by the law.

2. Every individual shall have the right to leave any country including his own, and to return to his country. This right may only be subject to restrictions, provided for by law for the protection of national security, law and order, public health or morality.

3. Every individual shall have the right, when persecuted, to seek and obtain asylum in other countries in accordance with the law of those countries and international conventions.

4. A non-national legally admitted in a territory of a State Party to the present Charter, may only be expelled from it by virtue of a decision taken in accordance with the law.

5. The mass expulsion of non-nationals shall be prohibited. Mass expulsion shall be that which is aimed at national, racial, ethnic or religious groups.

KAY HAILBRONNER

Comments On:
The Right to Leave, the Right to Return and the
Question of a Right to Remain

I. GENERAL REMARKS

The right to leave, the right to return and the question of a right to remain seem
to indicate the answer to the questions implied in the title. It will be relatively easy to show that public international law does recognize an individual's
right to leave a country, subject, of course, to some restrictions, while it is
at least doubtful whether a corresponding duty exists to receive somebody who
has made use of his or her right to leave. In between the two, there is a right
to return. In some way it belongs to the second, somewhat more doubtful
category of rights since it implies as well a duty of a country to receive the
person making use of a right to return.

Who are we talking about when we discuss individual rights in such
sensitive matters as territorial sovereignty, immigration and asylum law? The
individual rights and potential rights mentioned in the title obviously refer
to different categories of persons. The right to return seems to be related to
a State's own nationals, while the right to leave may apply to a State's own
nationals as well as to foreigners. Practical problems, however, will usually
arise only in relation to a State's own nationals. A State will rarely prevent
foreigners from leaving except for reasons of national security and public order.
The right to remain, on the other hand, raises primarily issues of immigration and refugee law. It is probably this topic where most legal problems
will arise. The question of temporary protection of civil war refugees and
the question of a right of permanent residence for refugees who have been
granted temporary protection after a certain period of time has elapsed
immediately comes to mind. But there is also a wide range of other issues
relating to the general legal status acquired by foreigners after some time,
particularly foreigners who have been born or raised in a foreign country. In
addition, the right to remain under exceptional circumstances may also arise
in relation to a State's own nationals.

In summary, there is a wide range of very different issues embracing the
humanitarian law of war as well as public international law principles on human
rights.

V. Gowlland-Debbas (ed.), The Problem of Refugees in the Light of Contemporary International Law Issues,
109–118.

What are we talking about in substance when we discuss individual rights in the context of public international law? The right to leave and the right to return are embodied in international human rights instruments widely ratified by States and therefore indicating an *opinio juris*. Nevertheless, one has to be careful in assessing the state of public international law merely on the basis of written texts. It is not sufficient to state a consensus on principles which are subject to very different interpretations and restrictions. Particularly in the field of human rights, general principles may turn out to hide a lack of common conviction on the substance of these principles. Restrictions based on different concepts may deprive an individual right of its substantive content altogether.

This is even more true when principles are discussed which are not even laid down in binding international instruments. Freedom of movement as well as a right to remain as such cannot be found in international human rights instruments, although there is frequent reference at least to the freedom of movement concept. Goodwin-Gill's paper is premised on certain doubts about the positive nature of the rights in question, and in particular about the right to remain. I fully agree with this assumption; it remains to be examined yet what right exactly for what category of persons and in what context we are talking about. It may well be that there is customary international law covering some aspects of that right while others may still be in the realm of claims and legal wishful thinking. There may not always be a strict distinction between customary international law, emerging customary international law and mere formulation of desirable legal policy; it is necessary, however, to be aware of the fact that customary international law is based primarily on the practice of States and their *opinio juris*. The concern for human rights and improvement of the living conditions of millions of refugees as such cannot replace a sober analysis of what States are prepared to accept as a legal duty under public international law in the field of immigration and refugee law. It is true that the international community is not limited to States anymore, but embraces other actors like international organizations, governmental as well as intergovernmental ones. The shaping of an international legal order in the area of refugee and migration law therefore is not exclusively a task of governments and their representatives. On the other hand, the present international order is still very much based on the principle of sovereignty of nations. Without a virtually uniform State practice reflecting a common legal consensus, new public international law will not come into existence.

Goodwin-Gill's paper represents a sober analysis of present international law and its possible future development. Some people will find it disappointing that public international law in terms of individual rights has so little to contribute to solving some of the most urgent problems of today's world. Migration and refugee movements continue to be one of the most important challenges for the international community. The general prospects for a solution of the migration and refugee movements in terms of individual rights are, however, not very good. States are increasingly reluctant to enter into new legal obligations restricting their sovereign rights to decide on the admission of foreigners. To a large degree, the legal literature on the subject can be understood as a plea for a stronger role of human rights for those leaving their home country and looking elsewhere for a decent living. In this sense, Goodwin-Gill has correctly described some of the rights in question as a legal concept indicating an umbrella term sufficiently wide to include the rights, emerging rights, as well as claims and interests.

II. THE RIGHT TO LEAVE

There is ample evidence to support the existence of a right to leave under public international law. Goodwin-Gill has rightly pointed to a number of international law instruments as well as national legislation confirming the right of a State's own nationals as well as the right of anybody else to leave a country.

The controversy is on permissible restrictions, and in particular, on restrictions based upon a wide concept of public order, national security, public health or morals.[1] Even within Western Europe it has been difficult to define generally where restrictions on the right to leave are necessary on grounds of public interest in a democratic society.

As regards the European Human Rights Convention, it has been rightly mentioned that the concept of a democratic society includes as essential components such fundamental principles as pluralism, tolerance, freedom of expression, access to independent courts exercising an effective control of State activities, and the rule of law.[2] This in effect means that limitations of the right to leave can no longer be based upon concepts of public order which do not fully take into account individual freedoms. A State's own national cannot generally be considered as a representative of that State and therefore made subject to "political image" restrictions when travelling abroad. It seems doubtful, therefore, whether limitations based upon the concept of preventing damage to a State's prestige abroad can be upheld.

An extensive study of the right to leave in public international law and national law[3] comes to the conclusion that the right to leave is in practice subject to several limitations applied in order to protect different, and in principle legitimate, State interests. To be lawful these limitations must be applied on the basis of a statutory provision, conforming with the criteria of accessibility, foreseeability and proportionality.[4] In addition, limitations will have to be based upon the proof that a legitimate national interest is, in fact,

---

[1] Cf. Art. 12 of the International Covenant on Civil and Political Rights.

[2] For a comprehensive discussion, see Hofmann, R., *Die Ausreisefreiheit nach Völkerrecht und staatlichem Recht* (The Right to Leave in International and National Law), Heidelberg 1988, p. 310.

[3] Hofmann, *op. cit.* (note 2), p. 310.

[4] Hofmann, *op. cit.* (note 2), p. 311.

endangered. As Hofmann has remarked, the yardstick has to be the principle that the exercise of the right to leave is the rule, and limitations of this right the exception. Exceptions, therefore, are lawful only if applied under special circumstances and based upon a restrictive interpretation of the grounds justifying the limitations of the right to leave.[5]

In addition to the concept of public order, it is the idea of national security that has frequently been used to justify limitations of the right to leave. National security in a narrow sense refers to threats to the territorial integrity and political independence of a State. Thus, in all States there are restrictions of the right to leave for people with special access to sensitive information. On the other hand, national security cannot be identified with a general and vague concept of national identity which may be endangered by a State national making use of fundamental freedoms, particularly the freedom of expression abroad.

There are also restrictions generally recognized in State practice on the basis of national duties including military service. Although the right of States to restrict the freedom of movement of their own nationals on this ground is generally recognized, one may ask whether there are limitations to this right in the context of a tolerated, even encouraged, emigration. A State which openly encourages its own nationals to move as migrant workers abroad may act contradictorily by subjecting its own nationals to duties which may be in conflict with the duties of the receiving State. Present international law, however, is still very much based on the concept of nationality and national sovereignty. The effect that large migration flows have had in changing the traditional pattern of national identity has not yet been fully taken into account in public international law.

Goodwin-Gill comes to the somewhat pessimistic conclusion that States feel free to impose those conditions and restrictions which they deem fit and that the majority of States accept that the passport may be used to control the movement of their nationals. It is hard to challenge this statement in principle. One has to realize, however, that international law has not been uninfluenced by factual developments. After the collapse of the Soviet Empire one has observed a growing recognition of the right to leave in the national legislations of many States which hitherto had deprived, in practice, their nationals of this right. There is a growing body of State practice defining more precisely legitimate and illegitimate reasons under which passports must be issued or prolonged. The CSCE declaration at the Copenhagen meeting of June 29, 1990[6] states that restrictions on the right to leave must have the character of very rare exceptions, and will be considered necessary only if they respond to the specific public need, pursue a legitimate aim and are proportionate to that aim, and are not abused or applied in an arbitrary manner.[7]

---

[5]   Hofmann, *op. cit.* (note 2), p. 315.
[6]   See Ermacora/Nowak/Tretter, *International Human Rights*, 1993, pp. 138, 140.
[7]   See at no. 9,5 of the Declaration.

III. The Right to Leave and Freedom of Movement

Goodwin-Gill's somewhat pessimistic remarks were aimed at freedom of movement in general rather than the specific right to leave one's own country. Freedom of movement is not equivalent to the right to leave. It implies a correlative obligation for States to accept those who have chosen to leave either their home country or their former country of residence. It is true that freedom of movement is something each government should guarantee to its own citizens, but not something in respect of which other States have any obligation. Recent State practice after the tearing down of the Iron Curtain does not point to an emerging trans-frontier freedom of movement.

The dilemma of a freedom of movement concept which receiving States did face when travel restrictions were abolished became obvious with a large flow of migration flows. States reacted with new visa restrictions and transport regulations to prevent uncontrolled and illegal entry of potential immigrants. Recent State practice, as well as the introduction of new legislation, demonstrates clearly a reluctance to enter into any freedom of movement obligations which may restrict the right of States to control entry and residence of foreigners in their territories. At the CSCE Copenhagen meeting the participating States affirmed that "free movements and contacts among their citizens are important in the context of the protection and promotion of human rights and fundamental freedoms". This clearly puts free movement into the context of other human rights but does not imply a freedom of movement. In addition, States will ensure that their policies concerning entry into their territories are fully consistent with the aims set out in the relevant provisions of the final act, the Madrid Concluding Document and the Vienna Concluding Document. In the context to implement and improve present commitments in the field of human context, including on a bilateral and multilateral basis, States will

> strive to implement the procedures for entry into their territories, including the issuing of visas and passport and customs control, in good faith and without unjustified delay. Where necessary, they will shorten the waiting time for visa decisions, as well as simplify practices and reduce administrative requirements for visa applications;
>
> ensure, in dealing with visa applications, that these are processed as expeditiously as possible in order, *inter alia*, to take due account of important family, personal or professional considerations, especially in cases of an urgent, humanitarian nature;
>
> endeavour, where necessary, to reduce fees charged in connection with visa applications to the lowest possible level;
>
> the participating States concerned will consult and, where appropriate, co-operate in dealing with problems that might emerge as a result of the increased movement of persons.[8]

[8]   See Ermacora/Nowak/Tretter, *op. cit.* (note 6), p. 142.

The wording of these provisions makes clear that freedom of movement has not acquired the dimension of an international human right. One may go one step further and doubt whether a right to move freely should be considered a desirable legal development to cope with the problems of underdevelopment, civil war, political instability and economic disaster in large parts of the world. State practice supports Goodwin-Gill's observation that the free movement of persons is only likely to be realized within regional arrangements based on homogeneous political and economic conditions.

Freedom of movement implying a correlative obligation of receiving States as an individual right thus becomes effective only when rights of foreigners already lawfully resident are affected. This is particularly the case with family reunion. There is a wide range of international instruments recognizing a right of family reunion, although in detail there are still a lot of questions as to the conditions and restrictions of such a right.

Immigration ministers recently passed a resolution on family reunion which shows that even in this area there are still a number of questions which have to be resolved.

IV. The Right to Leave and the Right to Seek Asylum

It is common knowledge that neither under the Geneva Refugee Convention of 1951 nor under public international law there is a right to be granted asylum. The right to seek and to enjoy asylum from persecution does not entail an obligation to be granted protection. The drafting history of the Geneva Convention as well as subsequent State practice show that the sovereign right of States to control admission to their territory is not restricted by the right to seek and to enjoy asylum. The prohibition of non-refoulement, laid down in Article 33 of the Geneva Convention and, with respect to torture and inhuman treatment, in Article 3 of the European Human Rights Convention and Art. 3 of the United Nations Anti-Torture Convention, is widely acknowledged in international practice. It may be considered as the only exception to the principle that States may restrict the admission of foreigners to their territory. It must be kept in mind, however, that the principle of non-refoulement can only be applied if certain conditions are met. One of these conditions is that a refugee is in fact in a situation in which he or she would be rejected or returned to the frontiers of a territory where he or she would face persecution for the reasons laid down in Article 1 A of the Geneva Convention. State practice supports an interpretation that the principle must be applied not only in case of expulsion and deportation but also in case of rejection at the border.

It is, however, very doubtful whether a further extension beyond the case of rejection at the border does find sufficient support in State practice. If one looks at the discussion during the drafting of the Geneva Convention, one can find numerous statements stressing that nothing in the Convention can be interpreted as an obligation to admit asylum seekers. Nevertheless, there is ample evidence that a State acts contrarily to its international obligations by rejecting an asylum seeker at the border if – as a result – she or he would face the danger of persecution. It is, however, very doubtful whether the principle of non-refoulement implies as well a general duty of States to organize their entry and immigration, visa and transport legislation in such a way that potential political refugees may use their right to seek and enjoy asylum effectively. A legal duty of receiving States arises only when and in so far as a potential refugee, claiming a danger of political persecution, has come within the scope of territorial jurisdiction of a State. It may be argued that it would be contradictory to provide for protection against rejection at the border or return, while making it, on the other hand, difficult, if not impossible, for potential refugees to achieve a situation in which the principle becomes applicable. It must be kept in mind, however, that an extension of the principle of non-refoulement to facilitate access to the territory and to grant exemptions from generally applicable entry and transport regulations means a completely new dimension with far-reaching consequences for the rights of States to control admission to their territories. The exercise of rights of control or the movement of persons with the sole intention of delivering potential political refugees to a fate of persecution or inhuman treatment may well be considered an abuse of the right of control. But that is not the issue in the discussion about carrier sanctions, visa restrictions and coast guard interventions on the high seas. The restrictions have not been introduced to prevent persons facing a danger of political persecution from seeking asylum. The legal issue is whether the principle of non-refoulement implies duties reaching beyond the individual return or rejection situation.

Recent State practice as demonstrated by the introduction of new asylum procedure legislation does not support in any way such an extension of the principle of non-refoulement. As a reaction to large migration movements a great number of receiving States have considered it indispensable to restrict the uncontrolled access of foreigners to their territory. Effective control of admission requires general restrictions on access. It is impossible to distinguish between persons who may be justified to claim a right or to be rejected or returned, and the large number of people seeking admission for other purposes. It follows that the prohibition of refoulement does not apply beyond the limited context of rejection at the border or expulsion or deportation.

V. The Right to Return

The right to return to one's own country is recognized in the Universal Declaration of Human Rights and in many other international instruments. As a right based on nationality it is, in principle, beyond dispute, as Goodwin-Gill has pointed out. There have, however, recently been some unsolved questions and problems in relation to the right of return.

One question is whether a right of return is really limited to a State's own nationals. Nationality may be doubtful and, in any case, States may be tempted to get rid of unwanted parts of their population by depriving them of their citizenship. Even beyond the question of a right of nationality and arbitrary nationality legislation one may ask whether public international law does not support a right of return for foreigners legally resident for a long time in the country. It is prohibited under public international law to organize mass deportations of people legally resident, regardless of their nationality. A corresponding right of return seems to be a logical consequence. Under this premise arrangements and agreements depriving people of their right to return are contrary to public international law.

There is another issue with respect to the right of return to one's own home country. Recently, States have imposed administrative and procedural difficulties to prevent the return of their own nationals. The practical operation of return agreements has frequently been impeded by bureaucratic obstacles and excessive requests concerning proof of nationality. There are a number of questions relating to the application of return agreements which are not yet satisfactorily resolved in public international law. The cooperation between receiving States and former home States of refugees is an underdeveloped area of public international law. So far, States have insisted upon their right to prescribe the conditions under which a right to return can be exercised. It is necessary, however, to look upon migration movements and the solution of problems arising from these movements from the larger perspective of public international law. There is an indication that States, regardless of specific provisions of return agreements, are obliged to cooperate in the solution of problems arising from the return of a State's own nationals. It is, however, difficult to postulate as yet precise rules defining the rights and obligations of the affected States.

VI. The Right to Remain

The right to remain has been rightly put by Goodwin-Gill into the context of civil war refugees. First of all, there is certainly a right to remain in the sense that people may not be forced to leave their own country or their country of residence. I also agree with his statement that international measures have been inadequate for the purpose of removing the causes for flight. Yugoslavia has clearly demonstrated the need for a more effective international machinery to prevent a policy of mass expulsion and mass deportation based on ethnic, religious or economic reasons. There is not only a need to make a more organized and calculated use of the possibilities provided for in Chapter VII of the United Nations' Charter. There is also a need for general guidelines and principles according to which no agreements will ever sanction a policy depriving large parts of the population of a right to remain.

The right to remain does, of course, arise as well in the context of individual rights of foreigners. In this connection the concept of temporary protection raises a number of as yet unresolved issues. The basic idea of this concept is that temporary refugees will return to their home country once the situation under which they had to leave their country has ceased to exist. The question arises, however, after how long a right of temporary refuge evolves into a right of permanent residency. People who have been granted temporary refuge cannot be left forever in a status of uncertainty. There must be a right to remain after a certain period of time taking into account all relevant factors like the duration of stay, connections with the receiving country and assimilation to its living conditions. Under what circumstances a right of temporary residence develops into a right of permanent residency is still a domestic matter. There may, however, be limits based on humanitarian considerations similar to those that have been developed under the European Convention of Human Rights with respect to the protection of family and marriage.

The European Court of Human Rights, based on Article 8 of the European Human Rights Convention, has considerably restricted the right of States to expel foreigners who have grown up or received most of their education in the receiving State.[9] The Court decided that a contracting State must not expel a young foreigner who is living with his family in the receiving State and who has spent most of his youth in the receiving State even if he has committed serious offences.

The European Court of Human Rights, however, has made clear that the European Human Rights Convention as such does not provide for a right to be granted entry or to remain. The right to decide on a prolongation of a residence permit remains essentially within the exclusive domain of each State. Unless a foreigner is facing political persecution, torture or inhuman treatment, residence rights are subject to national legislation. Bilateral and multilateral treaties on friendship and freedom of establishment usually provide for some kind of protection against expulsion after a certain period of time spent in a foreign country. It cannot be said, however, that customary international law has emerged from these conventions. Efforts to restrict the right of States to decide on residence rights have not been very successful. The United Nations Convention for the protection of migrant workers and their family members adopted on 18 December 1990 has not received a sufficient number of ratifications to enter into force.

One may well argue that public international law does not as yet sufficiently take account of the fact that millions of people live abroad for short or long periods. It might be considered as a legal deficit that – except under special circumstances – no right to remain can be found in any international instrument. It must be kept in mind, however, that nationality is still an essential

---

[9]   See the case *Moustaquim/Belgium,* Decision of February 18, 1991, no.31/1989/191/291= Europäische Grundrechtszeitschrift (1991), p. 149; case of *Beldjoudi v. France*, Decision of March 26, 1992, no. 55/1990/246/317.

feature of sovereignty. A right to remain is generally considered as an inherent part of citizenship. Foreigners, on the other hand, enjoy a right of residence only to the extent that they are admitted. It may be questionable whether this distinction reflects the reality of modern societies. State practice does not, however, indicate a trend towards an effacement of this distinction. In a homogeneous political and economic community like the European Union, European citizenship may replace partially the nationality of each Member State. In the process of a European integration this, however, does not really mean a departure from the traditional concept that a right to remain is linked to nationality. The answer to the question of a secure legal status of migrant workers as well as of permanent refugees therefore may well lie in a facilitation of the acquisition of nationality and citizenship.

RICHARD PLENDER

The Legal Basis of International Jurisdiction to Act with Regard to the Internally Displaced

I. The 1951 Convention and the Statute of the Office of UNHCR

The terms of Article 2(7) of the Charter of the United Nations, precluding the intervention of the organization in matters which are essentially within the domestic jurisdiction of States,[1] was foremost in the minds of the draftsmen of the Statute of the High Commissioner[2] and the Convention on the Status of Refugees.[3] In the immediate aftermath of the Second World War it was scarcely to be contemplated that the principal recipients of fugitives from East Europe would involve themselves in the movement of persons within the territories of the Soviet Union or the States located within its sphere of influence. The first international organization created by the United Nations was the International Refugee Organization, devised in response to a need recognized at the San Francisco Conference in 1945, where concern was expressed for *displaced persons who had not been repatriated* and were under the mandate of the High Commissioner of the League of Nations.[4]

The establishment of the Office of the High Commissioner, initially against East European opposition, was achieved with an explicit statement of the international nature of the problem of refugees: a statement which contained an implicit renunciation of any intention to engage in the internal affairs of the countries whose nationals became refugees. Thus, General Assembly Resolution 319 (IV), adopted on 3 December 1949, declared that,

---

[1] See also Art. 3 of the International Law Commission's Draft Declaration on the Rights and Duties of States, *YBILC* (1949), p. 286, which declares that 'every State has the duty to refrain from intervention in the internal or external affairs of any other State'. See further Trindade, 'The Domestic Jurisdiction of States in the Practice of the United Nations and Regional Organisations', 25 *ICLQ* (1976), p. 715.

[2] UNGA Res 428(V), 14 December 1950, Annex.

[3] Geneva, 28 July 1951, 189 *UNTS* 150; Protocol, New York, 31 January 1967, 606 UNTS 267. See generally Robinson, N., *Convention Relating to the Status of Refugees: Its History, Contents and Interpretation*, New York 1953.

[4] Holborn, L., *The International Refugee Organisation*, London 1954, pp. 1 and 29.

V. Gowlland-Debbas (ed.), The Problem of Refugees in the Light of Contemporary International Law Issues, 119–133.
© 1996 Kluwer Academic Publishers. Printed in the Netherlands.

the problem of refugees is international in scope and nature and that its final solution can only be provided by the voluntary repatriation of refugees or their assimilation within new national communities.[5]

The definitive resolution establishing the Office of the High Commissioner,[6] which also decided to convene a conference with a view to the adoption of a Convention, confined the principal definition of a refugee to those who were *outside their countries of nationality* and unable or unwilling to avail themselves of its protection for stated reasons.[7]

The element of expatriation has become so well established in the definition of a 'refugee' that it is often accepted among lawyers (although not among members of the public generally) as an indispensable prerequisite. According to Perluss and Hartman[8]

> Unlike a refugee, a person fleeing from internal armed conflict does not seek to disestablish his ties of nationality or allegiance to his country on a temporary or permanent basis . . . His need for relief, and therefore temporary refuge, lasts only until his government can ensure him *de facto* protection.

It was however the political circumstances prevailing at the time of the creation of the Office of the High Commissioner, not some inherent rule of law or logic, which confined the principal functions of the Office to cases of external displacement. Indeed, it was accepted from the outset that the definition given to a 'refugee' by the Statute and Convention was not intended to impose a constraint on the liberty of States to invest the High Commissioner with additional functions. The Statute of the Office of the High Commissioner itself directed him to

> engage in such additional activities . . . as the General Assembly may determine, within the limits placed at his disposal.

Recommendation E appended to the Convention expressed the hope that

> the Convention relating to the Status of Refugees will have value as an

---

[5]   The same resolution recommended that persons falling under the competence of the UNHCR should, for the time being, be refugees and displaced persons within the meaning of Annex I of the Constitution of the International Refugee Organisation, New York, 15 December 1948, 18 *UNTS* 53, together with such others as might be brought within the mandate from time to time.

[6]   See Plender, R., *International Migration Law*, 2nd ed., Dordrecht 1988, pp. 399–402.

[7]   'L'asile international diffère de l'asile intra-national en ce que dans ce cas le réfugié non seulement se soustrait à la persécution de la part d'un Etat (son Etat national), mais trouve protection auprès d'un autre Etat. C'est la deuxième limitation au sens large du terme asile, introduite pour arriver à la notion d'asile qui intéresse le droit international': Bolesta-Koziebrodzki, *Le droit d'asile* 1962, p. 56.

[8]   'Temporary Refuge: Emergence of a Customary Norm', 26 *Virg. JIL* (1986), p. 551 at 597–598. See generally Parrish, 'Membership in a Particular Social Group under the Refugee Act of 1980: Social Identity and the Legal Concept of Refugee', 92 *Colum. L. Rev.* (1992), p. 923.

example exceeding its contractual scope and that all nations will be guided by it in granting as far as possible to persons in their territory as refugees and who would not be covered by the terms of the Convention, the treatment for which it provides.

The functions and responsibilities of the High Commissioner, in particular situations, have been enlarged repeatedly by use of the concept of 'good offices'. The precedent was established by General Assembly Resolution 1388 (XIV) of 20 November 1959 – a measure designed for the assistance of Chinese refugees in Hong Kong, who were considered not to qualify under the mandate since it was theoretically open to them to avail themselves of the protection of the Republic of China. That resolution

> authorize[d] the High Commissioner, in respect of refugees who do not come within the competence of the United Nations, to use his good offices in the transmission of contributions designed to provide assistance to these refugees.

The precedent was followed late in 1961 when fugitives from Angola fled to the Democratic Republic of the Congo in such numbers that it was impossible to subject them to a determination procedure.[9] Successive resolutions of the General Assembly requested the High Commissioner to

> continue to afford international protection to refugees and to pursue his efforts on behalf of the refugees within his mandate and to those to whom he extends his good offices.[10]

The United Nations Organization first raised the question of institutional protection of internally displaced persons at the International Conference on the Plight of Refugees, Returnees and Displaced Persons in Southern Africa held in Oslo in 1988. In the following year the International Conference on Central American Refugees (CIREFCA) addressed itself to the subject. In 1990 the Economic and Social Council requested the Secretary General

> to initiate a system-wide review to assess the experience and capacity of various organizations, in the coordination of assistance to all refugees, displaced persons and returnees, and the full spectrum of their needs.[11]

The Commission on Human Rights[12] then requested the Secretary General to compile an analytical report on internally displaced persons. This was

---

[9]　UNGA Resolution 1673(XVI), 18 December 1961.

[10]　From 1965 onwards the two categories of persons were grouped within a single rubric. Thus UNGA Resolution 2039(XX) of 7 December 1965 requested the High Commissioner 'to pursue his efforts with a view to ensuring an adequate international protection of refugees and to providing satisfactory permanent solutions to the problems affecting the various groups of refugees within his competence'.

[11]　Resolution 1990/78 of 27 July 1990.

[12]　Resolution 1991/25 of 5 March 1991.

prepared by a consultant, Mr Jacques Cuénod, and submitted to the Economic and Social Committee.[13]

Following the Persian Gulf War, the French representative at the Security Council proposed Security Council Resolution 688 of 5 April 1991, which

condemn[ed] the repression of the Iraqi civilian population in many parts of Iraq, including most recently in Kurdish-populated areas, the consequences of which threaten international peace and security in the region

and

insist[ed] that Iraq allow immediate access by international humanitarian organizations.

Western governments interpreted the adoption of this resolution, by 10 votes to 3 with 7 abstentions, as authorization to establish safe havens in Kurdish areas.[14] Iraq initially objected to this action as a violation of its territorial sovereignty[15] but subsequently concluded a Memorandum of Understanding authorizing the provision of humanitarian assistance by United Nations personnel.

In July 1992 the High Commissioner formally requested States to extend 'temporary protection' to those in need of it in consequence of the conflict in former Yugoslavia. This became one of the seven elements of the Comprehensive Response to the crisis presented at the International Meeting on Humanitarian Aid for Victims of the Conflict in Former Yugoslavia on 29 July 1992. The proposals presented at that meeting and at the Second Follow-Up Committee Meeting in September 1992 emphasized the case for burden-sharing and solidarity in the face of a humanitarian need.

The Commission on Human Rights appointed a Special Rapporteur on Yugoslavia[16] and called for support from 'existing mechanisms'. General Assembly Resolution 2958 (XXVII) of 12 December 1992 commended the High Commissioner for Refugees

for her efficient role in the coordination of relief and resettlement operations of refugees and other displaced persons.

That resolution is of present significance; for the displaced persons mentioned therein were those *internally* displaced within the Sudan.[17]

---

[13]   E/1991/109/Add.1.

[14]   Harrington, 'Operation Provide Comfort: A Perspective in International Law', 8 *Conn. JIL* (1993) 635.

[15]   UN Document S/22459, 8 April 1991.

[16]   Resolution 1992/S-1/1, 14 August 1992.

[17]   See generally Moussalli, M., 'The Evolving Functions of the Office of the High Commissioner for Refugees', in *Problems and Prospects of Refugee Law*, Gowlland, V./Samson, K. (eds.), Graduate Institute of International Studies, Geneva, 1991, pp. 81–103.

The first explicit reference to internally displaced persons, in a resolution of the General Assembly dealing with the Office of the High Commissioner, was in one adopted in 1992[18] commending

> efforts by the High Commissioner, on the basis of specific requests from the Secretary General or the competent principal organs of the United Nations and with the consent of the concerned State, to undertake activities in favour of internally displaced persons, taking into account the complementarities of the mandates and expertise of other relevant organizations.

A subsequent resolution of the General Assembly[19] welcomed the decision of the Executive Committee of the Office of the UNHCR to extend, on a case-by-case basis and under specific circumstances, protection and assistance to the internally displaced and encouraged the Representative, through dialogue with governments, to continue her review of the needs for international protection of internally displaced persons and assistance to them.

That resolution was recalled by the Commission on Human Rights in 1994 when it adopted, without a vote, its Resolution on Displaced Persons.[20] That resolution called on the Department of Humanitarian Affairs, the United Nations High Commissioner for Refugees, the International Organization for Migration and other organizations to continue to cooperate with the Representative of the Secretary General on Internally Displaced Persons. On the same day, and again without a vote, the Commission on Human Rights adopted a Resolution on Human Rights and Mass Exoduses.[21] In contrast with previous years, when the corresponding resolution had concentrated on early warning, the resolution of 1994 placed greater emphasis on prevention and solutions. It welcomed the contribution made by the United Nations High Commissioner for Refugees to human rights bodies and invited Mrs Ogata to address the Commission at its fifty-first session; and encouraged States to accede to the Convention on the Status of Refugees.

The High Commissioner published Guidelines in 1993 governing the competence of the Office in respect of internally displaced persons. The latter emphasized the need for a specific request emanating from a competent UN authority, the availability of resources and the consent of the concerned State and (where applicable) other relevant entities. At the meeting of the Executive Committee in October 1993, 'most delegations expressed support for the guideline criteria developed by the Office'.[22] At the same meeting, the High Commissioner effectively ruled out any notion that the UNHCR could assist

---

18   UNGA Resolution 47/105.
19   UNGA Resolution 48/135, 20 December 1993.
20   UNGA Resolution 1994/68, 9 March 1994.
21   UNGA Resolution 1994/66, 9 March 1994.
22   UN Doc. A/AC.96/819, 5 October 1993, p. 6.

an internally displaced population without also seeking to protect and find a durable solution for them.[23]

From these sources it appears possible to identify three requirements that must be satisfied in order that the Office of the United Nations High Commissioner may provide assistance or protection to the internally displaced. First, there must be a specific request for involvement from the Secretary General or a competent United Nations organ. Second, the need to undertake additional activities should be a natural extension of the mandate of the Office: the case for the involvement of the UNHCR will be particularly strong where the functions to be discharged by the Office acting within its normal mandate are inextricable from those to be performed in the protection of internally displaced persons (as for instance where fugitives from the same event or course of conduct include many who succeed in crossing an international border and many who do not; or where the internal displacement of a population threatens to be transformed into an external displacement). Third, the concerned State should in principle consent to the UNHCR's involvement. (The High Commissioner's Guidelines countenance no exception to this principle, but it is submitted below that very exceptional circumstances may arise in which its consent is not required.) To these requirements of a legal character some practical conditions may be added: the Office of the UNHCR must have the necessary resources placed at its disposal, and it must be able to intervene directly with the governments concerned, so as to guard against erosion of the humanitarian and non-political nature of its task.

II. THE REPRESENTATIVE OF THE SECRETARY GENERAL

It was the situation in former Yugoslavia which caused the United Nations to examine and seek to define the functions to be exercised in relation to internally-displaced persons by the Organization in general and the High Commissioner in particular.[24] On 5 March 1992, the General Assembly requested the compilation of a study setting out the elements of debate on the position of internally displaced persons.[25] In July 1992, the Secretary General appointed a Representative on Internally Displaced Persons, Mr Francis Deng. A 'Comprehensive Study' on the issues raised by the General Assembly Resolution of 5 March was submitted by the Representative to the Commission on Human Rights at its forty-ninth session.[26] The Commission

---

[23]   *UNHCR's Role in Protecting and Assisting Internally Displaced People*, Nov. 1993, p. 11.

[24]   For a critical analysis of the functions exercised by the Organisation in that territory, see Higgins, R., 'The New United Nations and Former Yugoslavia', Martin Wright memorial lecture, 69 *International Affairs* (1993), pp. 465–483.

[25]   UNGA Resolution 1992/73, 5 March 1992.

[26]   *Comprehensive Study prepared by Mr Francis M. Deng, Representative of the Secretary-General on the Human Rights Issues related to Internally Displaced Persons*: UN Doc. E/CN.4/1993/35.

then requested the Secretary General to extend the mandate of his representative for two years.[27] In the same resolution the Commission requested the Representative to cooperate with the United Nations High Commissioner for Refugees and to coordinate his functions with those of the UNHCR. On 28 July 1993 the Economic and Social Council approved the request made by the Commission on Human Rights.[28] Following submission of a further report by the Representative[29] the General Assembly adopted without vote a resolution[30] encouraging the Representative to continue his review of internally displaced persons, including a compilation and analysis of the existing rules and his suggestions or recommendations with regard to institutional issues.

In a further report dated January 1994,[31] the Representative drew attention to the magnitude and scope of the problem. The global population of internally displaced persons was in the range of 25 million people, compared with a refugee population of around 18 million world wide. The most common and formidable causes of internal displacement were civil conflicts, communal violence, forced relocation and other gross violations of human rights. The international community was required to perform urgent humanitarian functions which national authorities were not in a position to discharge. The problems of internal displacement could only be solved by addressing its root causes, in particular, by the prevention of war. The Representative stated:

> Another task to be accomplished under the mandate is an assessment of the present situation with respect to existing international law to determine the degree to which it provides an adequate basis for the protection of the internally displaced.[32]

He reviewed certain provisions of international humanitarian law and concluded:

> Without prejudicing the issue of whether or not new normative standards are needed, it is generally recognized that even though the existing law appears to be adequate for the needs of internal displacement, a consolidation and evaluation of existing norms would be of value and would provide the basis for filling whatever gaps may exist. Building on the knowledge acquired from the practical experience on the ground, as well as the expertise of scholars with expertise in this area of the law, the proposed project would aim at the development of ideas for normative standards based on principles of existing international instruments. The goal would be to develop a doctrine of protection specifically tailored to the needs of the internally displaced. This requires first a compilation/

[27]   Resolution 1993/105, 11 March 1993.
[28]   Decision 1993/285, 28 July 1993.
[29]   A/48/579, September 1993.
[30]   A/48/135, 20 December 1993.
[31]   UN Doc. E/CN.4/1994/44.
[32]   Para. 19.

commentary of the existing norms and a further elaboration of the relevant standards (in the form, for instance, of a code of conduct) and eventually a declaration or other authoritative document.[33]

On the question of 'new normative standards', there is the proposal made by the Refugee Policy Group[34] for a declaration or convention to embody the right to access to humanitarian assistance, including the right to food. By such an instrument States might undertake in advance to permit the access of competent international organizations to their territories for the purpose of administering humanitarian assistance. The Under-Secretary General for Humanitarian Affairs, UNESCO, and the governments of Burkina Faso, Cyprus, Guatemala and Norway and the Russian Federation are also reported to have favoured the creation of a supplementary legal instrument on the rights of displaced persons. However, at the Diplomatic Conference preceding the Additional Protocols to Geneva Conventions

> States strongly opposed any reference to offers of relief, even emanating from neutral third parties, which might constitute an interference in their internal affairs. Only meagre provisions for relief are included in Article 18(2) [of Additional Protocol II].[35]

It is for consideration, therefore, whether the proposal advanced by the Refugee Policy Group might not be realized more easily by a simple amendment of Article 1(*b*) of the Draft Convention on Expediting the Delivery of Emergency Assistance,[36] which excludes from the definition of a 'Disaster' 'an ongoing situation of armed conflict'.

The Special Representative's proposal for 'a consolidation and evaluation of existing norms' is said to have general agreement. It would not be difficult to extract from the Charter of the United Nations,[37] the Universal Declaration of Human Rights,[38] the four Geneva Conventions,[39] the International Convention on the Elimination of All Forms of Racial Discrimination,[40] the International Covenant on Civil and Political Rights,[41]

---

[33]   Para. 28.

[34]   *Strengthening International Protection for Internally Displaced Persons*, December 1993.

[35]   Macalister-Smith, P., *International Humanitarian Assistance: Disaster Relief Actions in International Law and Organization*, Dordrecht 1985, p. 31.

[36]   UN Doc. A/39/267/Add 2 – E/1984/96/Add 2, 18 June 1984.

[37]   San Francisco, 26 June 1945, 1 *UNTS* xvi.

[38]   UNGA Resolution 217A(III), 10 December 1948.

[39]   Convention relative to the Protection of Civilian Persons in Time of War, 12 August 1949: 75 *UNTS* 135; Convention relative to the Treatment of Prisoners of War, 12 August 1949: 75 *UNTS* 135; Convention for the Amelioration of the Condition of the Wounded and Sick in Armed forced in the Field, 12 August 1945: 75 *UNTS* 31; Convention for the Amelioration of the Condition of the Wounded, Sick and Shipwrecked Members of Armed Forces at Sea: 75 *UNTS* 85.

[40]   New York, 7 March 1966: 60 *UNTS* 195.

[41]   New York, 16 December 1966, annex to UNGA Resolution 2200(XXI).

the International Covenant on Economic, Social and Cultural Rights[42] and from other texts, including regional instruments and the Declaration on Principles of International Law concerning Friendly Relations and Cooperation among States,[43] a body of principles which would much reduce the number of internally displaced persons if scrupulously observed by the States which have undertaken to be guided or bound by them. Indeed, a significant contribution to the resolution of the problem would be made if there were observance of Article 3 of the four Geneva Conventions, which prohibits violence to life and outrages upon the personal dignity of persons in the case of armed conflicts not of an international character; and Article 17 of Additional Protocol II to the Geneva Conventions[44] which imposes constraints on the movement of civilian populations in time of armed conflict.[45] The Declaration and Programme of Action for Human Rights[46] has already called for measures to strengthen existing instruments, including the creation of an international criminal court, and uttered condemnations of certain specific acts, including 'ethnic cleansing' which provoke the internal displacement of persons.

It will not be suggested that States and commanders of insurgent forces which are currently disinclined to observe existing norms, or to disregard the mechanisms proposed at Vienna, would be persuaded to act otherwise if there were a single, comprehensive, universally-applicable body of principles endorsed by the General Assembly. Nevertheless, the consolidation of existing principles into an accessible text may serve a useful political purpose in the formation of an international consensus, where those principles are manifestly violated.[47] It may also play a part in the definition of the functions of the international agency or agencies to be charged with responsibilities in this area.[48]

---

[42] New York, 16 December 1966, annex to UNGA res. 2200(XXX).

[43] 24 October 1970, annex to UNGA Resolution 2625(XXV).

[44] Geneva, 8 June 1977, 1977 *UNJYB* 95.

[45] The latter was ratified by Yugoslavia on 11 June 1979.

[46] World Conference on Human Rights, Vienna, 14–25 June 1993.

[47] 'The study finds that in so far as the principles of the law are concerned, there indeed appears to be fairly adequate protection under human rights and humanitarian law. There are, however, obvious gaps in the existing law with respect to the specific needs of internally displaced persons. Just as attention and protection are required for certain vulnerable groups such as minorities, women, children, the disabled or refugees, a specific regime for protecting the internally displaced would serve as a useful focus on their special needs': Deng, *op. cit.* (note 26), p. 68.

[48] The personnel of non-governmental organizations engaged in humanitarian relief may require convenient access to the established norms. For the benefit of the latter, a distillation of some of the fundamental principles has been undertaken by the Norwegian Refugee Council: Borgen, *The Protection of Internally Displaced Persons by NRC: Platform, Concepts and Strategies,* 1994.

III. The Consent of the Host State

Perhaps the chief difficulty of a legal character presented by the provision of humanitarian assistance to displaced persons is the question whether the consent of the host State is a *sine qua non*. Both as a matter of law and as a matter of practice, its consent is normally required.

The General Assembly Resolution of December 1991 on the Strengthening of the Coordination of Humanitarian Emergency Assistance[49] set out a basis for improving the humanitarian work of the Organization but it reaffirmed, in Article 3 of the Annex, the principle that assistance should be supplied only in response to an appeal from the affected State and with respect for its territorial integrity.

Recent international practice does not, however, support the proposition that humanitarian assistance can never be supplied without the consent of the host State. The general rule requiring the consent of the host State was not construed as an impediment to the provision of aid in Somalia, in the absence of a request from the Government. (It must be accepted however that the episode does not constitute clear evidence of a right to supply humanitarian assistance, since the United Nations' intervention was premised upon Article 2(7) of the Charter; and at the material time no Somali government was firmly established.) It was on the basis of a Memorandum of Understanding with the government of Iraq, dated 18 April 1991, that humanitarian operations were undertaken in the north of Iraq. That Memorandum was renewed on 22 October 1992 but there was an interval between the expiry of the first Memorandum and the conclusion of the second when humanitarian assistance continued to be provided without any formal consent on the Iraqi side. Further, Croatia did not consent to the continued stationing of UNPROFOR in Croatia in 1992: this was done by Security Council Resolution 743.

No principle of international law, and particularly nothing in Article 2(7) of the Charter, excludes action short of dictatorial interference undertaken with a view to the implementation of the purposes of the Charter. This, indeed, is the part of the significance of the word 'essentially' as it appears in Article 2(7). According to Sir Robert Jennings and Sir Arthur Watts:

> With regard to the protection of human rights and freedoms – a prominent feature of the Charter – the prohibition of intervention does not preclude study, discussion, investigation and recommendation on the part of the various organs of the United Nations.[50]

The reference is to Article 55(*c*) of the Charter, which imposes on the Organization in mandatory language the duty to promote universal respect for and observance of human rights. Thus, in rare and exceptional cases, the

---

[49]   UNGA Resolution 46/182, 19 December 1991.

[50]   Jennings, R. Y. / Watts, A., (eds.), *Oppenheim's International Law*, Vol. I, 9th ed., London 1992, p. 449.

prohibition of intervention must be taken not to preclude humanitarian action taken in pursuance of such investigations or recommendations. In the words used by Thomas Weiss, in an article this year in the *Washington Quarterly*[51]

A careful reading of even the quintessential government document, the UN Charter, suggests that territorial sovereignty is not as absolute and uncontested as is often implied by governments. Many cling doggedly to the seventh paragraph of the second article that supposedly shelters from international scrutiny 'matters which are essentially within the domestic jurisdiction of any State'. Long before the recent series of Security Council resolutions that overrode domestic jurisdiction by invoking Charter VII intervention, however, governments had agreed to respect individual human rights 'without distinction as to race, sex, language or religion'.

Other authors have identified the 'internationalization' of issues of human rights[52]; and some[53] go so far as to identify a 'new, constitutive human rights-based conception of popular sovereignty' which has made an anachronism of the view of sovereignty expressed in the *Tinoco* case.[54] It is not necessary to go so far in order to deny the right of the territorial State to prevent the international community from providing the essentials of life to nationals of that State forcibly displaced within its territory. Nor is it necessary to rely upon the controversial and contested 'right to humanitarian intervention'.[55] Whatever objections there may be to humanitarian intervention, these do not apply to humanitarian assistance to those in need in another State. In the words of Jennings and Watts:

even in a situation of conflict within a State, humanitarian assistance will not constitute intervention, so long as it is given (or perhaps is at least available) without discrimination between the parties to the conflict.[56]

The matter may equally be seen in another perspective, with similar results. The right of States to respect for territorial sovereignty must be observed; but in common with other rights of States in international law, this must be understood subject to the doctrine of *abus de droit*. The conferment and deprivation of nationality is a right which international law recognizes as being within the exclusive competence of States; but the abuse of it may give rise

[51] 'Intervention: Whither the United Nations?', 17(1) *Washington Quarterly* (1994), p. 106.

[52] Forsythe, D., *The Internationalization of Human Rights*, 1991; Donnelly, *Universal Human Rights in Theory and Practice*, 1989.

[53] E.g., see Reisman, M., 'Sovereignty and Human Rights in Contemporary International Law, 84 *AJIL* (1990), p. 866 at 870.

[54] UK-Costa Rica, 1 *UNRIAA* (1923) 369; 82 *AJIL* (1988), p. 459.

[55] See Brownlie, I., *International Law and Intervention*, 1988, pp. 338–342; Rodley, N., 'Human Rights and Humanitarian Intervention: The Case-Law of the World Court', 38 *ICLQ* (1989), p. 321.

[56] *Oppenheim's* (note 50), p. 444.

to an international claim.[57] By parity of reasoning, an arbitrary refusal to permit the administration of humanitarian relief to internally displaced persons, in violation of human rights, may constitute an *abus de droit* which cannot prevent the United Nations Organization from discharging the tasks conferred upon it by the Charter.

IV. THE DEFINITION OF INTERNALLY DISPLACED PERSONS

A publication prepared for the UNHCR in 1993[58] poses the question: "Could a legal definition of 'internally displaced person' be established in the same way that the 1951 Convention defines the refugee concept?"

More than one definition has been offered already. Referring to Economic and Social Council Resolution 78/1990, the Secretary General uses the term 'internally displaced person' to mean

> persons who have been forced to flee their homes suddenly or unexpectedly in large numbers, as a result of armed conflict, internal strife, systematic violations of human rights or natural or man-made disasters; and who are within the territory of their own country.

In referring to those fleeing 'in large numbers', that formula appears to anticipate that it is to be used for the purpose of defining a category of persons to whom an appropriate agency could supply the essentials of life in an emergency; and that such an agency could be called upon by the appropriate officer or organ of the United Nations to yield assistance as occasions arise. The formula would be less useful as a criterion for determining the eligibility of individuals for forms of protection such as travel documents.

The Cartagena Declaration on Refugees of 1984 states:

> displaced persons are those who have been forced to leave their homes – because their lives, security or freedom is endangered by general violence, massive human rights violations, on-going conflicts or other circumstances which seriously disrupt the public order but who have remained within their own country.

By contrast with the Secretary General's definition, the Cartagena Declaration does not confine itself to those fleeing *en masse*; but it does not extend to fugitives from man-made disasters other than those disrupting public order (for instance, ecological catastrophes).

The Friends World Committee for Consultation proposed the following version: "Persons who have been forced to flee their homes and have not

---

[57] See the Dissenting Opinion of Judge Reid in the *Nottebohm* Case, ICJ Rep. 1955, pp. 37–38 and *ibidem*, p. 408.

[58] *UNHCR's Role in Protecting and Assisting Internally Displaced People. Central Evaluation Section Discussion Paper:* EVAL/IDP/13/2 at 12.

crossed an international frontier." This is plainly unworkable: the language is so broad that it would even embrace fugitives from individualized threats such as domestic violence.

The Office of the High Commissioner has defined the categories of persons eligible for *temporary protection* as follows:

(i)   Persons who have fled from areas affected by conflict and violence;
(ii)   Persons who have been or would be exposed to human rights abuses, including persons belonging to groups compelled to leave their homes by campaigns of ethnic or religious persecution;
(iii) Persons who, for other reasons specific to their personal situation are presumed to be in need of protection.

The first two categories are defined with a workable degree of precision: the exclusion of those fleeing from natural and ecological catastrophes must be considered to be deliberate, as must the omission of any requirement of mass flight. The third category is intended to cover those whose need for protection was based on objective criteria other than place of origin; such as those seeking to avoid engaging in unacceptable military activities.[59]

The definition offered by the UNHCR draws attention, incidentally, to the fact that an internally displaced person is often distinguished from a refugee within the meaning of the Geneva Convention and New York Protocol *only* by the fact that the former remains within his State of nationality. Thus it has been held that a person who flees his country of nationality in order to avoid engaging in unacceptable military activities qualifies as a refugee: his conduct is an expression of 'political opinion', that is, adherence to principles established by General Assembly resolutions.[60] It is in view of this fact that the Secretary-General's Special Representative concluded:

> There is much to support the contention that the working definition of internally displaced persons should focus on those who, if they had left their own country, would be considered refugees.[61]

In the same Report the Special Representative concluded that the task of drafting an appropriate definition should be coordinated with the work of the Sub-Commission on the Prevention of Discrimination and the Protection of Minorities which[62] has appointed two Special Rapporteurs to prepare a preliminary study on the question.

The definition of internally displaced persons must depend on the purpose for which that definition is to be used, and in particular on the specific functions of any international agency to be charged with their systematic protection. It is thought, however, that those functions must extend not only to the

[59]   *UNHCR Background Note: Informal Meeting of Government Experts, Geneva 23 March 1994*, p. 2.
[60]   *Church v Home Secretary*, 16 March 1982, TH/69153/80 (2288).
[61]   Deng, *op. cit.* (note 26), p. 14.
[62]   By Resolution 1992/28.

distribution of the necessities of life (including shelter, housing, foods and medicine) but also more specific protection tasks, such as the issuance of travel documents to internally displaced persons who may be temporarily settled in foreign countries and the undertaking of efforts to secure family reunification. For these purposes it may prove useful to build upon the definition contained in Article 1A(2) of the Geneva Convention, the terms of which are well known and have acquired a degree of precision by their widespread application and frequent interpretation. Such a definition could read as follows:

> any person who, owing to well-founded fear of persecution or of death, bodily injury, deprivation of the freedom of the person or of basic necessities of life, attributable to military or paramilitary conflict or other circumstances which seriously disrupt the public order, has been forced to leave his or her home but is not unable to remain within, or to return to, the country of his or her nationality.

V. Institutional Arrangements

The *Note on International Protection* for 1992[63] draws attention to the complementary functions of protecting refugees and protecting internally displaced persons:

> From an examination of the common needs of the various groups for which UNHCR is competent, it is clear that, with protection at the core of UNHCR's mandate, displacement, coupled with the need for protection, is the basis of the UNHCR's competence for these groups. The character of the displacement, together with the protection need, must also determine the content of UNHCR's involvement.
>
> The Working Group considered that the same reasoning held true for persons displaced within their own country for refugee-like reasons. While the Office does not have any general competence for this group of persons, certain responsibilities have to be assumed on their behalf, depending on their protection and assistance needs. In this context, UNHCR should indicate its willingness to extend its humanitarian expertise to internally displaced persons, on a case-by-case basis, in response to requests from the Secretary General or General Assembly.

It is of course necessary that any functions undertaken by UNHCR should be discharged in cooperation with other agencies, so as to avoid duplication or confusion of responsibilities. In particular the Secretary General has stated in a communication to the Under Secretary-General for Humanitarian Affairs that:

---

[63]   UN Doc. A/AC.96/799.

The process has so far been practice-oriented but there is no doubt that the legal dimension is of great significance. The Commission on Human Rights should be encouraged to play a greater role in promoting and protecting the human rights of the displaced.[64]

The Special Representative of the Secretary General has canvassed the prospect of establishing a new United Nations agency devoted to the protection of the internally displaced.[65] The case for a separate agency has yet to be made out. There is no shortage of humanitarian agencies within the United Nations family devoted to assistance for displaced persons generally. These include, in addition to the Office of the High Commissioner for Refugees, the International Organization for Migration, the Department of Humanitarian Affairs and the United Nations Development Programme. Although none of them has at present a permanent mandate to act for the internally displaced, it is necessary to ask whether the creation of a separate agency for the purpose might not lead to duplication. Account must certainly be taken of a converse danger; that is, the risk that the authority of the Office of the High Commissioner for Refugees in seeking asylum for refugees within the meaning of the 1951 Convention might, in particular cases, be prejudiced if it were given the role of protecting fugitives within their countries of origin. The possibility cannot be discounted that Contracting States could be reluctant to grant asylum to those to whom the High Commissioner could give a degree of protection in the country of their nationality. This danger should not be overstated. The considerable experience of the Office of the High Commissioner in using good offices for the protection of displaced persons in their countries of origin, over several decades, has tended to augment rather than to reduce the moral or persuasive authority that it enjoys when it requests Contracting States to grant asylum; and of course the grant of asylum to a prospective refugee, remaining within his country of nationality, is not an obligation undertaken by Contracting States on acceding to the Geneva Convention.

The Office of the High Commissioner does not have an established jurisdiction to take action for the relief of internally displaced persons, other than by means of good offices in response to specific requests. It is known that there are many within the Office who entertain the gravest reservations about the enlargement of the functions of the Office that such a jurisdiction would entail, not least in view of the strain that it would place upon resources of the Office, which remain slender in relation to the existing functions. There are, however, no insuperable legal objections to the enlargement of the jurisdiction. Whether there is the will is a separate matter.

[64]   Quoted in *Comprehensive Study prepared by Mr Francis M. Deng, Representative of the Secretary-General on the Human Rights Issues related to Internally Displaced Persons*: UN Doc. E/CN.4/1993/35 at p. 28.
[65]   *Protecting the Dispossessed: A Challenge for the International Community*, The Brookings Institute, 1994.

VED P. NANDA

Comments On:
The Legal Basis of International Jurisdiction to Act
with Regard to the Internally Displaced

I. INTRODUCTION

The growing number of internally displaced persons signals the enormity of the challenge to the international community. In 1991, a study by the Refugee Policy Group estimated the number of people uprooted within their home countries by civil wars and ethnic tension to be 20 million,[1] while other estimates in the same year were also between 15 and 25 million.[2] Since then, the worsening situation in the former Yugoslavia, the tragedy in Rwanda, and the continuing conflicts in Liberia and Angola, among other places, have exacerbated the problem. More recently, in January 1994, the UN Secretary-General's Special Representative on Internally Displaced Persons, Francis Deng, placed the number "in the range of 25 million", caused primarily by "internal conflicts, ethnic and communal violence, forced relocation, and other gross violations of human rights".[3] Thus the question of providing both humanitarian assistance and protection to such large numbers scattered across the globe is of immense importance; consequently, the decision of the Graduate Institute of International Studies to study, in collaboration with the United Nations High Commissioner for Refugees (UNHCR), the topic, "The Legal Bases of International Jurisdiction to Act With Regard to the Internally Displaced", is commendable.

[1] See Cohen, R., *Human Rights Protection for Internally Displaced Persons*, Refugee Policy Group (June 1991), p. 1.
[2] D'Adersky, A-C., "UNHCR Facing the Refugee Challenge", 28 *UN Chronicle* (Sept. 1991), pp. 40, 42.
[3] CHR, *Internally Displaced Persons – Report of the Representative of the Secretary-General, Mr. Francis Deng, submitted pursuant to Commission on Human Rights resolution 1993/95,* UN Doc. E/CN.4/1994/44 (1994).

V. Gowlland-Debbas (ed.), The Problem of Refugees in the Light of Contemporary International Law Issues, 135–144.
© 1996 *Kluwer Academic Publishers. Printed in the Netherlands.*

II. Definition of Internally Displaced Persons

Of the various definitions offered for internally displaced persons,[4] there is much to recommend in the one proposed by the Special Representative, who supports "the contention that the working definition of internally displaced persons should focus on those who, if they had left their own country, would be considered refugees".[5] An equally acceptable alternative would be to use as the starting point the definition presently being used by the Secretary-General, with one major change. In the Secretary-General's words, the term means "persons who have been forced to flee their homes suddenly or unexpectedly in large numbers, as a result of armed conflict, internal strife, systematic violations of human rights or natural or man-made disasters and who are within the territory of their own country".[6] Under the change proposed here, the definition will not be limited to persons who flee "in large numbers", but will extend to any person who has been forced to flee his/her home "as a result of armed conflict, internal strife, systematic violations of human rights or natural or man-made disasters", and who is within the territory of his/her own country.

III. Legal Status of Internally Displaced Persons and Assistance and Protection to Them

A. *Historical Context*

Since the UNHCR mandate was limited to assisting and protecting refugees as defined under the 1951 Convention, viz., those who are outside the country of their nationality and who have a well-founded fear of persecution for reasons of race, religion, nationality or political opinion,[7] no international legal regime exists to assist and protect those who become displaced within the borders of their own States. The policy reason was that persons inside their own countries purportedly enjoyed the protection of their governments and consequently did not require other protection.

It is, however, worth recalling that following World War II, the proposers of the draft constitution of the International Refugee Organization recognized the prospect of persons losing the *de facto* protection of their government

---

[4]   For the various definitions, see Plender, *supra.*

[5]   *Comprehensive study prepared by Mr. Francis M. Deng, Representative of the Secretary-General on the human rights issues related to internally displaced persons, pursuant to Commission on Human Rights resolution 1992/73,* UN Doc. E/CN.4/1993/35 (1993), para. 50, at 14.

[6]   See ESC Resolution 78/1990, to which the Secretary-General refers for his usage.

[7]   See Article 1(a) (2) of the Convention Relating to the Status of Refugees, 28 July 1951, 189 *UNTS* 137; and the Protocol Relating to the Status of Refugees, 31 January 1967, 606 *UNTS* 167.

without having left the country's territory. The director of the Inter-Governmental Committee on Refugees, Sir Herbert Emerson, said that he "wanted to correct the impression that the term 'refugee' had invariably been used to describe a person who had left his country".[8] He added: "The term 'refugee' was generally used with reference to a person, whether inside or outside his own country, who did not enjoy the protection of the Government of his country".[9] To illustrate: the victims of Nazi Germany detained in concentration camps in Germany and Austria were just as persecuted as those who were able to leave the country and consequently attain refugee status.[10] However, there was no mechanism instituted to protect persons who remained within their country.

Notwithstanding the lack of a formal mandate to protect internally displaced persons, UNHCR has, however, long recognized the need to extend refugee protection to groups of persons based on their need rather than on a strict reading of the 1951 Convention definition. To illustrate: in 1957 and again in 1959 the General Assembly authorized the High Commissioner to use his good offices to allow UNHCR to provide protection and assistance to the refugees who did not meet the 1951 Convention definition.[11] Subsequently, in 1965, the General Assembly authorized the UNHCR to provide protection to non-Convention refugees on the same terms as Convention refugees,[12] and in 1975 it termed the situations of Convention and non-Convention refugees "analogous" because both were victims of man-made events over which they had no control.[13] Then, in 1985, the General Assembly urged all States to "support the High Commissioner in his efforts to achieve durable solutions to the problem of refugees and displaced persons of concern to his office".[14]

Based upon other similar statements of the General Assembly and the UNHCR activities pertaining to displaced persons, it appears that the terms "refugees" and "displaced persons" have been used synonymously[15] for the

---

[8]   ESC, *Summary Record of the Second Meeting of the Committee of the Whole on Refugees and Displaced Persons*, UN Doc. E/74, (17 June 1946), at 9. See also GA Res. 1388 (XIV) of 20 November 1959.

[9]   *Summary Record, op. cit.* (note 8), at 10.

[10]   See, e.g., ESC, *Report of the Special Committee on Refugees and Displaced Persons*, Special Supp., UN Doc. E/REF/75 of 1 June 1946, at 18–19. "(T)he majority of delegations considered that Jews detained in concentration camps should be [considered refugees]", *id., at* 19.

[11]   See GA Res. 1167, *UN GAOR*, 12th Sess., Supp. (No. 18) at 20, UN Doc. A/3805 (1957) (relating to Chinese refugees in Hong Kong); GA Res. 1388 (XIV), UN Doc. A/RES/1388, 20 November 1954.

[12]   See GA Res.2019, *UN GAOR*, 20th Sess., Supp. (No. 14) at 41, UN Doc. A/6014 (1965).

[13]   See GA Res.3454, *UN GAOR*, 30th Sess., Supp. (No. 34) at 92, UN Doc. A/10034 (1975).

[14]   GA Res. 40/112, *UN GAOR*, 40th Sess., Supp. (No. 53) at 471, UN Doc. A/40/53 (1985).

[15]   See Goodwin-Gill, G.S., "Non-Refoulement and the New Asylum Seekers", 26 *Virg. JIL* (1986), pp. 899–900. But see Hailbronner, K., "Non-Refoulement and 'Humanitarian' Refugees: Customary International Law or Wishful Legal Thinking?", 26 *Virg. JIL* (1986), pp. 897, 869–870.

purpose of providing assistance and protection to internally displaced persons. Thus, while the international community has in reality expanded UNHCR's mandate to encompass internally displaced persons, for practical reasons it has not formally expanded the definition of the Convention refugee to include them.

B. *The 1990s and beyond*

The 1990s have witnessed a spate of ethnic conflicts and collapsed States, where, because of the breakdown of the central authority, such as in Liberia and Somalia, or because of the intensity of internal conflict, as in the former Yugoslavia, the government purportedly providing protection to its nationals is unwilling or unable to do so, has disappeared or exists only in name. For example, as early as in 1990, the plight of the displaced within their home-lands because of civil war, ethnic persecution, or forced resettlement by their own governments was causing a great deal of international concern: more than 500,000 Liberians were uprooted and displaced because of the tragic internal conflict there,[16] and nearly 600,000 people were displaced within the boundaries of Yugoslavia because of the "fratricidal" civil war in that country.[17] Other recent examples include displaced persons in Angola, Mozambique, the Sudan, the former Soviet Union, Iraq, South Africa, Ethiopia, Myanmar, Cambodia, and Guatemala.[18]

Thus, the Economic and Social Council requested the Secretary-General to conduct a review "to assess the experience and capacity of various orga-nizations, in the coordination of assistance to all refugees, displaced persons and returnees, and the full spectrum of their needs".[19] And in June 1991, the High Commissioner, Mrs. Sadako Ogata, described humanitarian assistance to, and the use of the High Commissioner's good offices on behalf of, internally displaced persons:

> Very often, repatriating refugees return to areas with a significant inter-nally displaced refugee population. . . . [But they] are often unable to return to their *places* of origin and, in effect, may become displaced persons once back in their own countries.
>
> The Secretary General or the General Assembly has requested UNHCR's good offices on some occasions on behalf of [the] internally displaced (Cyprus, Vietnam and Laos). UNHCR has been asked to provide humani-tarian assistance to persons in Bangladesh, Lebanon, the Horn of Africa, Nicaragua and Uganda. Such requests for participation in UN humani-tarian efforts are based on UNHCR's specific expertise and experience

[16]   See U.S. Committee for Refugees, *Uprooted Liberians: Casualties of a Brutal War*, 1 (Issue Paper, Feb. 1991).

[17]   See U.S. Committee for Refugees, *Yugoslavia Torn Asunder: Lessons for Protecting Refugees from Civil War*, 1 (Issue Paper, Feb. 1991).

[18]   See Cohen, *op. cit.* (note 1), at 3–5.

[19]   ESC Res. 1990/78 of 27 July 1990.

with uprooted persons. [General Assembly Resolution 2956 (XXVII 1972); also Resolution 3455 (XXX, 1975) on Indochina; Resolution 42/110 (1987).] In some cases, where the emergency has been prolonged, UNHCR's initial emergency assistance has evolved into a search for more durable solutions to the problems of these uprooted persons.

Finally, UNHCR has contributed to broadly based UN humanitarian efforts to deal with the effects of war and civil strife in Southern Africa and Central America. . . . The groundwork has already been laid, and in the near future when political conditions permit, we hope to be involved in similar efforts elsewhere.[20]

As to providing protection for internally displaced persons, she added:

Protection, in one form or another[,] follows naturally from UNHCR assistance. If, for example[,] persons being assisted by UNHCR under its good offices experience difficulties, legal or otherwise, UNHCR must bring these problems to the attention of competent authorities or they will hamper the effective implementation of our humanitarian work. . . .

First and foremost, at no point must work with internally displaced [persons] threaten the institution of asylum, or interfere with our ability to protect and assist the refugees who are our fundamental responsibility. Establishing mechanisms that permit the international community to attend to the humanitarian needs of internally displaced [persons] is definitely a positive step. However, should the availability of such arrangements be used politically to justify the denial of asylum to persons in need, this would be tragic.

Second, it would be most unfortunate as well if internally displaced persons and refugees were seen to be in competition for funding. If the international community undertakes to provide institutional mandates for internally displaced persons, it must also provide funding for the operations that would be undertaken. Above all, it must be prepared to provide [the pertinent] institution with the capacity to respond.[21]

A 1991 UNHCR report[22] described five situations in which the Office could be concerned with internally displaced persons:[23] 1) returnee programs for the re-establishment of repatriating refugees;[24] 2) special operations pursuant to the General Assembly or the Secretary-General's request;[25] 3) arrange-

---

[20] Refugee Policy Group, *High Commissioner's Statement to the Refugee Policy Group*, in *Human Rights Protection for Internally Displaced Persons: An International Conference*, 24–25 June 1991, at Appendix 2–3 (1991), (emphasis in original) (citation omitted).

[21] *Ibidem*, at 4–6.

[22] See Jackson, I./Young, G., *The Role of UNHCR on Behalf of Internally Displaced Persons*, (Unpublished Report to UNHCR, 27 November 1991).

[23] *Ibidem*, pp. 2–4.

[24] See *ibidem*, Annex, pp. 1–5, for specific examples.

[25] See *ibidem*, pp. 5–7 for specific examples.

ments to provide humanitarian assistance in a particular region;[26] 4) situations exemplified by Kurdish refugees in Iraq; and 5) preventive efforts aimed at addressing the causes of refugee movements. The report concluded that, as a first step, there should be "a clearer definition of the Office's monitoring role regarding the causes of refugee flows with a view to their prevention".[27] The report, however, cautioned:

> Whether or not it would be appropriate for the Office to seek a *general competence* to protect and assist internally displaced persons is, of course, a complex issue. The High Commissioner's *general* and *automatic* competence to protect and assist refugees has been specifically recognized by the international community. Whether the international community would be prepared to underwrite a similar general and automatic competence for internally displaced persons would depend *inter alia* upon the political and financial issues involved. As against possible humanitarian considerations, it could well be claimed that internally displaced persons are the primary responsibility of their national governments and that intervention by the international community can only be justified on a case by case basis. From the standpoint of UNHCR, a general competence to deal with internally displaced persons might require the Office to become involved in action inconsistent with its purely humanitarian role. Moreover, a direct and clearly defined concern of UNHCR for internally displaced persons could have an adverse effect on the institution of asylum itself. It could, for example, involve the danger of governments considering that since UNHCR is required to deal with the problem of displacement in the country of origin, they have a lesser responsibility to grant asylum to those who leave that country as refugees. These various aspects of the problem would of course need to be further explored.[28]

Among other organizations, the International Committee of the Red Cross (ICRC) claims a right of initiative to render aid to displaced persons. This claimed right is derived from the provisions of common Article 3 of the Geneva Conventions.[29] This article also sets minimum standards for protection of civilians in non-international armed conflicts and is supplemented by the 1977 Protocol II "relating to the protection of victims of non-international armed conflicts".[30] Also, the United Nations International Children's

---

[26]   For example, the International Conference on the Plight of Refugees, Returnees, and Displaced Persons in Southern Africa (SARRED, 1988); International Conference on Central American Refugees (CIREFCA, 1989). See *ibidem*, p. 8 for details.

[27]   International Conference on Central American Refugees, *ibidem*, p. 5.

[28]   *Idem.*

[29]   See Art. 3, *TIAS* (1955), pp. 3362–3365.

[30]   For the text, see 16 *ILM* (1977), p. 1442. See also Meron, T., "Draft Model Declaration on Internal Strife", *Int'l. Rev. of the Red Cross*, Jan./Feb. 1988 (proposing non-derogable rights for those caught in civil strife).

Emergency Fund (UNICEF) has come to play a unique role in helping displaced persons during civil wars.[31]

Since 1991, the Security Council, the General Assembly, the UN Commission on Human Rights and UNHCR have been actively engaged in addressing the problem. To illustrate: the Security Council adopted Resolution 688 on 5 April 1991, which insisted that "Iraq allow immediate access" to international humanitarian organizations to assist the Kurds in northern Iraq, and that Iraq make available all necessary facilities for their operations.[32] Iraq, having initially objected to the Security Council action as a violation of its sovereignty, subsequently concluded a Memorandum of Understanding authorizing humanitarian assistance by UN personnel within Iraq.[33] Similarly, the Security Council adopted resolutions providing for humanitarian assistance to civilian populations uprooted by internal conflicts in Somalia[34] and the former Yugoslavia.[35]

The General Assembly adopted a resolution in 1992 commending the High Commissioner's efforts "on the basis of specific requests from the Secretary-General or the competent principal organs of the United Nations and with the consent of the concerned State, to undertake activities in favour of internally displaced persons . . .".[36] In December 1993 the General Assembly adopted another resolution on the subject, this time welcoming the decision of the Executive Committee of the Office of the UNHCR to extend protection and assistance to internally displaced persons.[37]

Earlier, in July 1992, to meet the General Assembly's request to compile a study on internally displaced persons,[38] the UN Secretary-General appointed Mr. Francis Deng as his representative on internally displaced persons. Mr. Deng submitted a "Comprehensive Study" on the subject to the Commission on Human Rights at its 49th session[39] and a subsequent one in January 1994[40] in which he identified the nature and scope of the challenge and outlined the need for an effective international protection system for internally displaced persons. He concluded that, "although the need for effective action is indisputable, the normative principles and the enforcement mechanisms for international action are clearly inadequate and ineffective".[41] To develop a

---

[31]   See 1991 Conf. Rep., *op. cit.* (note 20), pp. 4–5 (summary of an address by the Executive Director of UNICEF, James Grant).

[32]   SC Res. 688, *UN SCOR*, 46th Sess., 2982d mtg. at 2, UN Doc. S/RES/688 (1991).

[33]   *UN SCOR*, 46th Sess., UN Doc. S/22663 (1991). The Memorandum of Understanding is reprinted in 30 *ILM* (1991), at 860.

[34]   SC Res. 794, *UN SCOR*, 47th Sess., 3145th mtg. at 2–4, UN Doc. S/RES/794 (1992); SC Res. 814, *UN SCOR*, 48th Sess., 3188th mtg.at 1, UN Doc. S/RES/814 (1993).

[35]   SC Res. 743, *UN SCOR*, 47th Sess., 3055th mtg. at 2, UN Doc. S/RES/743 (1992).

[36]   GA Res. 47/105 (1992).

[37]   GA Res. 48/135 (1993).

[38]   GA Res. 47/73 of 5 March 1992.

[39]   Deng, F., *op. cit.* (note 5), Annex.

[40]   *Internally Displaced Persons, op. cit.* (note 3).

[41]   *Ibidem*, para. 62, at 15.

doctrine of protection, he considers the prerequisites to be: "first a compilation/commentary of the existing norms and a further elaboration of the relevant standards (in the form, for instance, of a code of conduct) and, eventually, a declaration or other authoritative document".[42]

The Commission on Human Rights adopted a resolution on displaced persons in 1994,[43] calling upon UNHCR, the Department of Humanitarian Affairs, the International Organization for Migration and other organizations to cooperate with the Secretary-General's Representative on Internally Displaced Persons.

In October 1993, at the meeting of the UNHCR Executive Committee, there was general support for the UNHCR guidelines governing the competence of the Office pertaining to internally displaced persons.[44] These included several requirements, including a specific request from a competent UN authority, the availability of resources, and the consent of the concerned State and, where applicable, of other relevant entities.

IV. Appraisal and Recommendations

Although a *de facto* expansion of UNHCR's mandate has already taken place, resulting in the provision of assistance and protection to the internally displaced on a case-by-case basis, the jurisdiction issue assumes special significance because the internally displaced remain within their homeland and the UN Charter expressly prohibits the organization's intervention "in matters which are essentially within the domestic jurisdiction of any state . . .".[45]

As to the legal bases for the international community to intervene in the absence of a government's request for assistance from the international community, or at least its consent, such assistance is clearly authorized as part of enforcement measures under Chapter VII. Beyond that, based upon recent UN interventions by the Security Council on humanitarian grounds in Iraq, Somalia and the former Yugoslavia, some preliminary conclusions can be drawn, although it is difficult to discern precise guidelines.

First, the Security Council could claim the right to intervene on the ground that the government's oppression of its own nationals constitutes a threat to international peace and security, as the Council did in the case of Iraq. Resolution 688, which the Security Council adopted in response to Iraq's brutal treatment of the Kurds, paved the way for humanitarian assistance to the

---

[42] *Ibidem*, para. 28, at 8.
[43] Resolution 1994/68 of 9 March 1994.
[44] See UN Doc. A/AC.96/819 (5 October 1993), at 6.
[45] UN Charter Art. 2, para. 7. The clause reads: "Nothing contained in the present Charter shall authorize the United Nations to intervene in matters which are essentially within the domestic jurisdiction of any state or shall require the Members to submit such matters to settlement under the present Charter; but this principle shall not prejudice the application of enforcement measures under Chapter VII".

Kurds[46] without Iraq's consent and even in the absence of the Council taking enforcement measures under Chapter VII. It could, however, be persuasively argued that the flow of Kurdish refugees from Iraq into neighbouring Turkey and Iran could conceivably have triggered an international conflict and hence there was a solid legal basis for the Security Council's blessing to create "safe havens" for the Kurds in northern Iraq.[47]

Second, a similar reasoning can be applied to a situation in which the persecution of a racial, ethnic or religious group within a State (but which is spread across several States) results in internal displacement and, even in the absence of the exodus of refugees across the State's borders, this situation could conceivably be determined by the Security Council as a threat to the peace because of the possible international repercussions of such persecution.

Third, force may be used to secure the delivery of humanitarian aid. Under Resolution 794 of 3 December 1992, the Security Council found a threat to the peace and, under its Chapter VII authority, authorized the use of force by neighbour States in Somalia "to establish as soon as possible a secure environment for humanitarian relief",[48] although with mixed results.[49] However, given the collapse of the State and breakdown of governmental authority, the situation in Somalia was considered unique, *sui generis*.[50]

Earlier, the UN intervention in the former Yugoslavia and the stationing of UNPROFOR troops there was in response to the suffering of the civilians in the tragic ethnic conflict and to provide humanitarian relief. To illustrate: Security Council Resolution 770 termed humanitarian assistance in Bosnia-Herzegovina as "an important element in the Council's effort to secure international peace and security in the area", and requested UN member States to provide relief by all necessary measures.[51] Security Council Resolution 771 specifically demanded that the ICRC have access to detention camps.[52] In sum, in situations where governmental authority and control and social order have broken down, accompanied by massive violations of human rights, pervasive hunger and the need of internally displaced persons for food and humanitarian assistance, and there is no government to invite such assistance, or even when an incumbent government refuses or resists such

---

[46]   SC Res.688, *op. cit.* (note 32).
[47]   See, e.g., *UN SCOR*, 46th Sess., 2982th mtg. UN Doc. S/PV.2982 (1991), at 6–7, 12–15. Several States, including the US and USSR, supported this reasoning.
[48]   SC Res.794, *UN SCOR*, 47th Sess., 3145th mtg. at 2, UN Doc. S/RES.794 (1992).
[49]   See, e.g., Richburg, K., "Aid Staffs Pull Out of Mogadishu: Violence that Killed 22 Soldiers Called 'Organized Ambush', "*Washington Post*, 7 June 1993, p. A-1; Richburg, K., "Stuck in Somalia?: American Mission is Unclear, Open-Ended", *Washington Post*, 21 September 1993, p. A-1.
[50]   Resolution 794 described the situation as "unique". *Op. cit.* (note 48). See also statements by several delegates at the Council debate on the situation, *UN SCOR*, 47th Sess., 3145th mtg., UN Doc. S/PV.3145, at 7 (Zimbabwe), 12 (Ecuador), and 16–17 (China).
[51]   SC Res. 770, *UN SCOR*, 3106th mtg. (1992).
[52]   SC Res.771, *UN SCOR*, 3106th mtg. (1992).

assistance, the Security Council may determine the situation as constituting a threat to the peace, especially if it would arouse world opinion and conceivably trigger a forcible reaction from other States. Also, Chapter VIII regional organizations might be called upon by the Security Council to undertake such humanitarian intervention.

Effective international action to provide a framework for assistance and protection to the internally displaced should include, initially, a declaration, and, eventually, a convention, clarifying and codifying the norms and affirming the firm commitment of the international community to assume responsibility for providing such assistance and protection.[53] Also, institutional arrangements must be clarified, identifying the pertinent international agency – whether UNHCR or another agency – to assume responsibility for the internally displaced. Similarly, it is essential that appropriate procedures be developed under which internally displaced persons would be provided assistance and protection.

The Secretary-General's representative has undertaken an exceedingly important task. His recent call must be heeded:

> If the international community is to rise to the challenge, then the mandate of the Representative of the Secretary-General must be seen as a catalyst and a leverage for the adoption of more effective measures. It is in this connection that the envisaged programme of activities can be expected to facilitate the development of a comprehensive strategy of international protection for internally displaced persons.[54]

---

[53]   See generally Refugee Policy Group, *Strengthening International Protection for Internally Displaced Persons* (December 1993) (proposing such a declaration).
[54]   *Internally Displaced Persons, op. cit.* (note 3), para. 63, at 15.

CLAIRE PALLEY

Legal Issues Arising from Conflicts between UN Humanitarian and Political Mandates – a Survey

Preparatory Remarks

Fastidious scholars may object that this essay covers a vast area, superficially glancing over many issues, each sufficiently complex to be the subject of learned disquisitions, with some being so perplexing that they can only be resolved by pronouncements of the International Court of Justice. The justification is an attempt to place the issues in an overall framework, to make sense of them and to give them perspective.

This has been effected by endeavouring to reconcile the concept of a world organization charged with the duties of enforcing world peace and security and promoting the observance of and respect for human rights with the concept of State sovereignty. More specifically, a way is pointed to showing UN human rights enforcement and humanitarian action to be consistent with State sovereignty. The attempt is based on the assumption that the UN Charter is a constitution for a world order. It is not necessary to go further in this respect than accepting that the Charter creates an international inter-Statal organization – although, even today, it is arguable that the UN can be seen as a very loose, still-evolving federation for security, humanitarian and human rights purposes, backed up by a constitutional court and with an executive Security Council able to take binding decisions for maintaining world peace and security. However, it suffices for the line of argument in this essay to treat the Charter as the United Nations Organization's constituent instrument which binds the organization to its member States.

Because this volume of essays is particularly concerned with UNHCR and "refugee" issues, and because practitioners, social scientists and lawyers of different specializations do not readily appreciate each other's standpoints, there is an attempt to lay a factual basis against which the theoretical discussion should be seen. That basis is briefly set out under the heading "Background" in relation to new Security Council and UNHCR assumptions of power. It is expanded in relation to UNHCR personnel, who perceive conflicts requiring them to choose between courses of action which partly frustrate the values they seek to further (*infra* under the heading "Characteristics of Certain Mandates

145

V. Gowlland-Debbas (ed.), The Problem of Refugees in the Light of Contemporary International Law Issues, 145–168.
© 1996 Kluwer Academic Publishers. Printed in the Netherlands.

in Practice and Confusions Which Have Arisen"). Finally, developments initiated by the Security Council, together with their purported doctrinal justifications, are described under the heading "Consequences of the Grant by the Security Council of New or Extended Mandates, Particularly of Mandates Operating in the Humanitarian and Humanitarian Law Spheres".

BACKGROUND

The post-Cold War activation of the UN Security Council's capacity to conduct itself as a guardian of world peace and security has resulted in a ferment of debate on old and new international law issues, many of which touch on the causes of refugee problems. Much of this debate has been triggered by a proliferation of Council decisions or recommendations, based on an expanded concept of "security", taking account of political, humanitarian, human rights, social and economic aspects, and also internal conflicts.[1] That broadened "security" perspective led to measures earlier either politically unlikely or thought to be beyond Council competence. Such new Security Council action should not be analysed as merely a shift in emphasis, with a little building on earlier precedents: the Council has greatly expanded the scope and the nature of the mandates it grants. The practical consequences have led the Council into new areas, notably new forms of peacekeeping and humanitarian intervention, and raised doctrinal questions about the legitimacy and legality of its action in the "humanitarian" sphere.

In parallel with the Security Council, UNHCR adopted additional functions, prompted by massive refugee and displacement problems following the revival of ethnic strife in former Communist federal States in Europe. Even greater problems arose in African States where the last semblances of control, formerly imposed on their "clients" by the competing Western and Eastern bloc powers, disappeared. Conversely, in some States where long-standing conflicts were settled, there were large-scale returns of refugees. UN member States responded financially to the resulting humanitarian problems, in part because of self-interest in discouraging refugee flows and instabilities likely to affect security, and encouraged UNHCR to assume an extended role. Although, by Article 2 of the Statute, the work of the High Commissioner was to be "of an entirely non-political character: it shall be humanitarian and social and shall relate, as a rule, to groups and categories of refugees," the High Commissioner was to engage in "such additional activities . . . as the General Assembly may determine" (Article 9).

---

[1] In its 31 January 1992 Summit Declaration, the Security Council declared that non-military sources of instability in the economic, social, humanitarian and ecological fields could lead to threats to international peace. Such elements were clearly enunciated in *An Agenda for Peace: Preventive Diplomacy, Peacemaking and Peace-keeping, Report of the Secretary-General*, UN Doc. S/24111 (1992), prepared at the Council's request.

A major new function of assisting displaced persons within States (i.e., persons who had moved or been moved but without crossing an international boundary) was now assumed in practice, financed by donor States and approved by General Assembly resolution 47/105 (1992). This welcomed:

> ... efforts by the High Commissioner, on the basis of specific requests from the Secretary-General or the competent principal organs of the United Nations, and with the consent of the concerned State, to undertake activities in favour of internally displaced persons, taking into account the complementarities of the mandates and expertise of other relevant organisations.

In conjunction with its new role of assisting internally displaced persons, UNHCR realized that the need for assistance extended to protection.[2] It appreciated that any action it could take was politically conditioned, whether as to causes of displacement or flow of refugees from the country of origin, in relation to possible return, or in respect of treatment of refugees in a country of reception. Increasingly, UNHCR acknowledged that, apart from natural disasters, human rights violations resulting from politically motivated action were the causes of refugee and displacement problems. UNHCR thus decided to concern itself with causes of problems, in particular violations of human rights, even monitoring these. It also decided to concern itself with conflict resolution by facilitating negotiations where it could, because only an agreed settlement can make durable arrangements possible.[3]

These decisions led UNHCR into political areas that were normally the concern of the UN's political organs. UNHCR also cooperated with other agencies, notably UNDP, WFP, WHO, UNICEF and FAO. Because mandates were different and time frames for action differently conceived (e.g., UNDP, being concerned with development, has a longer perspective and is not structured to deal with emergencies), and because of bureaucratic jealousies over jurisdiction, coordination became essential. This has partially been achieved by UN internal administrative restructuring, such as the creation of the Department of Humanitarian Affairs and its subsequent reorganization.

Unsurprisingly, the operationalizing of the world security system, accompanied by official UN aid bodies and specialized agencies expanding their activities into spheres touching on the political, has revealed conflict between mandates and a need for coordination and rationalization. This paper raises,

---

[2]   In Sri Lanka it created Open Relief Centres in conflict zones to house displaced refugees from India. In the former Yugoslavia UNHCR has cooperated with UNPROFOR in protecting displaced persons and in trying to assure voluntary return to safe areas. In El Salvador UNHCR has worked closely with UN observer missions (ONUSAL, deployed under Security Council resolution 693).
[3]   In the April 1993 UNHCR guidelines concerning activities on behalf of displaced people, it was stated that UNHCR might consider getting involved to attenuate the causes of internal displacement and contribute to conflict resolution through humanitarian action. Such action was normally to be supplementary to the UN's overall political or humanitarian efforts.

necessarily superficially, the many legal questions which have been exposed by the interaction and overlapping of functions and jurisdiction.[4]

THE NATURE OF THE LEGAL ISSUES

The legal issues can only be understood in the context of the constitution of the UN, the Charter.[5] No constitution, a mere document, can itself act. Thus, to be effective, it creates and authorizes new bodies or authorizes existing bodies to perform the functions and duties detailed in the constitution. Such authorizations, whether to bodies created by the constitution or to pre-existing bodies, are, legally speaking, mandates. In the case of the UN Charter, mandates arise at two levels. They are either granted directly by the Charter (explicitly or implicitly) or by Charter institutions (by virtue of Charter authority) in turn granting mandates within their competence. In all cases, the particular mandated body has responsibility to observe the conditions of its mandate and is accountable to its authorizing body irrespective of the mode of enforcement, be it merely political suasion or judicial declaration. Whether there is judicial review to pronounce on the validity of action under mandates to and by the Security Council, or merely a political process for ensuring conformity, is a hotly disputed issue.[6] Those opposed to review believe that this would emasculate the capacity of the Council to perform its security functions. They are not mollified by the fact that, even assuming power of review by the International Court of Justice to exist, bodies with mandates (such as the Council) have both provisional power to interpret their own competences as a necessary preliminary to action and power to take action unless restrained. The Court will be exceptionally cautious in substituting its own interpretation, whether literal or teleological, of the competences of executive bodies concerned with world security should these be challenged. It will certainly be more than reluctant to order provisional measures of an injunctive character.

Irrespective of whether judicial review is possible and what interpretative

---

[4] Reference should be made to the paper of Richard Plender (*supra*), for the legal basis on which UNHCR deals with internally displaced persons.

[5] See Gowlland-Debbas, V., "Security Council Enforcement Action and Issues of State Responsibility", 43 *ICLQ* (1994), p. 55; Watson, G.R., "Constitutionalism, Judicial Review and the World Court", 34 *Harv. ILJ* (1993), p. 1 and Reisman, W.M., "The Constitutional Crisis in the United Nations", 87 *AJIL* (1993), p. 83.

[6] See Franck, T.M., "The Powers of Appreciation: Who is the Ultimate Guardian of UN Legality?", 86 *AJIL* (1992), p. 519; Gowlland-Debbas, *loc. cit.* (note 5), at 68 *passim*; Reisman, "The Constitutional Crisis in the United Nations", *loc. cit.* (note 5), p. 83, who regards arguments in favour as "judicial romanticism"; Schachter, O., "United Nations Law", 88 *AJIL* (1994), at 1 *et seq.*; and Watson, G.R., *loc. cit.* (note 5). That the International Court has power of review is implicit from the judgments in the *Lockerbie Case: Questions of Interpretation and Application of the 1971 Montreal Convention Arising from the Aerial Incident at Lockerbie* (Libya v. U.S.) (Provisional Measures Order of April 14), ICJ Rep. 1992, p. 114.

techniques are employed, the mandates, i.e., the particular authorizations by the empowering instrument or body, must be analysed. The UN Charter, in creating organs with powers and functions, conditions such powers in the specific authorizing articles and also subjects all powers to certain general articles, most notably the Purposes and Principles set out in Articles 1 and 2, the latter being cast in mandatory language. In the case of the Security Council, Article 24.2 expressly requires the Council to act in accordance with the UN's Purposes and Principles. The Organization and its members, in good faith and in pursuit of the Purposes, are mandated to act in accordance with the Principles (Article 2). It is, here, inappropriate to analyse in depth the UN's Purposes (Article 1), but it can in short be stated that they require cooperation in solving problems of a humanitarian character; respect for human rights (a sphere much developed over the 49 years of Charter "life")[7] and for equal rights and self-determination of peoples; and conformity with the principles of justice and international law. Additionally, the Organization as a whole and member States in particular are required by Article 56 to take joint and separate cooperative action for achievement of the purposes set out in Article 55. Those purposes may shortly be described as humanitarian and as requiring observance of human rights, including the now-developed equal right of peoples to self-determination.

The Charter confers mandates not only on the organs it has created (and which in turn may create subsidiary bodies [Article 7.2]), but, it is somewhat controversially submitted, also on States members. Although the UN Charter is a treaty, it is also a constitution, established by the peoples of the United Nations through their governments' representatives (Preamble). By confirming the sovereign equality of members (Article 2.1), by requiring territorial integrity or political independence of States not to be subject to force or the threat of force (Article 2.4) and by safeguarding States from UN intervention in matters essentially within the jurisdiction of any State (Article 2.7), the Charter *confers* (as well as confirming) such powers on States. Whatever the *historic source* of member States' sovereignty, the *current source* of authority is the UN Charter. In short, the Charter accords mandates (irrespective of whether they be described as confirmatory or reservatory).

The Charter, as constituent instrument of the world political system, also prescribes the scope of State authority (i.e., sovereignty) and conditions upon which it is exercisable. The relevant conditions are, *inter alia*, conformity with the UN's Purposes and Principles. This in turn would require State respect,

---

[7] The Commission on Human Rights and its subordinate Sub-Commission on the Prevention of Discrimination and Protection of Minorities, established by the Economic and Social Council under Article 68 to promote human rights, are responsible for developing human rights concepts and standards, monitoring, reporting and procedures to encourage observance by way of States' reluctance to face ultimate public diplomatic examination in the Commission. The UN International Bill of Rights and the proliferation of human rights specialized treaties, providing for custodial treaty bodies, have resulted in widespread acceptance of standards and a degree of enforcement.

in good faith, for the self-determination of peoples, including the people of the State concerned,[8] and State cooperation internationally in encouraging respect for human rights (including within the State's jurisdiction).[9]

CHARACTERIZATION OF MANDATES

The Charter does not characterize the mandates accorded its organs, except in so far as conferring functions of a particular kind (such as responsibility for maintenance of international peace and security in Article 24.1) is a characterization. In contrast, the General Assembly resolution (GA Res.428(v) of 14 December 1950) establishing the Office of the High Commissioner for Refugees stipulated in Article 2 that "the work of the High Commissioner shall be of an entirely non-political character; it shall be humanitarian and social . . .". However, when discussing potential conflict between mandates, it is convenient to characterize them, even though the characterizations are not terms of art.

"Political" mandates would comprehend competences where the authorized body had to decide political questions. These would include security and economic questions, supervision of dispute settlement, preventive diplomacy and good offices.

Other mandates – and practice endorses this – can be characterized as "humanitarian" or as "human rights" mandates if the primary responsibility of the organ or body is concern with such functions or matters. "Humanitarian" is not confined to the sense in which aid workers use it, namely provision of relief, assistance, protection and humanitarian diplomacy. The principle of humanity, which has steadily become more significant than the original principle of reciprocity as a basis for the law of war, and which is reflected in Article 1 of all four Geneva Conventions, also underlies human rights and refugee law. Indeed, "humanitarian" and "human rights" mandates could be characterized as sub-species of a generic mandate, also "humanitarian", which relates to all concern for the well-being of the human person and respect for individuals.[10] Accordingly, all UN-authorized bodies concerned with human-

[8]   This contention is a variation on the revisionist position adopted by Reisman, W.M., in "Coercion and Self-Determination: Construing Charter Article 2(4)", 78 *AJIL* (1984), p. 624, and in "Sovereignty and Human Rights in Contemporary International Law", 84 *AJIL* (1990), p. 866.

[9]   This line of argument was put forward in respect of State responsibility for creating refugee problems by Guy Goodwin-Gill. See *The Refugee in International Law*, Oxford 1983, at 228. State responsibility and reliance on inter-State obligations were emphasized as the legal way forward, rather than rhetoric about human rights, in Garvey, J.I., "Toward a Reformulation of International Refugee Law", 26 *Har. ILJ* (1985), p. 483 at 493 *et seq.*

[10]   Feliciano, F.P., *International Humanitarian Law and Coerced Movement of Peoples Across State Borders*, International Institute of Humanitarian Law, San Remo 1983, p.6. Feliciano writes that the

itarian relief, assistance and protection or with human rights could be characterized as having "humanitarian" mandates.

Characterization is treated here as depending on the *nature of the powers* conferred. Alternatively, it could be based on the *objectives* for which such powers may be exercised or on the *effects* of their exercise (or non-exercise). However, all activity in society has political effects and it would thus be proper to describe every mandate as "political" in a broad sense. Conversely, "all action aimed at and motivated by concern for human beings is 'humanitarian'".[11] In short, all political action is humanitarian and all social activity is political. Conceived in that fashion, distinctions between mandates collapse. It is more fruitful, therefore, to concentrate on the primary responsibilities and functions of the body concerned, always admitting the possibility of mixed or dual mandates. The conflict may not merely be within the mandate of a single body, but within the overlapping mandates that different bodies often have. In either event, some degrees of conflict or inconsistency become inevitable. The significant question in each case is how a balance can be struck or conflicting functions reconciled.

THE CHARACTERISTICS OF CERTAIN MANDATES IN PRACTICE AND CONFUSIONS
WHICH HAVE ARISEN

Practitioners and lawyers have recently perceived what they see as confusion between the mandates of various bodies operating in the humanitarian sphere. Much of that confusion arises from generalizing principles from the history of particular humanitarian organizations, notably the ICRC and UNHCR. The ICRC, an independent organization which pioneered humanitarian relief and protection of combatants and non-combatants in armed conflicts, developed the concepts of neutrality, impartiality and independence. The ICRC's statutes reflect these concepts. A different wording governs UNHCR. Article 2 of the Statute of the Office of the UN High Commissioner for Refugees requires that the High Commissioner's work "shall be of an

---

principle of humanity . . . is utilised as a shorthand way of referring to a cluster of human values all relating in greater or lesser degree to the physical and moral integrity and well-being of the human person. So understood, humanitarian law would comprehend not only international law relating to the conduct of armed conflict, but also international law concerning refugees and displaced persons and as well much, perhaps most, of the international law of human rights.

See also Pictet, J., *The Principles of International Humanitarian Law*, ICRC, Geneva 1966, at 10. Pictet believed that international humanitarian law was constituted by all the international legal provisions ensuring respect for the individual and his well-being. Accordingly, humanitarian law covered both the law of war and human rights.

[11] Hocké, J.P., "Beyond Humanitarianism: The Need for Political Will to Resolve Today's Refugee Problem", in Loescher, G./Monahan, L. (eds.), *Refugees and International Relations*, Oxford 1990, p. 37 at 46.

entirely non-political character; it shall be humanitarian and social". This does not mean that as far as concerns the operational concepts, UNHCR should be equated with the ICRC. The latter's statutes are more specific as to its characteristics and the ICRC has evolved its operational principles over more than a century. In contrast, UNHCR is a body duty-bound to act as enjoined by the UN General Assembly and in cooperation, in certain cases, with other UN organs having jurisdiction (e.g., the Security Council in security matters and the Secretary General in preventive diplomacy). The operational principles developed by the ICRC and, in the last 40 years, by UNHCR are in reality not matters of legality (except in relation to Article 2 of the High Commissioner's Statute and the ICRC's statutes) but prudential matters, i.e., wise practice, promoting the bodies' images of legitimacy and their effectiveness in exercising their functions in difficult environments. Failure to apply such principles is not a question of acting unlawfully or improperly, particularly in UNHCR's case, when it has to act as part of the overall UN system. Be that as it may, in practice the inference has been drawn by practitioners that all humanitarian bodies must have the same attributes as the two major institutions.

Further confusion has afflicted discussion about recent UN peacekeeping operations in situations where humanitarian assistance was also being protected. Because the UN rules of engagement for earlier classical interposition peacekeeping operations required UN forces to be neutral and impartial, some have objected to changes in the rules even though the altered rules apply in different circumstances and for different kinds of operations, which are more complex and have different components. Surely, however, rules are made and re-made for specific situations and circumstances.

Yet more confusion has come from the fact that refugee law and humanitarian law have arisen in particular bureaucratic contexts, with their development and application being entrusted to particular sets of high priests with specialist lawyers as acolytes, all carefully guarding their own bailiwicks and resenting the intrusion of other custodians. Recently, the human rights lawyers have sought to intrude, but the more conservative international lawyers have been content to remain within their own doctrinal spheres as have, for the most part, the specialists commenting on UN Charter law. However, all these legal fields are parts of public international law, which needs to be seen as a seamless web. Only for convenience of exposition, or for necessary specialist function, should particular branches of law be hived off, while at all times their relevance and the possibility of systemic actors (such as UN organs) applying the relevant law must be kept in mind. Forgetfulness of interconnections may lead to reproaches that particular institutions are invading the spheres of the traditional custodians and failing to apply sacred principles.

It is appropriate now to analyse the principles developed by humanitarian institutions. "Neutrality" and "impartiality" to some extent overlap. "Neutrality" is a characteristic of not being ideologically or politically partisan, of not taking sides in respect of political objectives and of not engaging in hostilities. "Impartiality" is also a characteristic of not being partisan or of favouring one side, but it means more than that. "Impartiality" requires consistency and absence of arbitrariness (for example, no application of double standards). It dictates action to alleviate suffering, without reference to cause or person and without discrimination, and to meet the needs of various sides equally. UNHCR has not expressly been required to be "neutral" and "impartial", but in so far as UNHCR is required to be *"non-political"*, it is implied that its work must be "neutral" and "impartial". However, UNHCR must engage in "additional activities" should such functions be allocated to it by the General Assembly (Article 9 of the Statute). Functions of attempting conflict resolution and preventive functions in respect of human rights violations have been determined by the Assembly as being within UNHCR's revised mandate by its approval of the High Commissioner's good offices and reports on such activities. Paradoxically, that confirmation under Article 9 and the basic fact that UNHCR, as a body created by a General Assembly resolution, is part of the UN institutional system, necessarily make UNHCR both "political" and subject to any superior authority exercising its Charter competence. The result is that, when authorized to conduct a particular operation, UNHCR may well not be "impartial". For example, its mandate may be defined so as to require it to give greater aid to one group of persons than another, thereby discriminating against a group or groups of persons – as in Cambodia, where greater help was to be given to repatriated persons than to internally displaced ones.

Indeed, even without express arrangement, UNHCR may face a conflict between values and rights, both of which it is UNHCR's duty to further under its mandate. UNHCR is used to dealing with – but its personnel are unhappy about – such conflicts occasioned both by interpretative conflicts within mandates and the need to make practical choices between humanitarian duties: for example, whether to give humanitarian aid or not to do so, thus facilitating breaches of human rights; and choosing to further one human right or humanitarian benefit as opposed to another.[12] Such choices have necessarily become more frequent with UNHCR's involvement in internal armed conflicts. Should it afford assistance and protection in-country and avert "refugee" movements, or should it facilitate the right to seek asylum? Should it accept State policies of security in housing refugees or displaced persons in camps, or

---

[12] According to one analyst, "the better the High Commissioner performs the agency's protection function, the more seriously effective oversight of relief is jeopardised, since such action risks alienating the government on which UNHCR depends for its budget and its permission to operate": Loescher, G., *Beyond Charity. International Co-operation and the Global Refugee Crisis*, Oxford 1993, p. 138. Again, is "humane deterrence", in encouraging persons not to disrupt their lives unduly, compatible with the human right of freedom of movement? Only if there are carefully observed guidelines as to genuine lack of pressure and communication of information can this be a proper policy. See McNamara, D., "The Origins and Effects of 'Humane Deterrence' Policies in South-east Asia", in Loescher/Monahan, *loc. cit.* (note 11), p. 123.

should it reject such policies, unless needed for protection, as limiting freedom of movement and residence and effectively limiting individuals' right to seek asylum? Should it *encourage* voluntary repatriation or should it refrain from influencing refugees who believe themselves safer in countries of reception and think that return is premature? With what information should UNHCR provide refugees to facilitate individual choice?[13] Should short-term aid be the model for assistance rather than a longer process involving development aid? (The former produces dependency and undermines recipients' autonomy, whereas the latter supports it.) Should UNHCR afford persons relief, thereby enabling them to continue resisting in a civil war, thus prolonging their suffering? Should it provide persons with safe havens, thus encouraging them to leave their existing habitat and thereby incidentally facilitating policies of "ethnic cleansing"? Should it help persons move, thereby furthering policies aimed at forcible displacement? Should it persist with delivering relief if access is subject to a ransom and the surrender of supplies, which facilitate continued armed attacks and to some extent perpetuate the conditions which gave rise to the need for relief and under which human rights violations will continue to occur? Should it enlist military protection to ensure delivery of assistance? (Apparently even the ICRC has in some situations engaged paid protectors to ensure safe delivery of supplies and to protect aid workers, but it would never accept that supplies should be *forced* through. In the event of military protection being invoked, even without "forcing" supplies through, UNHCR necessarily loses its impartial image.) Should UNHCR and its personnel, as part of the UN system, be subject to involuntary and compulsory protection by UN forces? (Independent aid organizations may attempt to insist on freedom of movement, but they too, in the final analysis, are subject to the authority of any peacekeepers or UN civilian police force acting in terms of their mandates.) Should UNHCR, with its duty of protection, report on human rights violations and risk being perceived as antagonistic and thus less capable of negotiating protection on the spot for displaced persons threatened by persons responsible for the violations? (The question has been asked: when does silence become complicity?) None of these matters is simple or clear-cut: the civilian population requiring aid is often "hostage" to both governments and rebels or invaders (e.g., the resistance in 1993 to the attempt to move sick and wounded civilians from Srebrenica to Tuzla). These questions as to the priorities in competing humanitarian claims (either in relation to aid and protection or to human rights) have led "humanitarian professionals" to develop operational guidelines to assist them in taking difficult decisions. Over time, the ICRC has developed principles for this purpose. In 1992 the Providence Principles of Humanitarian Action in Armed Conflicts were proposed as norms which all international humanitarian institutions and

---

[13]   It is doubtful how many refugees would wish to be repatriated if the Lawyers' Committee for International Human Rights, *General Principles Relating to the Promotion of Refugee Repatriation*, New York 1992, were followed.

practitioners should strive to apply.[14] Similar principles were produced as the Mohonk Criteria for Humanitarian Assistance in Complex Emergencies.[15] The latter add "empowerment" to the earlier proposed criteria of "humanity, impartiality, neutrality and independence".[16]

"Independence", according to the Providence Principles, requires aid providers to be free of interference from home or host governments. The concept should be extended not only to any parties to conflicts, but also to donor governments. The latter extension is wise because of the often political aims of donor States and their encouragement in the generally prevailing "contract culture" of UN agency contracts with particular NGOs. In reality, full independence for UN-authorized bodies is impossible: the UN is a political organization, with member States granting aid for particular humanitarian projects; and UN bodies in the field often operate under the protection of the international security community. In these circumstances, "independence" must be restricted to meaning that there should not be undue influence by other interests, whether attempted to be exercised by home, host, donor or other governments or parties to any conflict. UNHCR always remains subject to the General Assembly's recommendations, while Security Council decisions will inevitably influence UNHCR conduct in the field if peacekeeping forces or observers are operating. Rather than absolute independence, which is not achievable, mutual self-restraint by the various UN organs and agencies in exercising their powers and in consulting at all times seems the best formula for providing "humanitarian space" and operational independence.

CONSEQUENCES OF THE GRANT BY THE SECURITY COUNCIL OF NEW OR EXTENDED MANDATES, PARTICULARLY OF MANDATES OPERATING IN THE HUMANITARIAN AND HUMANITARIAN LAW SPHERES

In order to provide background to the potpourri of legal issues raised by Security Council action, the following developments associated with UN forces are briefly listed. From limited classical peacekeeping (by way of verification by and neutral interposition of forces stationed by consent of the host State) the Council has moved to willingness to use force (as first shown in Namibia in April 1989 against SWAPO infiltrators) to full-scale war against Iraq after the latter's invasion of Kuwait, and then to lesser but still considerable use of armed force in internal and international armed conflicts in

---

[14]   The leading formulators were L. Minear and Weiss following discussions in the Thomas J. Watson Jr. Institute for International Studies, Brown University, and the Refugee Policy Group. The Principles are reproduced in Minear, L./Weiss, T.G. (eds.), *Humanitarian Action in Time of War*, Boulder 1993, at 20.

[15]   World Conference on Religion and Peace, New York 1994.

[16]   Empowerment reflects human rights values of autonomy and the ideas of professionals in the refugee field, who see relief as the first step in a continuum of relief, reconstruction, rehabilitation and sustainable development.

Somalia and in Bosnia-Herzegovina. Such uses of force have required alterations to the UN rules of engagement, and raised questions about the applicability of humanitarian law to UN forces,[17] in particular the permissible degree of force, the requirement of proportionality,[18] the prohibition against indiscriminate use of force impacting on civilian populations, the applicability of humanitarian law to protect UN personnel in conflicts or when captured, and the observance of human rights by members of UN forces or any UN administration.[19]

It is obvious that these issues have arisen out of conflict between the UN Security Council's political mandate and its mandate under the Charter to act in accordance with the UN's Purposes and Principles, which require the Council to respect human rights, to act in conformity with international law (i.e., including humanitarian customary law)[20] and to cooperate in solving problems of a humanitarian character. Similarly, when the Security Council authorizes peacekeeping (itself a humanitarian operation because armed conflict results in human rights violations and flows of displaced persons and refugees) the use of force has political effects, which may counteract the humanitarian objectives of such action. For example, force used to protect persons or in UN forces' self-defence involves direct confrontation with other armed forces or factions, thereby leading to rejection of the notion that UN forces play a neutral and impartial role. UN forces can no longer be seen as neutral where they have been given a protective role in the midst of armed conflict. The threat or use of force to protect "safe areas" and besieged towns likewise means that the UN forces will not be perceived as neutral. Similarly, reporting by peacekeeping forces of alleged crimes against humanity, war crimes and genocide means that the UN's political function of negotiating a settlement becomes more difficult. When the UN seeks to bring about a settlement, rather than seeing continuing or worsening violence, negotiators will in practice have to deal with persons allegedly responsible for such crimes and they will be tempted to ignore the violations, effectively tolerating impunity, itself a violation of human rights. Amnesty may well be demanded as part of a

---

[17]   See Amnesty International, *Peace-keeping and Human Rights*, London 1994, pp. 32–33 and notes 88–94.

[18]   See Gardam, J.G., "Proportionality and Force in International Law", 87 *AJIL* (1993), p. 391, at 403 *et seq.*

[19]   See Amnesty International *op. cit.* (note 17) note 15. Events in Somalia show that the UN administration was without appreciation of the human rights requirements for legal safeguards, a right to legal advice and due process for arrested persons.

[20]   See Gardam, J.G., *loc. cit.* (note 18), at 410, where it is suggested that the entire law of armed conflict applies to UN operations. However, the Geneva Conventions and the 1977 Protocols, except to the extent that their provisions reflect or have become customary law, do not, as treaties, bind the UN as such. They bind signatories, who must ensure that their contingents conform. Currently, the ICRC is devising an acceptable mechanism for the UN to accept the substance of the Conventions and the Protocols: Caratsch, C., "Humanitarian Design and Political Interference: Red Cross Work in the Post-Cold War Period", *International Relations* (1993), p. 301 at 312.

settlement – thence the recent development of "truth" commissions to establish guilt even though no prosecutions follow.

The Security Council has always encouraged negotation processes as a component of peacekeeping, usually by way of Secretary-General's good offices. (These negotiation processes themselves have often contained a major humanitarian component, agreed to by the parties.) Once the Secretary-General or negotiators accepted by concerned parties have proposed compromises to end particular conflicts, there is a serious risk of having to choose between restoring peace, and long-term observance of human rights. A settlement in Bosnia or Croatia which legitimated "ethnic cleansing", ethnic discrimination, grave violations of human rights and the fruits of covert aggression by Serbia would, were it endorsed by the Security Council, contravene the Purposes and Principles of the UN, as well as the purposes pledged by Article 56 to be achieved by joint and separate State action in cooperation with the organization.[21] In fact, in Security Council resolution 820 (1993) the Council commended the peace plan for Bosnia-Herzegovina and called on the Bosnian Serb party to accept the peace plan in full. At the same time the resolution (paragraph 7) endorsed the principle that all displaced persons have the right to return in peace to their former homes and should be assisted to do so. It is depressing to compare this resolution with the reality of non-implementation of such resolutions. Security Council and General Assembly resolutions on Cyprus, made in 1974, called for urgent measures to permit refugees who wished to do so to return to their homes in safety.[22] Such calls have, vainly, been reiterated by the Council in reaffirmatory resolutions for more than two decades.

Another remarkable development occurred in a sphere where the Security Council's political and humanitarian mandates intersect with the mandates of States to retain their sovereignty and normal incidents of that sovereignty unless there has been modification by the procedures stipulated in the Charter, e.g., amendment or an agreement. The Council determined that the commission of atrocities in the former Republic of Yugoslavia constituted a threat to the peace, and subsequently established machinery to prosecute and try in an international criminal tribunal individuals alleged to have committed crimes against humanity in armed conflict. The tribunal's establishment was considered by the Council to be a contribution to the restoration of peace, but it is arguable whether the Charter has given power to the Council to create judicial

---

[21]   In the Secretary-General's "set of ideas" for solution of the Cyprus problem, endorsed by the Security Council, these problems were skirted. The ideas largely recognized the ultimately enforceable rights to return to their homes and properties of Greek Cypriots displaced following Turkey's 1974 invasion. The "ideas" are silent on any rights of Turkish mainland settlers, because transfer of part of Turkey's civilian population into occupied Cyprus is in breach of Article 48 of the Fourth Geneva Convention. See *Report of the Secretary-General*, S/24472, 21 August 1992, pp. 6–7, 18–19, Displaced Persons.

[22]   General Assembly Resolution 3212 (XXIX), 1 November 1974, paragraph 5, endorsed by Security Council Resolution 365 (1974), 13 December 1974.

tribunals,[23] and even more doubtful whether it may deal with matters of *individual* responsibility.[24]

Anticipatory action, deterrence, countermeasures to restore or maintain peace and measures of reparation *potentially* conflict with other UN mandates, notably States' sovereign equality and legal rights preserved (and thus authorized in so far as not excepted by Article 2.7) by the Charter in Articles 1.2 and 2.1, in accordance with which the Security Council must act in discharging its duties (Article 24.2). Arguably, for example, Iraqi subjection to a reparation mechanism (by Security Council resolution 687 [1991]), with a Compensation Commission composed of 15 Security Council members, and the sequestration of Iraq's major natural resource contravene the Iraqi people's right freely to dispose of their natural wealth. When action is so extensive as to sequestrate a State's major resources, Article 1.2 of the Economic, Social and Cultural Rights Covenant may also be relevant. This provides that "In no case may a people be deprived of its own means of subsistence".

Political bodies have difficulty, when convinced that their objectives are "good", in seeing that they may be acting beyond their powers and invading the spheres of power or mandates of other competent bodies. Such an attitude may currently be affecting States members of the Security Council. Several decisions recently taken by the Council in order to restore or maintain peace are, arguably, not within its competence in so far as they invade the jurisdiction (mandates) of States and are not exceptionally permissible because the particular situation does not involve a threat to international peace.

The mode of using force decided upon by the Security Council may also be questionable. Because the UN, for different reasons at different times, has failed to utilize Charter Article 43 to have readily available armed forces at the Council's disposal, delegation of the use of force to powerful member States has become inevitable. Indeed, in the Gulf War, the Security Council failed to retain operational control or supervision itself, delegating excessive discretion to the major powers that participated. To purport to authorize States to use force against another State, not in self-defence, appears unauthorized by the relevant Charter provision: the alternative would be reliance on Article 51 and an artificial agreement for collective self-defence. Subsequent

[23]   O'Brien, J.C., "The International Tribunal for Violations of International Humanitarian Law in the Former Yugoslavia", 87 *AJIL* (1993), p. 639 at 692–694. O'Brien, for pragmatic reasons, dismisses the suggestion that consensual measures (either a treaty or a General Assembly decision) were necessary to establish the tribunal. O'Brien takes the view that the atrocities *constitute* a threat to the peace and that alternative remedies were exhausted. Does it make a difference if atrocities have ceased and order has been restored? Can such a tribunal only be established in *medias reas*? Can the Council at any time create *ad hoc* criminal tribunals so as to maintain peace? How long can such a tribunal continue to exercise jurisdiction over events which have occurred *after* the restoration of peace? Could the Council establish a permanent tribunal? See also Meron, T., "War Crimes in Yugoslavia and the Development of International Law", 88 *AJIL* (1994), p. 78, on the significance of the tribunal for humanitarian law.

[24]   Gowlland-Debbas, *loc. cit.* (note 5), at 68.

delegations authorizing the use of force in Bosnia have been made to NATO, an inter-State defence organization arguably not, in relation to Bosnia, a "regional arrangement" for the maintenance of international peace and security as envisaged by Charter Article 52. In Bosnia, the Council has employed NATO's capacity as a military instrument, but, because the Council is now observing the need for control of the use of force, there have been practical operational difficulties of coordination. Events indicate the necessity either of invoking Article 43 or of introducing new administrative arrangements to avoid "licensing" aggression against States or fictional collective defence arrangements.

"Unpopular" States have also faced the risk of having their sovereignty infringed by Security Council decisions. A case in point is Libya, and the economic sanctions resulting from its non-compliance with a Security Council mandatory call to surrender for trial two Libyan nationals accused of involvement in the blowing up of a Pan Am jet over Lockerbie. It remains to be seen whether the imposition of economic sanctions for Libya's non-compliance will be upheld as a lawful overriding of Libya's sovereign right to try its nationals for crimes allegedly committed by them, or whether Libya's failure to surrender them permitted the Council to determine this failure to be a threat to the peace, to call on Libya for compliance and to give effect to its decision under Article 41. Likewise, an unpopular regime has been subject to Council decisions to authorize the use of force to restore the lawful government in circumstances where a threat to international peace was not easily discernible, i.e., the authorization of force to restore President Aristide's government in Haiti.

Whereas the Council is authorized by Article 41 to impose measures interrupting economic relations (sanctions),[25] it is also mandated by Charter Article 1 to promote respect for human rights (including social and economic rights), to solve problems of a humanitarian character, and to settle international disputes in conformity with international law – this last comprehending humanitarian law. Sanctions imposed by the Council have indiscriminately impacted on civilian populations. Although sanctions regimes have provided for humanitarian exceptions, permitting, subject to the supervision of a Sanctions Committee, the delivery of foodstuffs, medical supplies, cooking and heating fuel and materials essential for civilian needs, humanitarian organizations report the infliction of suffering leading to hunger, malnutrition and deaths of vulnerable persons (children and the old). It is arguable that the Sanctions Committee does not obtain adequate information to enable

---

[25] *Ibidem*, at 55 *et seq.* for discussion of imposition of sanctions and other Security Council exercises of power under the Charter in the light of the legal institution of State responsibility and also of whether there are any limitations on the Council's powers of appreciation in characterizing a situation as one justifying the Council in overriding the legal rights of States. The standard work on sanctions is Gowlland-Debbas, V., *Collective Responses to Illegal Acts in International Law. United Nations Action in the Question of Southern Rhodesia*, Dordrecht 1990.

it to act promptly to suspend the operation of sanctions when undue suffering is being caused by an embargo on particular commodities.[26] A less serious, but nonetheless considerable, consequential impact of sanctions has been felt by the populations of third party States uninvolved in any conflict. This has made apparent the inadequacy of Charter Article 50 as a procedure to protect third party States and their populations from Security Council action.

The Security Council's assumption of a protective humanitarian role in securing delivery of relief for civilian populations, first in the former Yugoslavia and later in Somalia, was initially undertaken with consent in the former case and acquiescence by a non-functional government in the latter. This role was initially welcomed because the UN forces' logistical capacity and the degree of military deterrence they provided were seen as protecting humanitarian agencies' or organizations' relief convoys and personnel. Gradually, what was protection of relief supplies became protection of individuals facing violence in armed conflict, and peacekeeping took a step towards imposing order (not very successfully). Ultimately, the requirement of host State consent to the operations was replaced by the view that the situation constituted a threat to the peace and that Chapter VII, rather than Chapter VI, action was required. In Northern Iraq, action was taken against the wishes of Iraq[27] because Kurdish refugees were streaming towards the Turkish border. Such a characterization was well-founded, even if the real reason for action was humanitarian concern. Subsequently, somewhat more coercive mandates were granted, such as that for UNPROFOR in the former Socialist Federal Republic of Yugoslavia[28] and that for UNISOM II in Somalia.[29] These coercive measures of humanitarian intervention were effected by member States under Council authorization.[30]

---

[26] It must be assumed that the Security Council is unaware of or does not accept the existence of such deficiencies, or it believes that the conditions are being inflicted by the government of Iraq. If it were otherwise, the Council would be flouting a UN standard, namely Article 1 of the Universal Declaration on the Eradication of Hunger and Malnutrition (General Assembly Resolution 3348 (XXIX), of 17 December 1974), which proclaims the inalienable right of every man, woman and child to be free from hunger and malnutrition. The Declaration ends with an affirmation that participating States will make full use of the UN system to implement it.

[27] See Security Council Resolution 688 (1991) which established safe-havens in Iraq. Subsequently, on 18 April 1991, the government of Iraq agreed to a Memorandum of Understanding for UNHCR operations.

[28] The continued stationing of UNPROFOR in Croatia authorized by Security Council resolution 743 (1992) was without Croatian consent.

[29] Security Council Resolution 733 (1992). The latter is a less weighty precedent because of the absence of a State government.

[30] Individual States, or a group of States, may take coercive action by way of self-defence under Article 51 and notify the Council, but this paper is concerned with *UN* action. It is also confined to *coercion*. Measures such as debate in UN deliberative bodies, collective declarations and diplomatic protest are not covered, although they are in a sense coercive. Such a restricted scope of the concept of coercion is in accordance with the wording of Article 2.4, which prohibits the threat or use of force. The Netherlands Advisory Committee on Issues of International Law, in *The Use of Force for Humanitarian Purposes*, Report No. 15, The Hague

The abandonment of the requirement of State consent[31] for UN collective humanitarian intervention under Security Council authority has again raised questions concerning the scope of Article 2.7 (States' exclusivity of competence, authorized by the UN Charter, in matters essentially within their domestic jurisdiction).

The most radical approach to humanitarian intervention (or intervention following massive violations of human rights) has been put forward by American jurists.[32] Professor Reisman reinterprets Charter Article 2.4, which prohibits the threat or use of force against territorial integrity or political independence, so as not to preclude forcible assistance in pursuit of self-determination (certainly a construction consistent with assistance to overthrow colonialist regimes, something not contemplated by doctrine when the Charter was agreed, but developed later) or to maintain world order.[33] Taking a leaf from monographs on political thought, he also sees "sovereignty" as "popular", and not as "State" sovereignty, in the context of the ongoing development of the concept of self-determination. On Reisman's basis, assuming that refugee flows from the island of Haiti did not constitute a threat to the peace, forcible intervention would have been lawful because the people's right to self-determination had been thwarted by a military coup.[34] Conversely, an expansive

---

1992, p. 13, asserted that humanitarian intervention *by States* in extreme cases of violations of human rights was not impermissible if the UN itself were, for whatever reason, unable to take a decision. The Committee powerfully argued that to avoid confusion *UN action* should be referred to as "enforcement action for humanitarian purposes".

[31] These developments were summed up in *An Agenda for Peace* in the significant phrase that such operations had occurred "hitherto with the consent of all parties concerned". A carefully framed positive formulation of the right to collective humanitarian intervention appears in Jennings, R.Y./Watts, A., *Oppenheim's International Law*, Vol. 1, 9th. ed., London 1992, at 443. See the more radical approach of the Netherlands Advisory Committee on Issues of International Public Law, *The Use of Force for Humanitarian Purposes*, Report No. 7, The Hague 1992. A short but magisterial summary of the law is given by Greenwood, C., "Is There a Right of Humanitarian Intervention", 49 *The World Today* (1993), pp. 34–40. Fuller references to recent interventions and the current extensive literature appear in Hutchinson, M.R., "Restoring Hope: UN Security Council Resolutions for Somalia and an Expanded Doctrine of Humanitarian Intervention", 34 *Harv. ILJ* (1993), p. 624; Farer, T.J., "An Inquiry into the Legitimacy of Humanitarian Intervention", in Damrosch, L.F./Scheffer, D.J. (eds.), *Law and Force in the New International Order*, Boulder 1991, p. 185; and Damrosch, L.F., *Enforcing Restraint: Collective Intervention in Internal Conflicts*, New York 1993. For opposing legal and prudential arguments see Rumage, S.A., "Panama and the Myth of Humanitarian Intervention in U.S. Foreign Policy: Neither Legal Nor Moral, Neither Just Nor Right", 10 *Arizona Journal of International and Comparative Law* (1993), p. 1.

[32] See Reisman, *loc. cit.* (note 8) and D'Amato, A., "The Invasion of Panama was a Lawful Response to Tyranny", 84 *AJIL* (1990), p. 516.

[33] Reisman's views are powerfully criticized by Schachter, O., "The Legality of Pro-Democratic Invasions", 78 *AJIL* (1984), p. 645.

[34] UN involvement in Haiti came with the General Assembly's resolution of 12 October 1990. The later Security Council resolution (841 [1993]) reflects such arguments, namely the failure to reinstate the legitimate government of President Aristide, combined with a mass population displacement following on a climate of fear of persecution. (The careful wording

concept of self-determination may have the effect of precluding or invalidating intervention. The right to self-determination arguably encompasses the right of a people to survive in their current State and territory, and this requires the people and State to have the right to defend themselves. (Such a right is arguably a matter apart from Article 51, which allows self-defence *until* the Council has taken measures "necessary to maintain international peace" – objective wording implying that the right of self-defence persists if inadequate measures are taken.) It may be that the continued application of the arms embargo which the Security Council imposed (by Security Council Resolution 713 [1991]) on the former Yugoslavia, now extinct, can be characterized as a breach of Bosnia-Herzegovina's right to self-determination. Although raised, the issue was not dealt with in the International Court of Justice's Order following Bosnia's application for provisional measures, because the Court confined itself to examination of measures, and grounds for these, falling within the scope of the Convention on the Prevention and Punishment of the Crime of Genocide.[35]

Another approach has been put forward tentatively by Mr. Deng, the representative of the Secretary General on internally displaced persons. He proposes an international standard stipulating that:

> . . . any Government that fails to provide the most fundamental rights for major segments of its population can be said to have forfeited sovereignty and the international community can be said to have a duty in those instances to reestablish it.[36]

Sovereignty will have "collapsed" by virtue of the government's incapacity to prevent gross violations. If the world community intervenes to restore democratic self-government, the question is: how far may it go? May it

---

regarding "climate" was significant in relation to whether individuals would be able to show *personal* well-founded fear of persecution, thus entitling them to claim refugee status after leaving Haiti and arriving in the territory – or jurisdiction? – of another State.) An earlier example of State practice using thwarting of self-determination as justification for intervention was India's action in 1971 in East Pakistan. For further arguments and potential developments see Franck, T.M., "An Emerging Right to Democratic Governance", 86 *AJIL* (1992), p. 1.

[35] *Case Concerning Application of the Convention on the Prevention and Punishment of the Crime of Genocide* (Request for the Indication of Provisional Measures) (Order of 8 April 1993), reprinted in 87 *AJIL* (1993), p. 505 at 516.

[36] Deng, F.M., *Protecting the Dispossessed*, Brookings Institution, Washington 1993, at 140. Deng indicates that a duty is evolving for the world community to re-establish sovereignty (pp. 14–20), contending that protection and assistance of the internally displaced reconciles sovereignty with responsibility. At p. 119 he asserts that a government cannot invoke sovereignty for the deliberate purpose of starving its population or otherwise denying its people protection and resources vital to their survival and well-being. He suggests that if a government is incapable of providing protection and assistance, there is *a presumption* that the international community, either on invitation or by international consensus, *should act*. Deng considers such a presumption to be consistent with traditional views of sovereignty. Reisman's revisionist view faces no such need for presumptions or fictions.

establish a temporary government, or may it establish a constitution? In Somalia the Security Council has thought it inappropriate to take such steps, encouraging the various factions themselves to agree on such matters. If agreement is not forthcoming, should the Council be content with temporary restoration of order and then just remove the forces it has authorized, at which stage human rights violations and human suffering will recommence?[37]

An equally radical view of the right of humanitarian intervention, but one *excluding the use of force*, has been proposed by French humanitarian thinkers.[38] They claim that States have a right of unconditional free access to victims to safeguard life.

Admittedly, the General Assembly, in a series of resolutions (beginning with General Assembly Resolution 43/131 [1988]), has declared its concern about the suffering of victims of natural disasters and of emergency situations and emphasized the importance of humanitarian assistance. It has recommended that States in proximity to countries facing such situations facilitate such aid and has called for cooperation to this end (General Assembly Resolution 45/102 of 14 December 1990). This is not a recognition by the General Assembly of such a right.[39] However, the Assembly has welcomed the establishment by concerted action of temporary relief corridors for distribution of emergency aid (General Assembly Resolution 45/100) and subsequently indicated that State acquiescence, rather than a formal request, would suffice to permit the provision of aid to a population (General Assembly Resolution 46/182 of 19 December 1991). The Commission on Human Rights has gone further: it passed a resolution on Rwanda asserting the international community's right to provide humanitarian assistance and welcomed the Security Council's decision to give support for delivery of assistance and protection of persons, including persons in secure humanitarian areas (S-3/1 of 25 May 1994).

In the longer term, the duty of all member States to cooperate in solving humanitarian problems (Charter Article 1.3), and the duty (under Charter Articles 55 and 56) to promote solutions of economic, social, health and related problems and to achieve universal respect for human rights (including economic and social rights) may be seen as having two effects. First, imposing a responsibility on States to respect, as a minimum, the right to life of indi-

---

[37] It appears that ECOWAS may take a longer-term view in regard to Liberia than the UN has in relation to operations in Somalia. Regional organizations have an incentive to be more interventionist, because they are affected more severely by neighboring turmoil. Great powers have difficulty in finding the will to involve themselves in "distant lands", unless major strategic or economic concerns are relevant.

[38] See Bettati, M., "The Right of Humanitarian Intervention or the Right of Free Access to Victims", 42 ICJ *Review* (1992), p. 1, updating the arguments in Bettati, M./Kouchner, B., *Le devoir d'ingerence*, Paris 1987, and in Bettati, M., "Un droit d'ingerence", 95 *RGDIP* (1991), pp. 639–670.

[39] It could not competently create one. At best, a consensual resolution would be evidence of acceptance of the right as part of international customary law. There would also have to be general practice to that effect accepted as law. Recognition of a *duty* to intervene would be even more difficult to establish.

viduals, and, second, creating a correlative *right* by State actors in a world constitutional system with a human rights regime to intervene when there are large-scale threats to life. At that stage, rather than ritual references to obligations *erga omnes* and the *Barcelona Traction Case*,[40] to *ius cogens*, and to the Southern Rhodesian and South African precedents of mandatory sanctions based in part on failure to respect fundamental human rights, a legal doctrine of *international responsibility for enforcement* of human rights may develop (and may then be incorporated in a UN Charter amendment). Such development of doctrine will be facilitated if an *individual right* to seek humanitarian assistance and protection is recognized. (Such a right is a necessary implication of the *right* to life.)

By contrast, no question of a *duty* by States to take enforcement action can sensibly be contemplated. However, there can, and may already, be a duty to *consider*, in accordance with legal principles, whether such action is appropriate and likely to be effective. Currently, writers on humanitarian intervention are seeking to evolve such legal principles in order to avoid contemporary and apparently arbitrary exercises of discretion not overtly guided by recognized criteria.

Yet another humanitarian role undertaken by the Security Council is its assumption of power to grant "pacification" mandates, which can be seen as a new aspect of the Council's dispute-settling powers. In the post-Cold War era, with settlement of long-standing conflicts such as those in Cambodia, Namibia and El Salvador, the Council has, with the agreement of the States or parties concerned, granted variously mixed mandates, involving both security matters and humanitarian action, with effects going well beyond matters of "security" as traditionally interpreted. Other agencies, such as UNDP and UNICEF, as well as UNHCR, have been involved in working together in the field. These mixed mandates have required UN forces, observers and administrators to assist in transition to new democratic regimes, to monitor or hold elections, to administer, to enforce law and order (but without as yet establishing judicial machinery), and to deal with massive problems of resettlement of repatriated refugees and displaced persons. In such situations, the potential for conflict between political and humanitarian aspects of the mandates and long- and short- term aims is considerable. Quick moves to democracy with an absence of confrontation, as against enforcement of human rights and a blind eye to violations, is a charge levelled against the UN administration in Cambodia (UNTAC).

---

[40]   *Case Concerning the Barcelona Traction Light and Power Co. Ltd.* (Belgium v. Spain), ICJ Rep. 1970, p. 3.

SUMMARY OF THE LEGAL ISSUES RAISED BY CONFLICTING MANDATES

The above account of conflicts between and within mandates of the same or of different UN-authorized bodies raises, *inter alia*, the following legal issues:[41]

1. Are the UN and armed forces established by any organ bound by international humanitarian law, and to what extent? (There are a multitude of sub-issues such as proportionality, indiscriminate use of force or application of economic sanctions, reciprocal rights to protection of UN forces, capacity to act as quasi-protecting power and consequential duties of neutrality, etc.)

2. Are the UN and all its personnel, acting officially, bound by human rights law, and what is the content of the applicable law? (If so, how is a non-arbitrary principled balance to be struck between competing human rights and on what criteria?) Are human rights displaced in emergency circumstances of armed conflict in which UN forces are engaged?

3. Can the Security Council
    (i) establish a judicial tribunal with criminal jurisdiction in respect of crimes committed during armed conflict, and
    (ii) subject *individuals* to its jurisdiction?

4. Can the Security Council establish bodies with governmental powers within States and, if so, have such bodies duties to apply human rights and justice?

5. Can UN administrators tolerate "impunity" and general amnesties? Or is the doctrine against "impunity" sometimes not tantamount to a suicide pact, likely to prolong human suffering and to cause more loss of life?

6. Can the Security Council endorse, impose or recommend a political peace settlement legitimating human rights violations, crimes against humanity, genocide and the fruits of aggression?

7. Does the Security Council have power in situations where humanitarian assistance is required within State borders, without the consent or acquiescence of the host State, to

---

[41] Much of the material in this paper has been taken from two papers prepared by the writer for the Sub-Commission on Prevention of Discrimination and Protection of Minorities: see *Preparatory Document* and *Further Preparatory Document submitted by Mrs. Claire Palley on the question of the role of the United Nations in international humanitarian activities and assistance and human rights enforcement, bearing in mind the principle of non-intervention*, E/CN.4/Sub. 2/1993/39 of 19 August 1993 and E/CN.4/Sub.2/1994/39 of 15 June 1994. However, the views expressed are of a personal nature and do not represent the official views of the United Nations. The Commission on Human Rights, on the motion of Professor David Weissbrodt of the U.S.A.'s delegation, decided that, "having regard for the need for the Subcommission to avoid making judgements on issues that are within the responsibility of other United Nation's bodies and to avoid overloading its agenda . . . not to forward to the Economic and Social Council the draft decision of the Subcommission authorizing a study on the question of the implications for human rights of United Nations action, including humanitarian assistance, in addressing international humanitarian problems and in the promotion of human rights" (Decision 1995/107, 3 March 1995, Commission on Human Rights, Report on the Fifty-First Session, p. 291).

(i)   secure access for aid purposes;
(ii)   deliver aid;
(iii) employ measures other than force (e.g., economic sanctions) to enforce implementation of those purposes; and/or
(iv)   employ forcible measures to effect such purposes?

Can such power be inferred by teleological and purposive interpretation of the Charter in the light of developments in the sphere of human rights and the doctrine of State responsibility? Is this to be achieved by an unlimited power of appreciation of what constitutes "a threat to the peace"?

8. Are States members
    (i)   collectively entitled; and/or
    (ii)   duty-bound to consider whether to intervene to stop gross human rights violations such as genocide or massive threats to life? Does this extend to cases where self-determination has been thwarted by internal action? Which measures may be employed?

9. If States are accorded political mandates of sovereignty subject to any Charter limitations, is there judicial power to interpret Security Council decisions and evaluate their application in practice should there be proceedings before the International Court of Justice alleging a decision to be in conflict with such State mandates?

10. Does the Court have jurisdiction to pronounce on non-conformity of Council action or decisions with Charter provisions, and, if so, does this permit the Court to evaluate in terms of all or any of the elements (such as conformity with the principles of justice and international law, human rights, and solving problems of a humanitarian character) mentioned as UN Purposes and Principles in Articles 1 and 2 of the Charter?

CONSTITUTIONAL IMPLICATIONS OF THE VARIOUS LEGAL ISSUES

Quite apart from political resentment by small States at the predominance of the five Permanent Members of the Security Council, and the survival of only one superpower, States have raised doubts about the legitimacy[42] of the Security Council, the lawfulness of some of its decisions, the propriety and lawfulness of the Council's extended functions, Council selectivity in the exercise of its powers and, above all, the Council's non-democratic composition as opposed to that of the General Assembly with its strictly limited powers. This has placed UN constitutional revision high on the political agendas of many States members, with States considering whether the UN's administrative and constitutional structure needs revision because of lack of

---

[42] Legitimacy is used in the political and sociological sense and not to refer to observance of fundamental principles of legality such as certainty, consistency, non-retroactivity, etc., although non-observance of such principles will mean that the body concerned will not be appraised as having acted with legitimacy.

competence by principal organs in certain respects and/or because of lack of legitimacy by particular organs due to their *modus operandi* or composition.

To believe that revision will easily be achieved or that an amended UN Charter and improved administrative arrangements will ensure global security, good governance, protection of human rights and international justice would be foolish. Even so, improvement is possible. Much can be achieved by further improving administrative arrangements without attempting constitutional change. *Inter alia*, more coordination is needed through the Secretariat as between the Departments for Humanitarian Affairs, for Political Affairs and for Peace-Keeping, and with the new High Commissioner for Human Rights. Similarly, the Inter-Agency Standing Committee, at which the heads of UN relief and development agencies meet, could be given greater authority, especially in relation to activities on behalf of displaced persons.[43] Peace-keeping can be further re-conceived and re-shaped internally, with provision for a larger civilian component for field administration and with adequate training arrangements for both military and civilian peacekeepers. Mandates can, when granted, be made more specific. Internal guidelines, developing the rules of engagement and principles applicable when providing humanitarian assistance, can be internally formulated. Regional peacekeeping can be encouraged. Charter Article 43 can be utilized. Informal consultative bodies can be negotiated between UN principal organs, and so can greater access to the Security Council. More active consideration can be given by the appropriate bodies to developing binding human rights standards applicable to internally displaced persons, internal population transfers, the right to leave and return to a country and to effecting closure of the humanitarian law gap. The latter arises when much of human rights law is suspended at a time of internal emergency but the State concerned does not recognize the level of strife as amounting to armed conflict and thereby fails to bring humanitarian law into operation.[44] A significant step would be establishment by ECOSOC of an additional Sub-Commission to monitor humanitarian law. In sum, a great deal could be effected without constitutional amendment. In parallel, long-term constitutional revision could be considered along the various lines suggested by jurists and international relations experts.[45]

States members should be encouraged to take up questions of internal

---

[43]   This and other significant proposals for reform of administrative arrangements concerning protection for internally displaced persons and development of laws addressing their assistance and protection needs were made by Cohen, R., *International Protection for Internally Displaced Persons*, Refugee Policy Group, Focus Paper No. 2, Washington January 1994.

[44]   Meron, T., "On the Inadequate Reach of Humanitarian and Human Rights Law and the Need for a New Instrument", 77 *AJIL* (1983), pp. 589–606.

[45]   See, *inter alia*, Caron, D.D., "The Legitimacy of the Collective Authority of the Security Council", 87 *AJIL* (1993) , pp. 552–588; and Reisman, "The Constitutional Crisis in the U.N.", *loc. cit.* (note 6), at 96 *et seq.*

administrative change and possible long-term amendment by the wise words in June 1992 of Secretary-General Boutros Boutros-Ghali:

> The United Nations was created with a great and courageous vision. Now is the time, for its nations, peoples, and the men and women who serve it, to seize the moment for the sake of the future.[46]

---

[46]   *An Agenda for Peace, op. cit.* (note 1), at para. 86.

VIRGINIA A. LEARY
Rapporteur

Reflecting the Discussions

The papers presented at the Colloquium, as well as the commentaries on the papers, are reproduced elsewhere in this volume; my aim in these remarks is to reflect the richness of the discussion that followed the presentation of the papers and commentaries. It would be difficult – and tedious for the reader – to reproduce all the extensive comments that were made and I have not attempted to do so. Some participants may find, therefore, that their comments have not been specifically cited. I have, rather, attempted to integrate the diverse comments into a general summary which gives the tenor of the discussions and which will be useful to persons who did not attend the Colloquium.

The subject matter chosen by the organizers of the colloquium is one rarely discussed in the profuse literature on refugee issues: namely, the manner in which the problem of refugees stimulates rethinking of contemporary international law. In choosing "the problem of refugees in the light of contemporary international law issues" as the focus of the Colloquium, the organizers were suggesting that the problem of refugees cannot be resolved solely by existing refugee law but has repercussions and effects on, and implications for, a number of other aspects of contemporary international law.

It should be noted at the outset that the Colloquium was not confined to discussion of the problem of "refugees" in the narrow legal sense of that term. The term "refugee" in international law refers to persons who have crossed borders as a result of a well-founded fear of persecution and whose situation is covered by the Geneva Refugee Convention, but, despite their familiarity with the legal definition, participants, following the paper presenters, referred as frequently to persons in refugee-like situations as to refugees in the strict sense. Discussions focussed on the problems of internally displaced persons (away from their homes but within their own countries), returned refugees, persons in safe havens within the borders of their own country, and persons deprived of citizenship as a result of readjusted borders or the breakup of States.

The current international situation was perceived by participants to be

169

V. Gowlland-Debbas (ed.), The Problem of Refugees in the Light of Contemporary International Law Issues,
169–173.
© 1996 *Kluwer Academic Publishers. Printed in the Netherlands.*

Λ

responsible for the shift away from a narrow interpretation of the refugee problem, particularly the realization that there are presently more internally displaced persons in the world than "refugees", and the taking on of responsibilities for internally displaced persons and persons in safe havens by the Office of the United Nations High Commissioner for Refugees (UNHCR), at the request of the General Assembly. One of the major discussions (reported more fully below) related to the value or drawbacks of UNHCR assuming these expanded responsibilities.

Discussions on the international law implications of the problem of refugees centered on the following issues:

1. The relationship of the problems of refugees (in the broad sense of the term) to human rights law.
2. The role and mandates of international agencies (UNHCR, ICRC, UN human rights bodies)
3. The need (or lack of need) for new normative instruments relating to refugee-like situations such as that of the internally displaced. Relevance of the right to leave and the right to return.
4. State responsibility for violations of human rights.
5. Humanitarian assistance and humanitarian intervention. The principle of non-intervention.

Problems concerning internally displaced persons received special attention in the discussion, since, as was pointed out, their number far exceeds the number of refugees in the world. Discussion centered on the question of whether the internally displaced were a discrete category within the field of human rights law. Should the category also include returned refugees and persons in safe havens – all of whom shared some of the same problems as the internally displaced?

Some commentators pointed out that issues of the internally displaced do not fall within refugee law but general human rights law. They remarked that such persons are already protected by human rights law and that they should not be considered a special category. Others favoured regarding the internally displaced (and possibly returned refugees) as a particular group to be accorded special treatment within the general field of human rights.

A related question that was discussed was whether an international normative instrument, such as a declaration or convention, should be adopted on the internally displaced. Reference was made to the work of Francis Deng, Special Representative of the Secretary General for the internally displaced. He had suggested that such a normative instrument could consist of provisions already in other instruments, compiled into a separate instrument. Its value would be to focus special attention on the provisions in other instruments relating to the treatment of persons in the situation of the internally displaced. Several speakers stressed that action to assist such persons was more important than a new declaration. Others pointed out that a declaration could clarify issues and provide standards.

The topic of the internally displaced – as well as issues relating to returned refugees and persons in safe havens within their own countries – raised the issue of which organization or organizations should be responsible for their protection and assistance. A recurrent theme of the discussion related to the role of UNHCR. The changing international situation has thrust work and responsibilities on that body not envisaged at its founding. At the request of the General Assembly it has taken on reponsibilities for displaced persons (those who are away from their homes but have not crossed borders), returned refugees, and persons in safe havens within their own countries. These responsibilities have placed unusual stress on UNHCR.

Colloquium participants debated the setting up of a new organization to deal with persons in these difficult circumstances. Divergent opinions were expressed on this subject. Plender pointed out in his paper that it was political circumstances at the time of UNHCR's creation and not "some inherent rule of law or logic" which confined the functions of the Office to cases of external displacement. Participants accepted his view that there were no legal objections to the enlargement of the jurisdiction of UNHCR, but expressed concern that placing such diverse responsibilities on UNHCR would be too much of a burden on the organization: another organization should be created. One asked whether regional organizations might take over more of the responsibilities. It was pointed out that the proposal of one government that UNHCR should be given a standing invitation to involve itself in internal situations was rejected. Some thought that the responsibility of UNHCR for returned refugees required collaboration with governments which might be sending refugees back before the situation of the country of origin had stabilized, thus counteracting the work of UNHCR in protecting refugees.

While several participants expressed a preference for the creation of a new organization to handle these new refugee-like situations, the general opinion appeared to be that the creation of a new organization was not a practical solution. Echoing (more dramatically) the opinion of other participants, one member of the Colloquium commented that attempting to create another agency at the present political juncture was "crazy". Persons supporting this view emphasized UNHCR had long experience in humanitarian issues and that it had already, at the request of the General Assembly, taken on certain responsibilities in this area. Stress on UNHCR could be alleviated by the allocation of greater resources to its work.

It was also stressed that protecting persons suffering human rights violations within the confines of their own country was a responsibility of the State concerned. State responsibility for human rights violations on its territory should be emphasized. The role of UNHCR was to protect persons when they were unable or unwilling to have the protection of their own country. If a State failed to protect those within its borders, UN and regional human rights agencies already had the responsibility to deal with such issues. It was pointed out, however, that unlike UNHCR and the ICRC, human rights bodies normally did not have operational capacity.

The concept of the responsibility of the State of origin for the creation of refugees and internal displacement was also discussed, following presentations relating to the subject in several papers. Some felt it important to emphasize the responsibility of States in this regard; others felt emphasis on State responsibility distracted attention from the more important issue of preventing refugee situations and protecting those in such situations. It was also pointed out that State responsibility has little relevance in situations where State organs are effectively non-functioning, such as Somalia and Rwanda. Debate also centered on a newly important question: whether a State is required to give its nationality to those within its borders who might otherwise find themselves stateless. The recent dissolution of States and creation of new States has given this subject current relevance. Many pointed out that traditional international law, including the concept of "genuine link", provides little guidance on the subject of conferring of nationality.

The right to leave and the right to remain are international legal rules, but there was considerable discussion of their effectiveness and relevance. In some cases, the two seem to be conflicting. For instance, the creation of safe havens, viewed as implementing the right to remain, may be contrary to the right to leave and the requirement that other States provide asylum. And while the right to leave is a well-entrenched right, it only implies the right to seek and not to obtain asylum and hence may be meaningless. One commentator pointed out, however, that the right to leave had considerable relevance during the period of the Cold War and the situation in the USSR. Some pointed out that the right to remain did not relate only to refugees but also to settlers and persons of a different nationality who find themselves in a newly created State. It was suggested that it is not legal rules that are needed in this area but rather political solutions.

Considerable discussion followed the wide-ranging and comprehensive paper of Dr. Claire Palley on legal issues arising from conflicts between UN humanitarian and political mandates. The discussion deviated from the more narrow focus on refugees and persons in refugee-like situations and resulted in numerous reflections on the present international response to humanitarian crises. A number of commentators referred to the complexities of humanitarian situations and the inadequate international response. The conflict between practical considerations and principles of criminal responsibility were raised: how can the UN, on the one hand negotiate with persons who may be considered war criminals and, on the other hand, set up a tribunal to try war criminals. Several speakers referred to the concept of humanitarian assistance and distinguished it from humanitarian intervention. The problem of humanitarian intervention can scarcely be considered when no viable State is involved and humanitarian needs are overwhelming. The problem of judicial review of Security Council actions was raised. The discussion underscored the subject of the Colloquium: the essential link between the present humanitarian issues of refugees and general international law.

*   *   *   *   *

In pursuing the topic of the Colloquium, the organizers made the happy decision to bring together both activists and scholars concerned with refugee issues. Madame Sadako Ogata, UN High Commissioner for Refugees, and others from her Office, made valuable contributions based on the extensive experience of the Office, as did representatives from the International Committee of the Red Cross. The Colloquium participants included, however, a slightly larger number of international law scholars than practitioners. Although interesting papers were presented by both activists and scholars, the dicussion largely consisted of comments by the international law scholars. The inclusion of both scholars and practitioners at the Colloquium was an excellent initiative, but more interaction in the discussion between practioners and scholars would have enhanced consideration of the subject.

The Colloquium had an ambitious aim: to reflect on the problem of refugees in the light of contemporary international law issues. As the preceding report of the discussion demonstrates, the subject of refugees touches on innumerable important aspects of contemporary international law. Was the Colloquium successful in achieving its aim of focussing on those issues? Clearly yes. The papers and discussion raised many significant issues of international law relating to refugee situations. As the organizers pointed out in opening statements, the specificity of refugee law is being eroded and must be reconsidered in a broader context. Each of the issues raised in the papers and discussion would justify individual treatment in a future colloquium. The Colloquium was an academic exercise; its purpose was to stimulate intellectual consideration of the subject and not to arrive at practical conclusions. The high level of the papers and discussions accomplished that objective admirably.

List of Abbreviations

AFDI	Annuaire français de droit international
AJIL	American Journal of International Law
BYIL	British Yearbook of International Law
CIJ	Cour internationale de Justice
Colum. L.Rev.	Columbia Law Review
Conn. JIL	Connecticut Journal of International Law
GATT	General Agreement on Tariffs and Trade
Harv.ILJ	Harvard International Law Journal
ICJ	International Court of Justice
ICJ *Rev.*	Review of the International Commission of Jurists
ICLQ	The International and Comparative Law Quarterly
IJRL	International Journal of Refugee Law
ILA	International Law Association
ILC	International Law Commission
ILM	International Legal Materials
LNTS	League of Nations Treaty Series
PCIJ	Permanent Court of International Justice
RCADI	Recueil des Cours de l'Académie de Droit international
RGDIP	Revue générale de droit international public
RIAA	Reports of International Arbitral Awards
RSA	Recueil des Sentences Arbitrales
UN GAOR	United Nations General Assembly Official Records
UNJYB	United Nations Juridical Yearbook
UN SCOR	United Nations Security Council Official Records
UNTS	United Nations Treaty Series
Virg.JIL	Virginia Journal of International Law
YBILC	Yearbook of the International Law Commission
ZaöRV	Zeitschrift für ausländisches öffentliches Recht und Völkerrecht

List of Participants and Contributors

(Titles at the time of the colloquium)

Georges ABI-SAAB — Professor of Law, Graduate Institute of International Studies, Geneva

Rosemary ABI-SAAB — Chargée d'enseignement, Université de Genève, Ecole de Traduction et d'Interprétation, Geneva

Laurence BOISSON de CHAZOURNES — Chargée d'enseignement, Graduate Institute of International Studies, Geneva

Christina CERNA — Human Rights Specialist, Centre for Human Rights, United Nations, Geneva

Damien DESSALEGNE — Legal Adviser, United Nations High Commissioner for Refugees, Geneva

Alfred-Maurice DE ZAYAS — Centre for Human Rights, United Nations, Geneva

Jean-François DURIEUX — Chief, Promotion of Refugee Law Section, Division of International Protection, United Nations High Commissioner for Refugees, Geneva

Leonardo FRANCO — Director of International Protection, Office of the United Nations High Commissioner for Refugees, Geneva

Judith GARDAM — Professor, University of Adelaïde, Australia

Guy S. GOODWIN-GILL — Professor of Law, Carleton University, Ottawa, Ontario; Professor of Asylum Law, University of Amsterdam, Amsterdam; Editor-in-Chief, *International Journal of Refugee Law*

Vera GOWLLAND-DEBBAS	Professeur Suppléant, Graduate Institute of International Studies, Geneva
Peter HAGGENMACHER	Professor of Law, Head of International Law Section, Graduate Institute of International Studies, Geneva
Kay HAILBRONNER	Professor of Law, University of Constance, Constance
Wilbert van HÖVELL	Coordinator, Senior Legal Adviser, Special Operation in the Former Yugoslavia, Office of the United Nations High Commissioner for Refugees, Geneva
Michel IOGNA-PRAT	Senior Regional Legal Adviser for Central and Eastern Europe, Office of the United Nations High Commissioner for Refugees, Geneva
Iréne KHAN	Executive Assistant to the High Commissioner, United Nations High Commissioner for Refugees, Geneva
Karin LANDGREN	Senior Legal Counsellor, United Nations High Commissioner for Refugees, Geneva
Jean-Philippe LAVOYER	Member of the Legal Division, International Committee of the Red Cross, Geneva
Virginia LEARY	SUNY Distinguished Service Professor and Professor of Law, State University of New York at Buffalo, Buffalo, New York
Gil LOESCHER	Professor, Notre Dame University, South Bend, IN
Theodor MERON	Professor of Law, Graduate Institute of International Studies, Geneva, and New York University, New York
Václav MIKULKA	Member of the United Nations International Law Commission
Ved P. NANDA	Evans University Professor, University of Denver, Denver, Colorado

Huu-Thu NGUYEN	Professor of Law, Graduate Institute of International Studies, Geneva
Earl NOELTE	Director, Refugee Studies Program, Webster University, Geneva
Sadako OGATA	United Nations High Commissioner for Refugees, Geneva
George OKOTH-OBBO	Senior Legal Adviser, Regional Bureau for Africa, Office of the United Nations High Commissioner for Refugees, Geneva
Claire PALLEY	Member, United Nations Sub-Commission on Prevention of Discrimination and Protection of Minorities
Alain PELLET	Professeur à l'Université de Paris X Nanterre et à l'Institut d'Etudes Politiques de Paris, Membre de la Commission du Droit International des Nations Unies
Richard PLENDER	Queen's Counsel, London
Bertrand RAMCHARAN	Director, Secrétariat, International Conference on Former Yugoslavia, Geneva
Klaus SAMSON	Former Professor of Law, Graduate Institute of International Studies, Geneva
Brigitte STERN	Professeur à l'Université Paris I, Panthéon-Sorbonne, Paris
Alexandre SWOBODA	Director, Graduate Institute of International Studies, Geneva
Christian TOMUSCHAT	Professor of Public Law, Director of the Institute of International Law, Bonn; Member of the United Nations International Law Commission
Volker TURK	Legal Adviser, United Nations High Commission for Refugees, Geneva
Daniel WARNER	Deputy to the Director for External Relations and Special Programs, Graduate Institute of International Studies, Geneva

NIJHOFF LAW SPECIALS

MARTINUS NIJHOFF PUBLISHERS - THE HAGUE / BOSTON / LONDON